D1562477

Grammar for Writers

C. Beth Burch
Binghamton University SUNY

ARCHWAY
PUBLISHING

Scripture taken from the King James Version of the Bible.

Front cover design by Nathan JPS Burch (AU son) image taken by AU
Author photo by Goire Goodfellow Burch

Archway Publishing books may be ordered through booksellers or by contacting:

Archway Publishing
1663 Liberty Drive
Bloomington, IN 47403
www.archwaypublishing.com
1 (888) 242-5904

ISBN: 978-1-4808-3866-6 (sc)
ISBN: 978-1-4808-3867-3 (hc)
ISBN: 978-1-4808-3868-0 (e)

Library of Congress Control Number: 2016918814

Print information available on the last page.

Archway Publishing rev. date: 01/30/2017

For Paul-William, whose gentle heart and love envelop me,
sons Zachary and Nathan,
grand-girls Emma and Ami,
sister Ginger Kay,
Shanda, Falysiti, and Savannah
and
all our creatures great and small:
Goire, ITMB, The Flamingos, Georgiana Lena, Passie Irene
You make me whole in a world of fragments.
and
In memory of deceased parents, mentors, and
friends, all of whom I dearly miss:
Cynthia Sue Saulmon, sister
Doris Ellagwyn Saulmon and Charles H. Saulmon, parents
Passie Irene Hinden Burch, Vivian Cohen
Burch, & Jacob L. Burch, in-laws
Dr. Leonora Woodman, Purdue University, mentor and friend
Professor Leslie Field, Purdue University, mentor and friend

Contents

Preface, or What Goes Before

A thorough knowledge of grammar gives you more writing choices and makes you a more careful reader: it gives you power. Learning grammar does not guarantee that you will be a better writer, but it is a healthy intellectual pursuit in and of itself. More power over your prose, more power through language: those outcomes are what I seek to impart to you in this book.

I designed *Grammar for Writers* in a sequence intended to help you learn grammar most efficiently, and I created the book thinking specifically of the needs of writers. The book establishes big concepts first—sentence patterns. These basic patterns underlie sentences and verbal phrases. The book's chapters proceed in a sequence that breaks down sentence patterns into their elements—form classes and function words. Then finally you learn to combine the patterns. At any point in the book—or when you feel ready—turn to the chapters on figures (Chapter 6) and see how learning to use them can help you improve your style or at least help you be more conscious of how your writing reflects your ethos and writing persona. You will also find a chapter of well-written, interesting passages to analyze for practice, as well as two special reference chapters—one on usage and the other on punctuation. Finally, you can always refer to the glossary at the end of the book to get a quick definition of a term.

In *Grammar for Writers,* I do not assume that you possess intimate knowledge about such concepts as *subject, object, tense;* I explain and demonstrate such concepts. I do not attempt here to mimic the learning of language (and grammar) as native speakers acquire these. Rather I present a formal and hierarchical study of grammar, where concepts build logically, one upon the other, toward increasing complexity. Because this is a writing-intensive study of grammar, you are asked not only to recognize but also to construct the kinds of grammatical structures you are studying—in effect, to apply your knowledge. If you are working with nominative absolutes, for instance, you are likely to be asked to write perhaps twenty or thirty sentences demonstrating nominative absolutes. Writing your own examples of the structures requires you to internalize them, activating your brain's synapses and creating linguistic traces that you can revisit when a rhetorical or writing situation so demands.

The grammar in *Grammar for Writers* is linked to matters of rhetorical effect and style, as such connections are appropriate. When, for instance, adverbial clauses are introduced, you will also read about the emphasis that adverbial clauses demand. Does it matter where the adverbial clause comes in the sentence: at the beginning, at the end, or sandwiched in the middle? The text addresses not only these considerations but also those of punctuation: how are introductory adverbial clauses typically punctuated? And concluding adverbial clauses—how are they punctuated? If you violate conventions of punctuation, what rhetorical "message" do you send? In addition, you will learn about specific rhetorical figures so that you can consider the effects of strategies of balance, repetition, and coordination. In short, you will think about grammatical knowledge as relevant to writing. And you will become a writer more aware of and more sensitive to the nuances of language.

This book is a deep revision of my 2003 book *A Writer's Grammar.* Over the course of teaching from that book, I grew. I learned. Recently, I acquired the rights to that book, reconsidered and rewrote it, adding some chapters, deleting other, moving parts of the text around—just being a writer. I hope this result, *Grammar for Writers*, will smooth your writing path.

I would like to hear about your experience with this book. Write to me at bburch@binghamton.edu with your questions, comments, or ideas.

Chapter 1. The Shape of Things: Sentence Patterns

Grammar is a way of organizing what we know about language so that we can talk about and manipulate this knowledge. It is a framework for understanding sentences and explaining how they work. Much of our adult knowledge of grammar is intuitive and unconscious, acquired as we learned language as children. By trial and error and by imitation of the adults around us, we learned grammatical structures, how to organize speech to communicate our needs, to ask questions, to name the world. But there is also a *conscious* aspect to grammar, a reservoir of linguistic understanding that we can access when we speak and write. When we access this conscious information and make conscious choices about sentence form and organization and when we arrange words to create specific effects, we apply grammatical knowledge to create a rhetoric of the sentence. The study of rhetoric concerns the choices that writers make and the effects of these choices upon their readers. Using rhetoric means choosing what to write, how to express our thinking, how to order this expression, and what to emphasize—all within an ethical context. As writers and users of rhetoric, we consciously decide what to write; we determine how to order, arrange, and punctuate our words and sentences so that we can create a response in our audience. Thus, this book addresses not only grammar but grammar within a framework of rhetoric. Here I ask you to learn about grammar and also to consider the rhetorical implications of your grammatical choices.

Think of a sentence as a physical space, a site where a mini-drama unfolds: an actor or actors act or are acted upon in some place and situation, some details of which are known. The sentence is the heart of your prose, and it is a complicated and exciting place, which we will explore throughout this book. We will look at sentences through several different prisms or grammatical and rhetorical perspectives. Grammarians look at grammar, the structure and workings of a sentence, in more than one way: there is more than one grammar to describe a sentence's structure and functions. Think of it this way: a grammar is like a supermarket. Go to any supermarket, and you will find certain products in fairly predictable places: the Ben and Jerry's ice cream and the frozen spinach are going to be in the refrigerated cases; the fresh bagels are going to be near the Italian bread; most of the Coca-Cola and Pepsi will be down one aisle; and the pet food and supplies will be down another. Similar grocery products cluster together. That doesn't mean that you won't find a kind of product in more than one place in the store (you might find fresh bagels one place, frozen ones another), but it does mean that you can predict with some certainty that fresh green beans will be in the produce section—not with the soda and not with cleaning supplies. You also might find green beans in other parts of the store, according to how they are prepared: canned ones in one place and frozen ones in yet another.

Grammars are like this. Not every grammar is alike (just as every grocery store is slightly different from others), but there are some grammatical principles that operate consistently and predictably, regardless of the kind of grammar we may be discussing. Thus talking about grammar becomes a matter of understanding what things go together, under what circumstances they go together, and why. A **grammar** is a way of describing what a language does. **Rhetoric** considers the way that grammatical elements (or parts of sentences) work together to create certain effects. If you place a clause at the beginning of a sentence instead of at its end, for instance, you send readers a particular message and you emphasize a specific aspect of your message. But . . . let's begin with sentence patterns, the major structures into which most English sentences fall.

You will read material in this chapter that is very familiar to most students who pass through the public school system in the United States. But you will also be asked to think about this familiar material in a new way. Take in all this new information; add it to what you already know as a speaker and nascent student of grammar and the English language. And be patient: although some of the information seems easy, it is more challenging than it appears (and more subtle). Allow yourself the time to be confused but also think purposefully about the material so that it all begins to gel. By book's end, you will have a considerably more supple understanding of how to use the language in your writing and speaking.

In this chapter, you'll find a description of the basic ways that English sentences fit together—the **patterns** of English—and you'll think about the effects of using each one.

An important concept underpinning most English grammars is this: that patterns exist in the ways that we speak and write. Over and over the same structures occur, with regularity. One major feature of all English patterns is that English is a **verb-medial** language: this means that verbs typically occur in the medial or middle position in the sentence. In English, as in many languages, the verb is the key player in the sentence: the verb determines the pattern of the sentence. So we will pay special attention to verbs as we consider patterns, and we will *scrutinize the verb first*: the verb is the key to the pattern of the sentence. English has **transitive verbs, linking verbs, and intransitive verbs**—and a number of patterns for each kind. Let's look at some basic examples of patterns for each kind of verb.

Transitive Patterns

Look at the bare-bones sentences below this paragraph. What structural similarities do you see? How are the sentences similarly built? What elements or major parts do they have in common? Use the language of nouns and verbs, adjectives and adverbs that you may recall from elementary school to describe the pattern you see here. You may experience a curious and somewhat maddening phenomenon: that to explain a grammatical structure, you have to use grammatical language, which may not be clear or even available to you until the grammatical concept is clear. This means that all the concepts may become clear all at once and that often you may be working with an imperfect understanding of what is being discussed. Be patient and be willing to be confused temporarily. Eventually the concept will become clear. Try to explain what each word seems to be *doing* in these short sentences.

1. Nothing surprises me.
2. We have your book.
3. The killers hit the bishop.
4. Frost wrote a letter.
5. My best friend Sarah likes the indispensable black travel dress.

To begin, each sentence has at its front a noun, noun substitute or pronoun, or **noun cluster** (a noun plus its attendants, the words that pattern with it, modify it, or describe it). Nouns are, you will recall, naming words, words that we use to label objects, people, and ideas. This front or initial noun or noun cluster tells what the sentence is to be about, its **subject**: *nothing, we, the killers, Frost, My best friend Sarah*.

Then, each subject is associated with a **verb**: *surprises, have, hit, wrote, likes.* Verbs express or refer to action in a sentence, to what is happening. Each verb implies a question—*Who? Whom?* or *What?*—and needs something more to complete it. Finally, each verb doesn't sound quite finished without the answer to the question *Whom?* or *What?* Nothing surprises *whom*? We have *what*? The killers hit *whom*? Frost wrote *what*? My best friend Sarah likes *what*?

Finally, note that each sentence has a noun or pronoun to answer that question, "Who?" or "What?": Nothing surprises *me*; We have *your book*; The killers hit the *bishop*; and Sarah likes the *dress*. The nouns that follow the verb and complete its meaning by answering the question *Whom?* or *What?* are called **direct objects**, which are part of a larger class of words called **complements** or completers. Complements, including direct objects, work with subjects and verbs to impart information and to create *complete* grammatical structures or *sentences*. Notice that direct objects, like all **objects** when we speak in the language of grammar, are always nouns or noun substitutes. Thus the word *objects* is a clue here to the kind of word that fits the pattern: a noun.

Direct Object Pattern

So we call this pattern **S-V-O: subject-verb-object**. In an S-V-O sentence, a subject does something to or acts upon an object. In this pattern, some kind of action (either physical, emotional, psychological, or intellectual) is transferred from the subject through the verb to the object. We call these verbs *transitive* verbs, verbs that *take* an object and that *transfer* some kind of action from subject to object. The subject of each of these direct object sentences is also an **agent***. *Agent* is a cognate of the Latin verb *ago, agere*, which means *to do*. Thus an agent is a do-er, and typically the subject also does something, acts. The object, on the other hand, is acted upon: somebody does something to the object. S-V-O is the most common pattern in English: readers are accustomed to reading about the subject first, then the verb, then the object. Any time you interrupt or subvert or rearrange this basic arrangement, you draw the reader's attention and emphasize the idea that is being interrupted, subverted, or rearranged.

When you choose an S-V-O pattern, then, you are presenting events directly, showing an actor and describing what the actor did to something or to someone. The rhetorical effect is directness and, usually, clarity. It is obvious what was done and who did it.

Sentence patterns manifest themselves in all kinds of places. Look at the sentences in the "Mr. Woofard" cartoon caption below to see two examples of S-V-O patterns: *You / will like / Mr. Woofard* and *He / has / disorder.*

"You will like Mr. Woofard. He has an attention-deficit disorder."

Mr. Woofard

The repetition of this sentence pattern is very directive (one student tells the other what to do) and at the same time reminiscent of the language of elementary reading books, which often repeat patterns for emphasis and improved comprehension. The use and repetition of the direct object pattern helps to create the humor of the caption.

About Prepositional Phrases

Let's interrupt the discussion of patterns a moment to consider **prepositional phrases**. Prepositional phrases remain outside the S-V-O structure (or the structure of any pattern) and are not considered elements or constituents of the pattern (those things that constitute or compose the pattern). Prepositional phrases enhance the pattern, elaborate the pattern, make the pattern more interesting. But they are not part of the pattern, nor do they change the pattern. So here's a tip: when you are trying to distinguish the pattern of a sentence, **ignore prepositional phrases entirely**. Prepositional phrases are added to basic patterns to expand, develop, or modify them. Pattern elements or main parts (the S, V, or O) are NOT found within prepositional phrases. This is an important idea to understand as you work to understand how sentences fall into various patterns.

Take a few minutes to review prepositional phrases because you need to recognize them as you identify patterns. A **prepositional phrase** is built of a preposition plus its object, which is a noun or a noun cluster: *for + low-income housing, of + daily therapeutic care, during + the past five years, at + the eleventh hour, in + the injected knee, off + the roof.* Some of the most common prepositions are these:

around
at
beneath
beside
between
by

down
during
for
in
of
on
through
to
toward
with
within
without

If the object has modifying words clustered around it, the cluster or string is part of the prepositional phrase.

Sometimes prepositions themselves occur in phrases, thus creating **phrasal prepositions**. Prepositions can pattern together and act as a unit to create variations on the original meaning of the preposition. Consider this partial list of phrasal prepositions:

according to
along with
as for
because of
except for
instead of
next to
thanks to
by means of
in back of
in charge of
in spite of
on behalf of

Phrasal prepositions make possible subtle variations of meaning and delicate levels of explanation and understanding; when you use a phrasal preposition, you express a complex grammatical relationship. Each phrasal preposition functions or acts just like a single-word preposition and when patterned with a noun or noun cluster of its own, creates a prepositional phrase:

in spite of / my friend's best efforts,
according to / the rules of the game,
instead of / vegetable lasagna.

It is important to understand that in English several words can—and frequently do—function as a unit expressing one idea. We are accustomed to hearing these clusters or units in English and making perfect sense of them. But when we see them in print, on the page, we tend not to see the units but rather to think of individual words. As you build grammatical understanding, you may find it helpful to think of *concepts as residing in phrases* rather than in individual words.

Remember that as valuable as prepositional phrases are to the development and even the subtlety of a sentence, they are *not* part of the sentence pattern. When you are trying to determine the pattern of a given sentence, consider striking out the prepositional phrases so that you can see the skeletal pattern elements better exposed.

~~~~~~

FOR DISCUSSION: DIRECT OBJECT PATTERN

In your study group, talk about the following S-V-O sentences, identifying what words function as subjects, verbs, and direct objects. Be prepared to explicate or explain fully any of the sentences to the class at large after the small-group discussions. Your group should discuss the relationships among the words, how the subject is related to the object—and vice versa. You should also explain how each subject is an agent, what it does. The elements of the pattern (that is, the S, the V, and the O) are frequently headwords of larger clusters that include many modifying or enriching words (that we'll examine more closely later). Observe also how the sentences are punctuated, or in this case, not punctuated, except for end punctuation. These sentences are correct without internal punctuation because *we do not separate the simple elements of a pattern with punctuation.* Don't break up a simple pattern with punctuation between any of the basic elements. No punctuation goes between subject and verb or between verb and object, for instance.

1. In the sometimes rancorous discussion, Cinderella maintained calm.
2. These books explain the writer's creative processes to the layman.
3. Jones savored the victory.
4. Old friends celebrated their memories with joy.
5. The Ferrari delivers power.
6. Full resort amenities include golf for amateurs and professionals, tennis, a fitness center, and a spa.
7. Edward Jones crunched the numbers.
8. The bull market was drawing con artists.
9. By Web or by phone, scamsters can tell lies.
10. The Sioux would not desecrate graves.
11. German police in Bavaria found a vast weapons cache.
12. I believe the songs.
13. He ends his tour with an outdoor show in Newark, Delaware.
14. He's muffed his share of big moments.
15. Many movies put their heroes through life-changing experiences.
16. The survivors confront a pack of hungry wolves.
17. The gourmet cook includes some enticing recipes here.

18. Try this new weight-loss diet for 90 days. [The subject in this sentence is understood, thus not stated. Imagine a *You* at the beginning of the sentence.]
19. I need more hours in the day.
20. We've packaged a unique set of tools.
21. An eloquent ad campaign can turn around a troubled company within months.
22. Ferrari announced an initial public offering (IPO) of stock.
23. You can engage your clients in a relevant, one-to-one conversation.
24. My grandmother makes hats for children.
25. Ancient Tibetan mandalas symbolize wholeness.

~~~~~~

Compound Elements in Patterns

All parts of the pattern can be **compounded**. You can, for instance, create a compound subject:

Stan
and   *will hide the valuables in a paper bag*
Ollie

Here you have two subjects that are attached to one verb phrase. Stan will hide the valuables—and so will Ollie. In the next sentence, you will see a compound verb, where one subject patterns with two separate verb phrases:

              washed the dishes
Sammy   *and*
              pressed his white shirt.

Here Sammy completes two actions, washing dishes and pressing a shirt. In this sentence, each verb phrase happens to have the same pattern, a transitive verb plus a direct object. It is possible to have compound verbs that have different patterns. You'll read more about those later. You may also write or read sentences with all sorts of compound elements. Here's an example of a sentence with compound direct objects:

the posters

All evening Nathan drew   *and*

the charts.

As long as only some elements of a pattern are compounded, you still have one pattern.

For Writing

Now it's time for you to practice writing the S-V-O pattern. In your writer's notebook (either paper or electronic), compose 25 S-V-O sentences. To make the task interesting, include the name of a person from history, either living or dead, in each sentence, either as subject or direct object. Example: *Napoleon loves eclairs* or *Many presidents have admired George Washington.* In at least three of the 25 sentences, include a compound sentence element. When you finish your sentences, check to see that each verb is transitive, that is, that it takes an object and that the subject acts as or is an agent. Then review your sentences with your writers' group. Your sentences don't have to be historically correct, by the way!

Indirect Object Pattern

The S-V-O pattern is not the only transitive pattern. There are others. Take a look at the following skeleton sentences with an eye toward detecting similar structures in the sentences. What sentence features do you see?

1. We'll send you a string of pearls from Tiffany's.
2. My aunt gave us girls a Vignelli dinner plate.
3. Gram made us some chocolate chip cookies.
4. The new Corvette shows true fans its stuff.
5. The lieutenant is giving Sam the bad news.

In these sentences you can probably make out the subject clusters (*We, My aunt, Gram, The new Corvette, the lieutenant*), the verbs (*send, gave, made, shows, is giving*), and the direct object noun clusters that answer the question *What?* or *Whom?* implicitly raised by the verb—*a string of pearls, a Vignelli dinner plate, some chocolate chip cookies, its stuff, the bad news*. And you probably also detected the presence of another noun or noun substitute located between the verb and the direct object: *you, us girls, us, true fans, Sam*. These elements intervening between the verb and direct object are **indirect objects**. They answer the questions *To whom was something done or given?* or *For whom was something done or given?*

We write the indirect object pattern **S-V-IO-DO**. Note the location of the indirect object: between the verb and the direct object. This is its required place. There is no other place in the sentence where it can exist and still remain an indirect object. If, for instance, you revise the indirect object sentence

The lieutenant is giving Sam the bad news

to read

The lieutenant is giving the bad news to Sam,

an indirect object does not exist in the revised sentence. The revision changed the pattern to S-V-O, and the indirect object becomes the object of a preposition and part of a prepositional phrase modifier, *to Sam.* (Some grammarians disagree with this analysis; they maintain that it is only not the position of the noun but its function or the task it performs in the sentence that makes it an indirect object. Nevertheless, the form changes dramatically.) In the revised sentence, the grammatical importance of the original object *bad news* decreases because it has moved to mid-sentence, a place of little emphasis.

The importance of the indirect object *Sam* increases when the indirect object is moved to the prepositional phrase because it falls at the end of the sentence, a place of natural emphasis. *Giving Sam the bad news* buries *Sam,* the receiver of the bad news, in mid-sentence. As a writer, you choose where the emphasis should be. This is a **rhetorical** choice. A note: observe that three separate **noun clusters** (also called **N-groups** by some grammarians) exist in this pattern: *lieutenant, news,* and *Sam* all have modifiers clustering around them. Each noun refers to a separate entity. In *Gerry gave her friends a cookie,* the nouns *Gerry, friends,* and *cookie* refer to three separate entities. We say that these nouns have separate **referents** because each noun **refers to** something separate or different.

~~~~~~

FOR DISCUSSION

Analyze the following S-V-IO-DO sentences in your writer's group. Identify what words function as subjects, verbs, indirect objects, and direct objects. Discuss the relationships among the words, how the subjects are related to the objects and the indirect objects—and vice versa. Observe that, as in an S-V-O sentence, each subject is still an agent, that it still performs an action—in this pattern, the subject performs an action to or for someone. The elements of the pattern (that is, the S, the V, the IO, and the DO) are frequently headwords for larger clusters that also include modifying or enriching words and phrases like determiners, possessives, adjectives, adverbs, intensifiers, and even prepositional phrases (more about these kinds of words later).

Remember: when you sort out the pattern of a sentence, **ignore prepositional phrases entirely**. Prepositional phrases are added on to a basic pattern to expand, develop, or modify it. Pattern elements (the S, V, IO, or DO) are **not** found in prepositional phrases. Here, then, are some indirect object sentences for your group to prepare for the whole-group discussion:

1. Aunt Tobi taught the brat a lesson.
2. Paolo's kiss gave me shivers.
3. The waiter poured me coffee in a flashy silver mug.
4. You can save me time and stress.
5. Our psychology professor assigned us a paper and a project.
6. Nixon forwarded his secretary the message.
7. I gave Emily a blue notebook with a denim cover.
8. The florist sold him a yellow rose.
9. Paul bought me a gold Claddaugh ring in Galway.
10. With glee, Preston gave Drew a black eye.
11. The real estate agent showed Joe the big brick house.
12. Ralph handed her the pencil.
13. In legal documents, Engelbert granted me his power-of-attorney.
14. The grocer sold the customer a fruit basket of lemons, limes, grapes, and apricots.
15. Goldie built her puppy a doghouse from a cardboard box.
16. I wrote my friend Cynthia a letter on expensive stationery.

17. An anonymous donor sent the school a new computer and printer.
18. I purchased Ginger a scented candle for her birthday.
19. The tourists sent them pictures of azure oceans and purple mountains.
20. The nurse passed Harold a milky concoction.
21. The Jolly Green Giant handed the shopper a can of beans.
22. Jimi Hendrix played his fans "Purple Haze" with gusto.
23. The soldier wrote his love a syrupy letter.
24. The inventive witch sent the warlock a poisoned letter in the U.S. mail.
25. The veterinarian prescribed the poodle some medicine for her headaches.

~~~~~~

Verbs for the Indirect Object Pattern. Did you notice that the verbs in the indirect object pattern have similar meanings? These verbs are a rather small class of verbs like give. We call them **give verbs**. You will find that there are considerably fewer verbs that fit in this class and that your options for composing indirect object sentences are slimmer than your verb choices for the direct object pattern. Here are some of the most common give verbs for indirect object patterns:

award
buy
give
grant
hand
leave
make
play
pour
purchase
sell

send
serve
show
teach
tell
write

FOR WRITING

Now it's time for you to practice writing this pattern. In your writer's notebook (either paper or electronic), compose 25 S-V-IO-DO sentences. To make the task interesting, include a noun that begins with the letter G somewhere in each sentence; you'll want to include the noun in any one of the noun slots (subjects, indirect objects, and direct objects can all have nouns or noun clusters). Example with a "g" word: *The goonies handed the robber a shiny coin.* Remember: as you write these sentences, you will find that you are choosing verbs from a considerably smaller pool than with S-V-O sentences. Do not be concerned if you seem to use the same or similar verbs over and over.

Objective Complement Pattern

Besides their patterning with direct and indirect objects, transitive verbs can pattern in English sentences in still another way. Study the following examples to see the relationships among elements in these sentences:

1. My child believes me ridiculous.
2. The class found the professor intolerable.
3. Everyone considered the event successful.
4. Question six left me puzzled.
5. She probably thinks me rude.

and these:

6. The boss called me her colleague.
7. His friends nicknamed him Oscar.
8. The workers elected Hoffa president of the union.
9. The Green Party considered Michael Pollan an ally.
10. The sportswriters named the successful quarterback most valuable player.

Once again, you see the familiar S-V-O structure. In this pattern, though, the direct objects tend to answer the question *Whom?* more than *What?*—*The class found whom? Everyone considered what? The boss called whom? The workers elected whom?* Even though a direct object is present, the pattern remains incomplete until the final complement is added *after the direct object.* This final complement completes the relationship founded upon the subject-verb relationship. This kind of complement (or completer) of the direct object is called the **objective complement** or the completer of the object.

We write this pattern **S-V-DO-OC** for subject-verb-direct object-objective complement. Notice how in the first group of examples the objective complements are adjectives that refer to, describe, or modify the direct objects: *a ridiculous me, intolerable professor, successful event, a puzzled me, rude students.* In the second group of examples, the objective complements are nouns that refer to or rename the direct object: *her = colleague, him = Oscar, Hoffa = president, Ralph Nader = ally, quarterback = player.* In both these cases, we say that the direct object and the objective complement have the same **referent**, that is, they *refer to* the same person or the same thing. The subjects have totally different referents than the direct objects or their objective complements. In *The workers elected Hoffa president of the union,* the subject *workers* refers to one group of people, and the direct object *Hoffa* and its complement *president* refer to another person totally separate and apart from the first: thus they have different referents.

FOR DISCUSSION

In your writers' group, prepare to present an analysis of any two of the following S-V-DO-OC sentences to the class as a whole. Identify what words function as subjects, verbs, direct objects, and objective complements. Discuss the relationships among the words, how the subjects are related to the objects and how the direct objects and the objective complements are related, and whether the objective complements are nouns or adjectives. As in all kinds of transitive sentences, each subject is an agent because it does something. The elements of the pattern (that is, the S, the V, the DO, and the OC) are frequently part of larger clusters that include determiners, possessives, adjectives, adverbs, intensifiers, and even prepositional phrases—more about those in the next chapter. Remember that when you sorting out the pattern of a sentence, **ignore prepositional phrases entirely**: prepositional phrases are added on to a basic pattern to expand, develop, or modify it. Pattern elements (the S, V, DO, and OC) are *not* found in prepositional phrases. Here are some objective complement sentences to talk about:

1. The Marilyn Manson groupie painted his lips black.
2. First-year college students and older students too called the cafeteria food garbage.
3. Betsy believed the book about the princess scandalous.
4. In 1963, Bob Dylan's political anthems made him the voice of the Movement.
5. Critics may proclaim this record the best.
6. This album might make him hip again.
7. The reviewer called Johnny Depp clever.
8. The board named Shelley's daughter a National Science Scholar.
9. The magazine Fortune will vote one company Most Generous Company in America.

10. This new voice-activated device makes commute time and downtime productive time!
11. Together we can make the planet better for everyone.
12. Vanity Fair called the actress a minor-league Marilyn Monroe.
13. My friends consider the reform ideas ludicrous.
14. At one time Texas voters considered him a political lightweight.
15. Most of us believe statistics unreliable and unbelievable.
16. His habits make me uneasy.
17. That class left me clueless.
18. The inspector and the engineer deemed the bridge safe.
19. You made your Democratic friends proud with this issue.
20. The police called the suspect a liar.
21. Sue dyed her shirt red.
22. The height and the angle of descent made me dizzy.
23. Nikolai called the officers imperious.
24. Diners at Number 5 find the Cobb salad delicious.
25. I consider this sentence the end.

FOR WRITING

Now it's time for you to write this pattern. In your writer's notebook (either paper or electronic), compose 25 S-V-DO-OC sentences. As you write these sentences, you will find that you are choosing verbs from an even smaller verb pool than the verbs you could use with S-V-IO-DO sentences; so if you believe that you are using the same verbs repeatedly, you probably are—but you haven't much latitude. After you write the sentences, check to see that in each sentence, your direct object and objective complement have the same referent. Here is a list of the most common verbs in objective complement sentences:

believe
call
choose
color
consider
deem
elect
find
make
name
paint
proclaim

~~~~~~~~~~~~~~~~~~~~~~~~~~~~~~~~~~~~~~~

Possible Confusions: Appositives

Sometimes appositives look like objective complements, and it's easy to confuse the two because the difference is subtle. **Appositives** are nouns patterning with and renaming other nouns. Generally, appositives are **in apposition with** the nouns they relate to—this mean that they are literally *in position with* their nouns, side by side. Here are some examples of transitive sentences with appositives:

Our friend, the new chef at Le Jardin, makes wonderful cherry tarts.

Friend and *the new chef at Le Jardin* are in apposition; *the new chef at Le Jardin* renames *friend*. This is still an S-V-O sentence, and the pattern has not changed; the subject just has an appositive.

The panel of chefs awarded our friend, the new chef at Le Jardin, the prize for best cherry tarts.

Friend and *the new chef at Le Jardin* are still in apposition; now they are functioning as the indirect object and appositive in an S-V-IO-DO sentence. Note that their relationship is still the same, even though the pattern of the sentence changes.

It's easy to confuse appositives with other sentence elements that are nouns. It is particularly easy to confuse appositives with objective complements as in a sentence like this: *We welcomed our friend, the new chef at Le Jardin.*

In this sentence, *friend* and *the new chef at Le Jardin* are direct objects in an appositional relationship. *The new chef at Le Jardin* is an appositive to the noun *friend* —and *friend* serves as the direct object of the verb. The relationship is fundamentally different than that between direct object and objective complement, where the object and its complement still have the same referent but where the action and power of the verb extend across the entire sentence. In this S-V-O sentence, the verb's power ends with *friend,* its object. The verb has no impact on *the new chef at Le Jardin,* the appositive that merely renames the direct object. The sentence seems and sounds complete as it is.

But in an S-V-DO-OC sentence like *The panel of chefs named our friend winner!* The action of the verb is not completed when we get to *our friend* in the sentence; the panels named *our friend* something—*winner*—and until that information is presented, the verb is not complete and the reader doesn't have the whole idea of the sentence. *In other words, you can omit an appositive but not an objective complement without changing the meaning of the sentence.* Understanding the concept behind the objective complement will help you to sort out the differences between appositives after direct objects and objective complements.

FOR DISCUSSION

Here are some more sentences (some are adapted, mostly shortened, from the originals) with appositives for you to study. What principles of punctuation for appositives can you deduce from these examples?

1. "The tennis player Martina Navratilova is unique in professional sports for having come out at the height of her career." —Margaret Talbot. From "Game Change."

2. "Late one recent morning, the door opened on a thirty-seventh-floor suite in the Waldorf Towers, where Imelda Marcos, the former First Lady of the Philippines, lived in the eighties, during her reign and subsequent exile." —Michael Schulman. From "Bling Ring."

3. "In 1988 he opened a pub, the Wynkoop Brewing Company, in an area of abandoned warehouses called Lower Downtown." —Ryan Lizza. From "The Middleman."

4. "American officials have tried to make sure that sophisticated weapons—particularly portable anti-aircraft missiles, often called by their military acronym, MANPADs—do not leak out." —Dexter Filkins. From "The Thin Red Line."

5. "He had evidently been inspired by Emma Goldman, the prominent anarchist rabble-rouser." —Kelefa Sannah. From "Paint Bombs."

6. "'She' is Helen, a struggling single mother and casino worker living in London." —James Kelman. From Rev. of Mo Said She Was Quirky.

7. "F. Scott Fitzgerald cabled Max Perkins, his editor at Scribners, and demanded to know if the reviews were good." —David Denby. From "All That Jazz."

8. "Gerard Depardieu plays Donissan, a country priest with literally self-flagellating faith." —Richard Brody. From Rev. of *Under the Sun of Satan*.
9. "Judith Long, the magazine's copy chief, agreed to look for the issue."—Ian Parker. From "Navasky Lives."
10. "One day last fall, Tom Mauser, the father of one of the victims of the Columbine shooting, came to visit." —Ryan Lizza. From "The Middleman."

Linking Patterns

The transitive patterns present scenarios where subjects act upon or do something to objects—to some*thing* or some*one* else—and variations on this pattern: giving something to someone else, doing something for someone else, calling or naming somebody something. The linking patterns present an entirely different concept. Take a look at the sentences that follow and see if you can explain the relationships you see between the subjects, the verbs, and the complements.

1. Tom Thumb is a Delaware builder.
2. His departure from Sportscenter is an obvious career move.
3. Judith Exner was Sam Giancana's girlfriend.
4. A trip to the office means trouble!
5. El Nino was a freakish, destructive disruption in worldwide weather.

Predicate Noun Pattern

The complements or sentence completers following the linking verbs in these sentences are all nouns. We call them **predicate nouns** (nouns that rename the subject and occur in the predicate, after the verb). We name the pattern **S-LV-PN** for subject-linking verb-predicate noun.

The purpose of predicate noun sentences is to identify and name; the complements rename the subjects (they are often called **subjective complements** or completers of the subject). **Linking verbs** join or link the subject to the complement. In these sentences, the subjects and complements have the same referents: *Tom Thumb* and *the Delaware builder* are one and the same person; *Exner* was the *girlfriend*, and *El Nino* was the *disruption*. Compare, for instance these sentences:

Judith Exner criticized Sam Giancana's girlfriend

The transitive verb *criticized* takes the direct object, *girlfriend*. *Exner* and *girlfriend* refer to two different people; we say that they have different *referents*—

and

Judith Exner was Sam Giancana's girlfriend

The linking verb *was* takes the complement or predicate noun, *girlfriend*. *Exner* and *girlfriend* now refer to the same person and have the same *referent*. Now take a look at the following sentences and determine how they are like the first set of linking sentences above—and how they are different as well:

1. Her skin is clear.
2. Her joints feel fine.
3. Olbermann is glib.
4. School has been easy for Matthew French.
5. He's also famous for his daring paintings.

Predicate Adjective Pattern

How are these **subjective complements** different from the ones in the first group of sentences? These complements are **predicate adjectives** that describe or modify the subject—skin = clear, joints = fine, Olbermann = glib, School = easy, he = famous. Like predicate nouns and their subjects, predicate adjectives and their subjects have the same referent. Like predicate nouns, predicate adjectives are joined, linked, to their subjects via linking verbs.

You may find it useful simply to memorize the major verbs that can function as linking verbs so that you can recognize them more easily. *These verbs don't always function as linking verbs, but they most frequently do.* Here they are:

- **forms of the verb *be*:** *am, is, are, was, were, be, being, been* (including *has been, have been, had been, is being, will be,* etc.)

- **the verbs naming the senses**: *looks, sounds, smells, feels, tastes*

- **and an odd assortment of verbs** like *seem, appear, become, remain,* and *grow*

As you memorize these most frequently used linking verbs, remember that these verbs *may* be linking but that they are *not necessarily always* linking and that other verbs may sometimes function as linking verbs. In *The shrimp gumbo tastes spicy,* the linking verb *tastes* links *gumbo* and *spicy*: *spicy* and *gumbo* have the same referent and refer to the same entity. But in *Bubba tastes the gumbo, tastes* is a transitive verb: *Bubba* and *gumbo* are clearly different entities with different referents, and *Bubba* acts upon the *gumbo*, does something to the *gumbo*—he tastes it.

Not all adjectives that occur in the predicate are predicate adjectives; only adjectives that modify or pattern with the subject are predicate adjectives. The sentence *The students are diligent* contains a predicate adjective, *diligent,* that patterns with and describes the subject, *students*. But the sentence *They are diligent students* does not contain a predicate adjective because *diligent* (an adjective occurring in the predicate part of the sentence) modifies or describes or patterns with the predicate noun *students,* not with the subject *They.*

~~~~~~~~~~~~~~~~~~~~~~~~~~~~~~~~~~~~~~

FOR DISCUSSION

Analyze the S-LV-PN and S-LV-PA sentences below for presentation in a whole-class discussion, identifying what words function as subjects, verbs, predicate nouns, and predicate adjectives. Discuss relationships among words, how subjects are related to complements, whether complements are nouns or adjectives. In this pattern, subjects are no longer agents; rather in these sentences subjects are being described, renamed, amplified—completed—through and by means of the complement. Notice also that the elements of the pattern (that is, the S, the LV, the PN or PA) are frequently headwords of larger clusters or word groups that include determiners, possessives, adjectives, adverbs, intensifiers, and even prepositional phrases (more about these kinds of words in the next chapter). Observe how the sentences are punctuated. Notice that we do not use punctuation to separate the main parts of a sentence pattern. Also remember that when you are sorting out the pattern of a sentence or even first composing a sentence of a certain pattern, **ignore prepositional phrases entirely.** Prepositional phrases are added on to a basic pattern to expand, develop, or modify it. Pattern elements (the S, LV, PN, and PA) are not found in prepositional phrases. Here are some linking pattern sentences to talk about:

1. "*Time Out of Mind* is a spare, spooky-sounding album."—Benjamin Hedin. From *Studio A: The Bob Dylan Reader.*

2. I feel afraid.

3. The movie is preposterous—and hugely entertaining. [Do you see the compound complements?]

4. Their issues are Social Security and the cost of prescription drugs. [More compound elements]
5. The gentlest things for your skin are aloe vera, cocoa butter, and pure merino wool. [Again, look for compound complements.]
6. White House aides are aghast.
7. He's an intellectual heavyweight.
8. I was awake before dawn on my birthday in 1995.
9. The saga of the ghost rider is edifying entertainment.
10. Education is the most important issue for all citizens.
11. These marvelous glasses are heavy.
12. Guiseppe is a daring Italian pilot with a handsome mustache.
13. This flower is a gardenia.
14. He was a clairvoyant.
15. Sam Adams is famous for a few things.
16. Life will be a little more glamorous with a Cadillac.
17. Lewis was a clear winner in the poll.
18. Your comments are an exaggeration.
19. Ella was graceful and gentle and articulate. [Notice the compound elements.]
20. The poodles were sleek and elegant.
21. We are hip!
22. Kubrick may be unique among directors.
23. This is not a question of screen violence.
24. These private scenes became embarrassing and disgusting.
25. DiMaggio was the classic player of our century.

FOR WRITING

Now you practice writing these patterns. In your writer's notebook (either paper or electronic), first compose 25 S-LV-PN sentences and then write 25 S-LV-PA sentences. To make things interesting, use only predicate adjectives beginning with the letter *M* in the S-LV-PA sentences. As you write these sentences, remember to use linking verbs and remember that your complements—the predicate nouns and the predicate adjectives—must refer to (or have the same referent as) the subject. After you write the sentences, check to see that in each sentence your subject and subjective complement (predicate noun or predicate adjective) have the same referent.

The Intransitive Pattern

A third kind of sentence pattern centers on the **intransitive verb**, the verb with no complement whatsoever. This means that it has no complement or object, that the verb is complete in itself. Check out these sentences.

1. Negotiations came to a halt.
2. You should stroll in Central Park.
3. Over the last several years, crime in New York City has dropped.
4. I'm speaking out now.
5. Around here, time doesn't stand still.
6. The toddlers laugh, smile, and play in the sun.

The major elements in these sentences are simply subjects and verbs. Yes, there are sometimes prepositional phrases used adverbially (*to a halt, in the sun*) or adverbial words (*now*), but you will learn more in a subsequent chapter about how adjectives, adverbs, and prepositional phrases can constitute part of a cluster around a noun or verb but (except for the predicate adjective) do not constitute elements of the sentence pattern. Rather they are modifiers that add to what is known about the elements, words that expand, develop, enhance, limit, or modify them. All the verbs in these sentences are **intransitive complete**—that is, verbs not taking or requiring an object or complement-completer, verbs complete in themselves: *came, should stroll, has dropped, am speaking, does stand, laugh, smile, play.*

We write this pattern **S-V** or **S-V(adv)** to show that an adverbial element in any form (single word or phrase) is an option.

Many verbs can be both transitive and intransitive. For instance, consider the verb *walk*. In this sentence, *walk* is intransitive: *All the players walked casually onto the field.* The verb has no complement, only an adverbial modifier (*casually*) and a adverbial prepositional phrase (*onto the field*). But in the next sentence, *walk* is transitive because it takes compound objects, *poodles* and *golden retrievers: Sister Ellen walked the poodles and the golden retrievers together.*

~~~~~~

FOR DISCUSSION

In your writers' group, discuss the following S-V sentences in preparation for a presentation to the class as a whole. Identify what words function as subjects and verbs. If there are adverbials, point them out. The elements of the pattern (that is, the S and the V) may frequently be part of larger clusters that include determiners, possessives, adjectives, adverbs, intensifiers, and even prepositional phrases. Remember that when you sort out the pattern of a sentence, **you ignore prepositional phrases entirely**; prepositional phrases are added on to a basic pattern to expand, develop, or modify it. Pattern elements (the S and V) are NOT found in prepositional phrases. As you talk about the sentences, don't forget to observe how they are punctuated. Here are some intransitive sentences to talk about:

1. Residential streets blend with the world's most fashionable drives.

2. Bits and bytes and ones and zeroes zoom through the atmosphere. [Observe the compound subject.]
3. We should meet at one o'clock at Bloomingdale's.
4. Tennessee Williams entered the literary world as a short story writer.
5. This offer will expire soon.
6. Then the phone beside him rang.
7. Letters arrived at Smith & Wesson headquarters.
8. She never wavered in her belief in the dream.
9. Mary Cassatt painted by day's natural light.
10. Love dies hard.
11. The black poodle stretched out languidly on the white carpet.
12. Fifi White screamed at the mouse.
13. He played in center field.
14. Many of us are worrying.
15. A California congressman and some journalists flew to the Congo.
16. The hunter was aiming in the right direction.
17. These moments pass so quickly!
18. She frets about her husband's decision.
19. Everyone will retire for the night in a fancy, insulated tent.
20. Sammy rises with his knapsack over one shoulder.
21. The home runs in his imagination never died.
22. During World War II, a group of Americans parachuted into the war zone.
23. Many French generals and ministers came to Dien Bien Phu.
24. One thinks of William Faulkner, the great novelist and chronicler of Yoknapatawpha County.
25. I had arrived in Vietnam eight weeks earlier as a private.

FOR WRITING

Now you practice writing this pattern. In your writer's notebook (either paper or electronic), compose 25 S-V sentences. As you write, remember to use intransitive complete verbs and remember that your sentences will not have complements—but they may have adverbial constructions, either single words or prepositional phrases. To make it interesting, add one prepositional phrase to each sentence and make one of the nouns in each sentence begin with the letter *T*.

The There-V-S Pattern

An easily recognizable pattern looks like this:

1. There were fantastic schemes.
2. There is a babyishness to his speech.
3. There is a good deal of anguish and angst in his music.
4. There is never any minimum charge.
5. Here are your rhinestone tap shoes.
6. There's only one place big enough for Earth's biggest selection of shoes.
7. There are no guns in this town.

Each sentence begins with the word *there* or *here* and is then followed by a verb—*were, is,* and *are* in these sentences. All these verbs are, in fact, forms of the verb *be,* by far the most common verb in this pattern. It is possible but not typical for other verbs to function in this pattern. Following the verbs are nouns—*schemes, babyishness, deal, charge, tap shoes, place, guns*—that act as the subjects of the sentences. These subject nouns are what the sentences are *about.*

We write this pattern as **There-V-S**. The elements in this pattern are the word *there* (or sometimes *here*) and then verbs followed by subjects—a reversal of normal word order. There-V-S sentences are almost always intransitive, but you may find an occasional exception. Note also that, as in other intransitive patterns, there are sometimes prepositional phrases used adverbially (*to his speech, in his music, for Earth's biggest selection of shoes, in this town*). In these sentences *there* is considered an **expletive**, that is, a word that fills a space without contributing any meaning. Expletives are placeholders. They take up space that other words might occupy—and they give the writer a chance to delay a word, perhaps to gain greater impact by using it later in the sentence. The *there* front-loaded in the sentence tells the reader that something emphatic and interesting is coming later, thereby lending more importance to the subject that is wrenched from its normal place in the sentence anyway. These are typically ontological statements, sentences that declare being or a state of being, sentences that describe something that merely exists. *There* isn't the only word that functions in this place. *Here* is also common (notice the one *here* sentence). When you use this transformation, you can delay the reader's knowledge of the subject. Remember that in this pattern, the subject follows the verb; this is an inversion of the typical English sentence order.

FOR DISCUSSION

In your writer's group, discuss the following There-V-S sentences to prepare for a whole-class discussion to follow. Identify what words function as subjects and verbs. If there are other interesting sentence features, point them out. Remember that when you are sorting out the pattern of a sentence or even first composing a sentence of a certain pattern, **ignore prepositional phrases entirely.** And don't forget to observe how these sentences are punctuated—no punctuation separates a simple verb from its subject. One more thing—the subject and verb still agree, even though the subject follows the verb. If a subject is singular, the verb form is singular. If a subject is plural, the verb form is also plural.

1. There is no end to her patience.
2. Here is the culprit.
3. There was the sheriff.
4. Here goes nothing.
5. There can't be any fun today.
6. There is a boy with a Coke and some Doritos.
7. There is a bug on the saucer.
8. There might be some cheese in the refrigerator.
9. There are clouds to the west of us.
10. Here is your change.
11. There is no cure for Lou Gehrig's disease, or ALS.
12. There might be time for lunch.
13. There was an explosion in the countryside.
14. There has been a big mistake.
15. There are many commercial advertisements on television.
16. Here waits the chariot.
17. There are too many commercials on MTV.
18. There is plenty of information for your report in the library.
19. There is too much screaming on that program.
20. Here is the rescue boat.
21. There is a billion-dollar problem.
22. There are several coupons in my purse.
23. There was a feud between those prominent families.
24. There could be more room in this house.
25. There are extremely low temperatures in the northeast part of the state tonight.

Pattern Odds and Ends

As we end our discussion of sentence patterns, let's consider a few oddities about the language, details that may affect how we view, understand, or analyze a sentence. Let's look specifically at the ideas of the modes of discourse and the imperative mode and nouns of direct address.

The Modes of Discourse are the **declarative mode**, the **interrogative mode**, the **subjunctive mode**, and the **imperative mode.** When we make simple statements or declarations, we declare ideas and we are in the declarative mode: *That power saw makes a lot of noise.* Most English sentences are declarative.

When we ask questions, we use the interrogative mode: *Why does that power saw make so much noise?* You will read more about how we form interrogatives in a subsequent chapter about transformations.

The subjunctive mode expresses something wished for, imagined, or contrary to fact—*If I were queen, there would be more dancing.* Obviously, this statement is contrary to fact because I am not queen, and this expression articulates a wistful desire for things to be other than they are. Notice how the verb changes from the normal *I was* to *I were* when it is preceded by the *If*, which immediately signals that what follows is not factual. This is the traditional (and preferred) way of indicating the subjunctive. The subjunctive mode is, however, falling rapidly out of use, and it is increasingly common to read or hear a sentence like *If I was a rich man, I would throw dollar bills from my high-rise apartment.* If you want to show your grammatical and linguistic *savoir faire*, however, use the subjunctive mode and sound elegant.

The imperative mode is the command mode, used to tell someone to do something or to command:

1. Watch out for that falling piano!
2. Do your homework.
3. Sing beautifully of days of yore.
4. Pay your income tax on or before April 15.
5. Take the first left turn past the Old Soldier monument.

Notice that none of these sentences has a stated subject, but all of them are addressed to someone in the vicinity of the speaker, an anonymous *you*. We understand that *you* is the subject for all these sentences, and we speak of sentences in the imperative mode as having *the understood you* as the subject. So if you see a sentence without an apparent subject, try inserting *you* as the subject—and check to see whether someone is being exhorted to do, be, or say something. Insert the *you* into the sentence so that you can then see the whole pattern.

Another sentence strategy that may seem like an oddity is the *noun of direct address*. You will see this when the speaker or writer is writing or speaking directly to a specific and named audience, as in these sentences:
1. George, you need a new coat.
2. Students in the front row, move back.
3. Parents, do a better job of watching your children.
4. Officers, be safe!

Notice that the person or persons or class of persons being addressed is mentioned first in the sentence and that this noun or name is set off by a comma. When you are determining the pattern of a sentence beginning with a noun of direct address, just ignore the direct address noun as you figure out the sentence pattern:

~~George~~, *you need a new coat* = *you* (S) *need* (V) *coat* (O) or S-V-O

~~Students in the front row~~, *move back* = understood *you* (S) *move* (V) *back* (adv.) or S-V

Parents, do a better job of watching your children = understood *you* (S) *do* (V) *job* (O) or S-V-O

Officers, be safe! = understood *you* (S) *be* (LV) *safe* (PA) or S-LV-PA

The Big Picture: Looking at All the Patterns

Let's summarize now the sentence patterns. Here's a list presenting each pattern and a key example for each pattern:

S-V-O—The United States inculcated democracy in postwar Germany.

S-V-IO-DO—Tom's of Maine gives you a better fluoride toothpaste.

S-V-DO-OC—A prominent politician called the New York prison boom stupid.

S-LV-PN—You are the expert witness for this case.

S-LV-PA—Language is very complex.

S-V—The correctional facility sits near the town.

There-V-S—There goes my baby.

~~~~~~

FOR DISCUSSION

Working with your writers' group, read the sentences that follow and identify the pattern of each. Talk about how the parts of the sentences fit together. Be prepared to discuss your findings with the class as a whole.

1.   Mr. Carlton became my most important mentor in high school.

2. She had better control of her temper tantrums after therapy.
3. I lift my microscope down from the shelf.
4. A huge gap appeared in the fabric of time.
5. In the South, cicadas have a breeding cycle of 13 years.
6. There were spiders in the hot, dusty attic.
7. The wedding party drove idly into the city.
8. The railroad made the Industrial Revolution accomplished fact. —Peter Drucker. From "Beyond the Information Revolution."
9. Read these prospectuses carefully.
10. Holy Cross Monument shone atop a nearby mountain.
11. Memory is sometimes mystical.
12. There is a flaw in her logic.
13. The Church has become more conscious of its role in key events of the century.
14. Dogs can think.
15. Elaine has the face of an angel.
16. The technology committee faces another issue.
17. The collapsed buildings were shoddy.
18. The educational environment was hostile to reform.
19. This is a poignant story.
20. Accidents happen.
21. New Yorkers once elected Guiliani mayor.
22. The desert glistened with water.
23. I shut my eyes tightly.
24. Gary followed the other passengers through the golden arches.
25. Savor the aroma of our fine tea.

You should know that not all grammarians agree that these seven patterns best describe how English happens on the page. Some grammarians describe more patterns; some, fewer. Some use other designators:

for instance N-V-N rather than S-V-O. I have found, though, that the **functional** labels like S-V-O, labels that describe the *function* or *job* of each sentence component, serve the purpose of describing sentences well. And I have also found that these seven patterns are all we need to characterize whatever sentences we may find or create. It is important, though, that you realize that other grammars, other texts, other grammarians may describe or label these ideas in other ways—and that the differences don't mean that some of us are wrong.

Something else to consider is the reiterative nature of these patterns, which occur again and again in different ways. For instance, in future chapters you'll see how the patterns manifest themselves in verbal phrases (such as infinitive, gerund, and participial phrases) and in clauses. In grammar, everything is tied to everything else; thus you'll revisit this idea of patterns (as well as the important notion of clusters, about which you will read in future chapters) throughout this book. If the concepts remain a bit fuzzy now, you'll encounter them again later. If you believe you are seriously confused, though, now is the time to reread the chapter, try the assignments again, and talk to your professor.

What you have been working with so far are simple sentences in the strictly grammatical definition of the word: that is, one independent clause, a complete pattern with a noun cluster and a verb or predicate cluster, fairly unadorned except for prepositional phrases and occasional adjective and adverb cluster or phrasal modifiers. Chapters that come after this will explore how we expand or amplify these patterns by adding other structures and how we combine patterns to create compound and complex sentences, structures to fit and display the complexity of our thinking and the relationships we observe in the world. In short, we'll explore how your rhetorical choices multiply as your understanding of grammatical structures deepens.

Soon, in fact, we will look at ways to expand these patterns—not only with single-word modifiers like adjectives and adverbs but also with verbals and verbal phrases. Coming up: a chapter on form classes and function words—and more about prepositional phrases.

Chapter 2. Noun Clusters, Verb Clusters, Function or Structure Words

English is a binary language with two major players: nouns and verbs. Everything else in the sentence bows to and gathers round nouns and verbs. Certain kinds of words and structures in the adjective family cluster around nouns, and certain kinds of words and structures in the adverb family tend to cluster around verbs. Other kinds of modifying structures called **free modifiers** relate to the idea of the sentence as a whole. Together, noun clusters and verb clusters make up patterns, sentences, paragraphs, and eventually, whole units of discourse and communication. Each kind of cluster, noun and verb, has an important linguistic function. This chapter introduces you to all the form classes and the function words, those ingredients that constitute clusters. For each kind of cluster, we will examine its typical construction and notice how much of the word order of our language is not, as native speakers may think, errant or optional, but rule-governed. Our ears and brains are so accustomed to the structure of noun clusters and verb clusters that we take them for granted—when actually they are very nuanced.

Clusters accumulate into patterns. When you can see the structure of entire noun clusters and verb clusters, you can more easily see the nature of sentence patterns and from there make reasoned decisions about punctuation or additional sentence development.

The **form classes** are the major sentence building blocks. The **function or structure words** are the cement that joins the form class words and makes their relationships clear. First we'll take up the form classes.

Form Classes

The building blocks of syntax or sentence structure are the form classes and structure words. In traditional grammar, both form classes and function words are called the **parts of speech** (and there are traditionally eight parts of speech—noun, verb, adjective, adverb, preposition, conjunction, pronoun, interjection). For several decades now, grammarians have understood that the traditional parts of speech are not, however, quite sufficient to describe what goes on in an English sentence, so this book adapts the original labels and terms used in school grammar and introduces some new grammatical terms so that we can describe sentences more completely and specifically. *Instead of talking about the parts of speech, then, we will speak of form classes and structure words or function words.*

Form classes and structure words are two very different kinds of word classes, two different kinds of sentence building material: bricks and mortar. The bricks—the form classes—give the structured sentence its essential character—its tone, shape, color, and primary meaning. The mortar—the structure words—pattern with the form class words to show the relationships among the form class words and to hold the ideas in place. Of course, structure words also carry meaning, and that fact makes the English language challenging as well as infuriatingly precise. In this chapter, we'll look first at the two form classes that comprise noun clusters—*nouns and adjectives*—and see what other kinds of words congregate to form noun clusters. Then we will continue our look at the form classes of *verbs* and the often accompanying *adverb* family. Finally, we will review structure words.

Nouns and Noun-ness, Nominals and Naming

Nouns name. Naming the world is the purpose of nouns. In traditional grammar you may have heard words like *nominal* and *nominative*—words that have as a root the Latin *nominalis*, meaning *name*. Nouns are naming words, words that designate objects, people, places, feelings, phenomena, theories. How do we understand the quality of being a noun—or nounness? How do we recognize nouns? There are several ways that we identify nouns, besides simply memorizing them.

Position of Nouns in the Sentence. One major way that we recognize any word is by its position in a sentence. Nouns regularly occur at certain places in a pattern:

- before a verb (as the subject of a sentence, *My **cat** meows noisily*);

- after a verb (as the direct object or predicate noun, *My turtle eats **lettuce***), answering the question "What?" or "Whom?" raised by a verb;

- after a preposition (as the object of the preposition), as in *at **school*** or *in my **sandwich***;

- after a determiner such as *a, an, the, first*, as in *a **kitten**, an **orange**, first **try***.

Look at the positions of the boldface words in these sentences from John McPhee's *Heirs of General Practice*:

1. "**Nellie Burns** has a fast-growing **tumor** in her **stomach**."
2. "The **Conklings** now live in a **cabin** up a **trail** in a **forest** far from **town**."
3. "A **woman** takes her **husband** to an **internist** because he's been having **pain** in his **chest**."

4. "Duodenal **ulcer,** for example, is not a surgical **problem** unless you bleed, perforate, obstruct."

Many of these nouns occur at the very beginning of sentences (*ulcer, woman, Conklings, Nellie Burns*) in the subject position. Other nouns come after verbs and seem to complete them (*tumor, husband, problem*)—in the complement or completer position as direct objects, indirect objects, predicate nouns. These terms that describe how nouns function will be explored in a later chapter; you have probably heard them, however, before. Try to hold any questions or confusion about these terms in your mind for now and focus on just the nouns themselves. Some nouns follow prepositions to create prepositional phrases—*in his chest, from town.* Still others tend to come close on the heels of **determiners,** what we used to call articles or article adjectives—*a problem, **her** husband, **an** internist, a cabin, a tumor, a trail.* Our ears and brains are accustomed to these patterns or structures in sentences. We look for nouns in certain places within patterns, particularly in the subject position, the complement position, and the object-of-the-preposition position.

Nouns' Plural Potential. Many nouns name specific, countable things and as such may have **number**; that is, they may refer to one item or to more than one item. If a noun refers to more than one specific item, it is plural and ends in *-s* or *-es,* for the most part. Some words (like *deer, woman*) have irregular plurals. In the McPhee sentences, we see the already plural noun *Conklings.* And we see other words that could be made plural: *tumor, stomach, cabin, trail, woman, husband, internist, pain, chest, ulcer, problem.* This is a class of nouns called **count nouns**. Not all nouns can be made plural, you understand, but the possibility of plurality is one feature of many nouns.

Proper Nouns and Capital Letters. You'll also note that some nouns, names of specific families or countries or places (*Conklings*), begin with capital letters; these are **proper nouns**, nouns that refer to the name of a very specific or particular person, place, organization, or thing. But be careful! Not all capitalized words are proper nouns; some aren't even nouns.

Nouns and the Possessive Possibility. Many other nouns, specifically those referring to people, may have a **possessive** form (this is also called **possessive case**): my *sister's* coat, *Janet's* new briefcase. The possessive case, indicated by an apostrophe plus an *s*, doesn't always have to mean possession of a material object; it can simply describe—as in *a day's wages for a day's work.* In speech, possessive nouns sound just like plural nouns because they both have the *s* marker or *s* sound, but you can distinguish between them when you write. Just keep the notion of singular and plural distinct from the idea of possessive. That is, to make a singular noun possessive, add an apostrophe plus *s*. If the singular noun already ends in *s*, you may still add apostrophe *s*.

To make a plural noun possessive, add an apostrophe after the final *s* at the end of the word. If the plural form does not end in *s*, add apostrophe plus *s* (as in *children's* toys or *men's* clothing). Consider, for instance, the plurals and possessive forms of *boy:*

Singular noun—*boy*—(the unadorned, singular noun)

Singular possessive—*boy's*—(singular noun plus apostrophe and *s*)

Plural noun—*boys*—(singular noun plus *s*)

Plural possessive—*boys'*—(plural noun already ending in *s*, plus apostrophe)

Just plain singular nouns and just plain plurals don't require apostrophes. A common error in commercial signs is the unnecessary apostrophe: *Get your doughnut's here!* reads (incorrectly) a sign in a local doughnut shop.

Now take a look at the plural and possessive forms of the proper noun *Ross,* whose singular form ends in *s*:

Singular noun—*Ross*

Singular possessive—*Ross's* new boots

Plural noun—the *Rosses* (a whole family of people with the *Ross* surname!)

Plural possessive—the *Rosses'* summer home

Now put your understanding of possessives to work by filling in the chart that follows. This work will give you practice in using possessives correctly.

~~~~~~

WORK WITH POSSESSIVES

Study the first few rows in the Practicing Possessives chart, then fill in the empty slots by determining the pattern of plurals and possessives.

Practicing Possessives

Singular	Singular Possessive	Plural	Plural Possessive
boy	boy's	boys	boys'
family	family's	families	families'
student	student's	students	students'
evening	evening's	evenings	
dog		dogs	dogs'
	mouse's		
house		houses	
bus			
			moments'
deer		deer	

Singular	Singular Possessive	Plural	Plural Possessive
			friends'
	ass's		
wife			
		flowers	
			barkeepers'
cat	cats		

Being able to differentiate plural from possessive is key to choosing the appropriate form in writing, particularly when you are revising a piece. Remember that if the word you wish to make possessive is singular, simply add an apostrophe plus an s. If the word is already plural, add the apostrophe only if the word already ends in s. If it does not end in s, add apostrophe plus s.

FOR WRITING

Choose one row from the chart above and write four sentences, one using each form of the noun correctly. Be sure to include enough contextual clues in your sentences to make the nouns make sense.

Noun Suffixes. Another way that we identify nouns, perhaps even subconsciously, is by certain suffixes that typically mark nouns:

- *-er*, meaning *one who does a certain action* or *one who represents a certain quality*. Added to a verb base form, -er produces *teacher* (teach plus *-er*), *writer, dancer, lamplighter, joker, lover, fighter*. The **base form** is the verb form without any endings; the base form is the same as the present tense form for all verbs except *be*. A variation of this *-er* suffix is the *-or* suffix: *favor, rumor, advisor*. Be careful: not every word ending in *-er* or *-or* is a noun:

think of *slower*, for instance, or *freer*, which are not nouns; they do not name anything.

- *-ness*, meaning *state, quality, condition,* or *degree of being.* Added to an adjective, *-ness* produces *happiness, greediness, emptiness, wariness, loveliness.*

- *-ity*, meaning *state* or *quality of being*, as in *probity, rarity, charity, alacrity*

- *-cy*, also meaning *state, condition,* or *quality* as in *bankruptcy, lunacy, idiocy, truancy, fluency*

- *-dom*, meaning *state, condition, domain,* or *a particular office or position*, as in *kingdom, freedom, boredom*

- *-ment*, designating an *action or process* or *the result of an action or process*, as in *excitement, embarrassment, judgment, accomplishment, embezzlement*

- *-tion*, meaning *a state, quality,* or *condition*, as in *abbreviation, accumulation, action, direction*

- *-ure*, meaning *act, process,* or *function*, as in *departure, aperture, closure, fissure, rupture*

Test Sentence for Nouns. In *Understanding English*, linguist and grammarian Paul Roberts identified test sentences for all form classes. Once you think you have identified a noun, you can try it in Roberts' noun test sentence:

I lost my _____.

Almost every noun you can think of, concrete or abstract, count or non-count, will fit into this sentence:

I lost my <u>money.</u>

I lost my <u>joy.</u>

I lost my <u>happiness.</u>

I lost my <u>books.</u>

I lost my <u>card.</u>

I lost my <u>purse.</u>

I lost my <u>enthusiasm.</u>

I lost my <u>love.</u>

I lost my <u>England</u>. (Only metaphorically!)

I lost my <u>Smith</u> (maybe at the family reunion where there are several Smiths!).

Adjectives: The Form Class and the Noun Cluster

Nouns are rarely solitary. They tend to occur in clusters, with specific kinds of words clustered or gathered around them. **Adjectives** and **determiners** specifically hang around nouns to create noun clusters. A **noun cluster** is a noun plus any modifiers or words that pattern with the noun or relate to it in some way, words that enhance or restrict or define or amplify the meaning of the noun. A noun cluster may be as small as two words: *the essence.*

Within a noun cluster, the most common and important of the modifying words is the **adjective**, a form class most closely related to nouns and most likely to occur in a noun cluster. The function of adjectives is to describe and to limit, to tell us more about the noun in question. There are several ways you can identify adjectives:

Position of Adjectives in the Sentence. Most adjectives in English occur very near to nouns, typically (but not always) *before* nouns: the *yellow* dress, her *dirty* hair, a *fresh* flower, a *weary* soldier, a *friendly* smile. Another position where you'll often find adjectives is following a *be* verb (*am, is, are, was, were, be, being, been*) or other verbs that function as **linking verbs** as part of an **S-LV-PA pattern**. Linking verbs link or join the **subject** and a sentence completer or **complement**. Look for the adjectives following the linking verbs in these sentences and notice how the adjectives actually describe or refer to the subject:

1. The child is young. Child = young.
2. A dog is rabid. Dog = rabid.
3. We will be late. We = late.
4. The food was fresh. Food = fresh.
5. Our fire will be hot. Fire = hot.
6. The journey seems long. Journey = long.
7. Fred's voice sounded raspy. Voice = raspy.
8. The lawyers have been dilatory in pursuing the case. Lawyers = dilatory.

So we can predictably find adjectives in two positions, pre-noun (before the noun) or post-linking verb (after a linking verb). Sometimes, however, adjectives surprise us and move to a position right after nouns. In such cases, adjectives occurring in such unfamiliar sentence positions attract extra attention from readers and listeners alike because they are more rhetorically **emphatic**. When this is the case, the adjectives are frequently paired:

The road, **hot** *and* **dusty** *beneath our feet, stretched far into the horizon.*

We ate the peaches, **succulent** *and* **warm***, as quickly as we could.*

The rhetorical effect of paired adjectives after the noun is two-fold: the adjectives slow down the sentence, creating a sentence-interrupting phrase; and they lend emphasis to the noun as the recipient of the attention from the set-off words. These adjectives also draw extra attention because they are not in their usual place in the sentence. So if you want to be sure that your readers attend to a particular noun, an idea or thing or phenomenon, use a pair of adjectives following it to draw more attention to it.

Adjectives and the Potential of Degree. In addition to its position in a sentence, an adjective can be identified by its ability to express degree or intensity. For instance, we can say "I am *rich*; but John is *richer*; and Frances is *richest* of us all." When you compare two items, use the *-er* degree or **comparative** form or the word *more* (with most words of more than three syllables). When you compare more than two items, use the *-est* degree or **superlative** form of the adjective or the word *most* (also with most words of more than three syllables). Sometimes we use *more* and *most* with the basic form of the adjective simply because the sound is more euphonious or pleasing. Look at these series of adjectives for examples of varying degrees of adjectives:

afraid, more afraid, most afraid

cheap, cheaper, cheapest

friendly, friendlier, friendliest

late, later, latest

lonely, lonelier, loneliest

maudlin, more maudlin, most maudlin

sanitary, more sanitary, most sanitary

tall, taller, tallest

ugly, uglier, ugliest

weary, wearier, weariest

Adjective Suffixes. Like nouns, some adjectives have characteristic endings. We just looked at the adjectival suffixes that signal degree, *-er* and *-est*. Other suffixes typical of adjectives are in the list below. All of them add the meaning of "the quality of being" or "full of" or "characteristic of" or "concerning" to the base word.

-ly, as in *lovely, lonely, friendly*

-y, as in *blurry, teary, mopey, dirty, flirty*

-able, as in *comfortable, lovable, huggable*

-ful as in *playful, sorrowful, mournful*

-ish as in *bookish, waspish, greenish*

-ous as in *dangerous, virtuous, bounteous*

-ic as in *scientific, horrific, beatific*

-less as in *friendless, useless, worthless*

Test Sentence for Adjectives. We can also identify adjectives with a test sentence. To test whether a word is an adjective, try putting it in another of Roberts' test sentences. Here is his test sentence for adjectives:

A(n) _____ something is something that is _____.

An *old* something is something that is *old;* a *sanitary* something is something that is *sanitary;* a *red* something is something that is *red;* a *tall* something is something that is *tall.* Try a noun in the slot: a <u>chair</u>

something is something that is <u>chair</u>—it doesn't make sense. Try a verb: A <u>run</u> something is something that is <u>run</u>. This option doesn't make sense either. But some forms of verbs, the ones called **participles**, the ones that end in *-ed, -en,* or *-ing, can* function or act as adjectives to pattern with nouns: A *running* something is something that is *running*. In most cases where participles pattern before nouns, the difference between the participle and an adjective that would occur in the same position is not clear—and is simply not significant. If it does the job of an adjective and fits in the test pattern, call it an adjective. This is one of the principles of structural grammar. Although items can often be identified by form (their physical shapes) as well as by their functions (what they do or how they act) and although both form and function matter in ascertaining form class, *function is more important than form in understanding and labeling words.*

Other Parts of the Noun Cluster: Determiners

Determiners are structure words that also signal nouns and are vital parts of the noun cluster. (You can also read about them in the later section in the discussion of structure words.) Determiners help to *determine* or *specify* nouns. Some determiners are these:

a, an, the (called *articles* in traditional grammar)

her, his, my, our, their (*personal possessive pronouns* in traditional grammar)

this, that, these, those (*demonstrative pronouns* in traditional grammar)

some, any, many, few, most, least (quantitative words)

Any time you see a determiner, look for a noun soon to follow.

Other Parts of the Noun Cluster: Noun Adjuncts

In noun clusters, sometimes nouns pattern alongside other nouns: *the computer lab, a time machine, a dust cloth, a bicycle rack, a test case, a hat rack, skin diseases, bush pilots.* In these phrases, words ordinarily considered nouns (like *computer*) pattern with other nouns (like *lab*) to restrict and define the original nouns. The first noun in each pair functions adjectivally, even though it doesn't quite fulfill the criteria for a true adjective: it's a noun masquerading as an adjective, a **hybrid grammatical structure**, part noun and part adjective. We call these modifying nouns **noun adjuncts**, nouns functioning as adjunct to other nouns (or alongside them in a supporting role). These noun adjuncts function only *before* the noun, not in post-noun or post-verb positions as complements. For instance, we can say *The patient has a* **skin** *disease* but not *The patient has a disease* **skin** or *The disease is* **skin.** Incidentally, many noun adjuncts eventually end up as compound words: *fireplace, lamppost, thumbnail, bonfire* (originally *bone + fire*).

~~~~~~

FOR DISCUSSION—RECOGNIZING NOUN ADJUNCTS

In your writers' group, discuss the following sentences, all of which contain a variety of adjectives, determiners, possesive nouns, and noun adjuncts in their noun clusters. Be ready to explain the components of the noun clusters to the class as a whole.

1. Jerry's wild swing broke the flower vase.
2. Our small investment group bought mostly tech stocks.
3. The computer center has three green walls.
4. Aunt Bea gave Opie her mother's antique china cabinet.
5. Janet's small clothes closet is stuffed with long coats.

FOR WRITING—NOUN CLUSTERS WITH NOUN ADJUNCTS AND DETERMINERS

Create a noun cluster by adding a determiner plus an adjective and a noun adjunct or perhaps a possessive noun to each of the following nouns. In some clusters, try a pair of post-noun adjectives. A few examples are done for you.

1. case = a Sony camera case, worn and dirty
2. agent = Jane's rich insurance agent
3. worker = three Pittsburgh iron workers
4. markers =
5. zone =
6. friend =
7. teeth =
8. inspector =
9. quality =
10. babies =

Other Parts of the Noun Cluster: Prepositional Phrases

Another common component of the noun cluster is the prepositional phrase. A prepositional phrase is built of a preposition and its object, a noun, and any words that may cluster around the noun object. If the noun object has modifiers or is part of a noun cluster, all the modifiers in the cluster are *constituent*—that is, the modifiers and the noun object *constitute* part of the prepositional phrase and are thus considered part of the prepositional phrase. When prepositional phrases occur in noun clusters, they serve nouns. This is called *patterning with* or *modifying* the noun. It is possible to have prepositional phrases within prepositional phrases within prepositional phrases—and noun clusters within noun clusters within noun clusters.

There are many prepositions in English, and they are important in the scheme of the sentence, for they express relationships between words and ideas. Often these relationships are spatial (as signaled by *near*, *over*, *around*). Some common prepositions are

above

around

at

below

beneath

beside

between

by

down

during

for

from

in

near

of

on

through

to

toward

with

within

without

In English, we also have **phrasal prepositions**, several prepositions patterning together with a noun to create a prepositional phrase. Some phrasal prepositions are

according to

ahead of

along with

because of

but for

by means of

except for

in case of

in front of

in spite of

instead of

next to

on behalf of

out of

thanks to

Each phrasal preposition functions or acts just like a single-word preposition and, when patterned with a noun or noun cluster, creates a prepositional phrase: *in spite of my friend's best efforts, according to the rules of the game, instead of vegetable lasagna.* It is important to understand that several words can—and frequently do—function as a unit in English. Remember to look for phrasal prepositions when you are analyzing sentences and remember to use them to show particular relationships within the sentence.

A Word about Word Order in Noun Clusters

Word order is important in English, particularly in noun clusters where the kinds of modifiers appear in a fixed word order that native English speakers have internalized. Consider the scrambled items below, for instance, and arrange them into a noun cluster that makes sense:

stack, fifteen, of, stories, dense, horse-choking, long, a

You've probably come up with *a stack of fifteen long, dense, horse-choking stories,* a noun cluster that includes another noun cluster as object of the preposition *of.* What generalizations can you make about the order of determiners, nouns, adjectives, and prepositional phrases?

EXERCISE WITH NOUN CLUSTERS

Try arranging these groups of words into noun clusters:

- first-term, the, failures, biggest, administration's, diplomatic

- squares, collars, silver, the, their, on

- of, coffee, a, cup, large, black

- enchanting, a, blonde, girl, with, hair

The noun cluster is typically ordered this way: determiner, intensifier (optional, depending on adjective), true adjective (may be more than one), compound adjective, proper adjective, noun adjunct, prepositional phrase or *a very large, wooden-looking Acme chicken coop with no chickens.*

~~~~~~

FOR DISCUSSION—MORE PREPOSITIONAL PHRASES

For each noun cluster below, discuss in your writer's group how the prepositional phrase functions or operates. Consider how the prepositional phrase changes or enriches or restricts or develops the idea presented by the noun headword. Some of the phrases have phrases within them. Make note of determiners, adjectives, possessive nouns, and noun adjuncts in the noun clusters in your discussion as well—and be prepared to present some of your discussion to the class as a whole.

1. . . . an ordinary inspector **in a paper bag factory**
2. . . . a dirty plastic bottle **of about two hundred plain white pills**
3. . . . something **about the whole village**
4. . . . a shrill sound **of pain**

5. ...a fatal accident in **the gravel quarry**
6. ...some nasty rumors **about deaths from sickness**
7. ...the greenhouse effect **of pollution**
8. ...a report **from the commodities market**
9. ...the soft sound **of waves on the shore**
10. ...a wad **of cotton**
11. ...a quart **of light beer**
12. ...a new battery **in the radio**
13. ...the carpets **of the sitting room**
14. ...an electrified fence **inside the electrified fence around the perimeter**
15. ...the light **over the shaving mirror**

For Writing—Finding Noun Headwords

Look at the following simple noun clusters and see if you can, first, point out the noun headword or word that all the other words tend to cluster or gather around; and second, identify the other kinds of words that make up each cluster:

1. the delta of a small stream
2. a shiny, fast automobile
3. the unusual rate change
4. the small, sleepy female bear
5. some yellow, curling sycamore leaves
6. those boring chords
7. the famous Henry James
8. literary embarrassment
9. a bad mustache with sprinkles of gray hair
10. four towns within missile range

Summing Up: Noun Clusters

Nouns and noun clusters most likely constitute our first contact with language. For babies learning to talk and navigate their environments, naming the world about them is the first step to becoming a being with oral or spoken language. Thus nouns are usually the first words uttered: *mama, dog, dada, milk, bug.* Nouns are indeed a large part of our vocabularies; they are essential for communication, for they name what we are talking, thinking, and dreaming about. But nouns and noun clusters are only half of written and oral expression; verbs are the other half. Now let's consider verbs and verb clusters, and then later we will take up the structure words that help hold sentences together.

Verbs: The Heart of the Sentence

Verbs are the other major building block of English syntax or sentence structure, the other half of the noun/verb binary. Together, nouns and verbs constitute most of the content or meaning in a sentence. Nouns are naming words, essentially static words expressing *what.* Verbs, however, are rooted in a concept of time; they express the *how*, frequently through action or the description or reflection or trace of action—action that may be physical, psychological, emotional, or social. Think of these verbs: *do, working, be, grabbed, remain, fretted, arguing, sign, will meditate.* Some of them (like *working*) evoke a physical action; others, a mental one (*meditate*, for example). But all imply that something is happening, occurring, in some variable state of energy. **In short, verbs animate nouns.** Verbs move ideas. Verbs make sentences go. Verbs differ greatly from nouns; verbs complement or complete nouns. Together these two binaries within the English sentence create complete ideas and utterances.

How can you identify verbs? In many of the same ways that you can identify nouns: by their positions in sentences, by their suffixes, and by their making sense in a test sentence. But verbs also differ from nouns in an important way—their ability to have tense. Let's begin our work with verbs here, with tense.

Verbs' Ability to Have Tense. One way to identify a verb is to realize that it can express an element of time. All English verbs can express both present and past time. Past time is expressed in **past tense**. We articulate past tense by adding a suffix to the base verb or making an internal change to the base verb. What is the **base verb**? The base looks like the present tense, singular, form of the verb: *add, work, listen, imagine*. Sometimes you may see the base verb referred to as the **verb stem** or the **infinitive.** Many verbs form past tense simply by adding an *-ed* to the **base** of the verb: *added (add + -ed), worked (work + -ed), listened (listen + -ed), imagined (imagine + -ed)*. On the other hand, many verbs form past tense by adding *-t* or other endings or by vowel changes inside the word: *teach-taught; buy-bought; see-saw; go-went; do-did*; and so on. Regardless of how past tense is formed, the fact that it *can* be formed means that the word in question is a verb. To test whether a word is a verb, then, see if you can make it past tense.

Another identifying characteristic of verbs is the fact that they have principal parts or main forms or versions with which to form various tenses. You may remember in elementary school rehearsing the **principal parts of verbs**. Some of the principal verb parts combine with auxiliaries or helping words to form what we call verb tenses—and to articulate the **modes** and **aspects** of the verb. The principal parts include (1) the base or infinitive or present tense form, (2) the past tense form (usually signaled by *-ed*), (3) the past participle form (usually ends with *-ed, -en, -n,* or *-t*), and the (4) present participle form (ends always in *-ing*). Often, in regular verbs (those that form their past tense by adding *–ed*), the past tense form (2) and the past participle form (3) are identical. It may be useful to recall some principal parts of verbs by working through the next writing task. Here are the principal parts of the verb *choose:*

Base form—*choose,* as in *I choose my clothes carefully each morning.*

Past tense form—*chose,* as in *Jack chose a blue shirt for the party.*

Past participle—*chosen,* as in *The team has chosen to kneel.*

Present participle—*choosing,* as in *Annie is choosing her wedding gown now.*

Note that both participial forms of the verb require an auxiliary verb; we don't say *The team chosen to kneel* or *Annie choosing her wedding gown now.*

FOR WRITING—PRINCIPAL PARTS OF VERBS

Fill in the chart Principal Parts of Verbs below with the missing principal part of the verb. If you can't recall some of the forms of these verbs, you can look them up in a dictionary under the verb in question. The first few are completed as examples.

Principal Parts of Verbs

	Simple Present 1st Person	Past Tense	Past Participle	Present Participle
1	(I) look	(I) looked	(I) have looked	(I) am looking
2	run	ran	run	running
3	emphasize	emphasized	emphasized	emphasizing
4	drive		driven	
5				sneaking
6	treat	treated		
7	go		gone	
8				roasting
9	dive			
10		lay	lain	lying
11	lay		laid	laying
12	wear	wore	worn	
13		loved		
14	grade			grading

	Singular Possessive	Plural	Plural Possessive	
15	abjure			
16		had		
17			believed	
18				frying
19	open		opened	
20				agitating
21		devised		
22				munching
23	do			
24			chosen	
25				snoring

Verbs and Agreement

English verbs and their subjects have very close, even symbiotic, relationships. Thus, a verb must reflect (or match or *agree with*) the person of its subject. This means that the form of a verb may change if your discourse changes from first-person (*I, we*) to second-person (*you*) or to third-person (*he, she, it, they, the teacher, Sam*). To clarify: **first person** refers to the person speaking or doing the acting: *I* or *we*. **Second person** refers to a person being addressed or spoken to: *you*. **Third person** refers to a person spoken of or talked about, as if the person were not present: *he, she, it, miners, Tom Swift, Barack Obama, lambs, my piano teacher* (more about this later with conjugations).

A verb must also reflect or agree with the number of its subject. **Number** refers to how many people or items are embodied in the subject—but English distinguishes only two levels of number: one and more than one—or singular and plural. Thus we learn from childhood to say *Doug Flutie was* (not *Doug Flutie were*) and *The birds fly* (not *The birds flies*). English verbs change as their subjects change: if a subject is singular, the verb must reflect that singularity or *agree* with the number of its subject.

Verbs and Mode

English verbs also have several other ways of presenting themselves. Grammarians say that verbs have, for instance, **mode** (also called **mood**): **indicative**, **imperative**, **interrogative** and **subjunctive** (also called **conditional**). Don't let the language of these terms distract you.

Indicative is the mood of the simple statement. You might think of its association with *indicate* (meaning *to point out*); verbs in the indicative mode simply point to some phenomenon, stating ideas or facts or presenting information. This is the usual (and most common) verb mode.

A second mode is the *imperative* or command mode. Here you can just remember an *imperious* person telling or commanding someone else what to do: *Take out the trash! Revise that poem!* Imperative mode verbs give orders. Notice that the subject is typically omitted or ellipted and is usually the understood *you*.

The *interrogative* mode is simply the mode of asking questions. In interrogative utterances the verbs move around and swap places with the subject; auxiliary verbs also play a part. You will read considerably more about the interrogative mode in the next chapter when you study the question transformation. Examples of the interrogative mode are *Do you want cream with your coffee? Are you hungry?* or simply a phrase or utterance with a question mark, pronounced with rising intonation— *Going to class this morning?*

The *subjunctive* mode is the least used and the least known. Geoffrey Pullum, Professor of Linguistics at the University of Edinburgh in Scotland, defines English subjunctive clauses as "finite yet tenseless clauses with their verb in plain form." *Plain form* means the present tense form of the main verb, also known as the infinitive. Pullum points out that the way that the subjunctive appears most commonly in contemporary English is as a **mandative subjunctive**, that is one that accompanies a verb or adjectives indicating some necessity, demand, or mandate. Examples are "It's vital that he be more punctual" and "Jill insists that Jack wear shoes." Notice in both examples the plain, infinitive form of *be* instead of the declarative form *is*. Also notice the nature of the sentence; there is *necessity* (*it is vital*) and *demand* (*Jill insists*).

The subjunctive mode also chiefly expresses ideas contrary to fact, ideas in the realm of the imagined, ideas articulating something wishful or anticipatory: *If I were you, I'd cut my hair* or *Were this my boat, I would get a bigger motor.* Pay attention to the *If I were* structure: *be* has an important role in the subjunctive mode.

In general, people make less of a fuss about the subjunctive mode than they used to, and as fewer educated people know about and understand the subjunctive, fewer people use it still. Indeed, so esteemed a publication as the *New York Times* has all but abandoned the subjunctive: witness this sentence in an article by Jacob S. Hacker and Paul Pierson appearing in the April 3, 2016 issue: "If it [a Republican defeat] **was** catastrophic enough, it could lead to changes in party strategy." So you will indeed hear educated people say *If I **was** that lottery winner, I'd invest in Microsoft* or *Jill insists that Jack wears shoes.* It's good to know the difference, though, and you may find situations where using the subjunctive is the perfect and appropriate grammatical choice.

Verbs and Aspect

You should also know that verbs have still another quality called aspect: **aspect** refers simply to whether the action of the verb is completed or ongoing. You'll read more about this when you work with perfect and progressive aspects, which are often also called perfect and progressive tenses. The perfect aspect is created with a form of *have* plus the past participle of the verb (*have shopped, had done, will have written*); the

progressive aspect is created with a form of *be* plus the present participle of the verb (*is shopping, had been shopping, will have been shopping*).
When you package all this information about person, number, mood,
aspect, and tense, you have a verb conjugation. When you chart out
these forms of a verb, you *conjugate* that verb. Let's put all these elements of verbs into a rubric, then, and look at some **conjugations**.

Conjugation of Verbs

Here is an active voice, indicative mood conjugation of the regular verb
open, with all the simple tenses laid out for you to see.

Conjugation of *Open*, Simple Tenses

Singular	Plural
Present Tense	
I open	We open
You open	You open
She opens*	They open

*The third person singular form of the verb always ends in *-s* in English.

Past Tense	
I opened	We opened
You opened	You opened
He opened	They opened

This regular verb forms its past tense by adding *-ed.*

Future Tense

I shall open	We shall open
You will open	You will open
She will open	They will open

Historically, *shall* has been used with 1st person future tenses; *will*, with 2nd and 3rd persons—but rarely these days. Here its usage reflects the history of the structure.

Conjugation of *Open*, Perfect Tenses

Perfect tenses (also *aspects*, you'll remember) are formed with the appropriate tense of **have** plus the past participle (ends in *-ed, -en,* or *-n*) of the verb being conjugated. In this case, the past participle is *opened.* The *perfect aspect* of the verb shows that the action of the verb was ongoing but is now completed. Don't forget that *aspect* simply refers to whether the verb's action is completed or ongoing.

Present Perfect

I have opened*	We have opened
You have opened	You have opened
He has opened	They have opened

*Note the *-ed* form of the verb or the past participle, paired with the present tense of *have.* The present perfect describes an action, here the act of *opening* that has taken place repeatedly in the past and continues into the present—*He **has opened** that cellar door every day for the last twenty years.*

Past Perfect

I had opened	We had opened
You had opened	You had opened
She had opened	They had opened

Derive the past perfect of *open* by pairing the past tense of *have* with the past participle of *open*. Past perfect refers to an action that was begun and completed in the past: *The children had opened their presents by one o'clock.*

Future Perfect

I shall have opened	We shall have opened
You will have opened	You will have opened
He will have opened	They will have opened

To form the future perfect tense of *open*, use the future tense of *have* plus the part participle of *open, opened*. The future perfect refers to a future time when something will be completed: *By the time the next watchman makes a round, the thief will have opened the vault.*

Conjugation of *Open*, Progressive Tenses

Progressive tenses are formed with the appropriate tense of *be* plus the present participle (ends in *-ing*) of the verb being conjugated—in this case, *opening*. Progressive tenses, which illustrate the *progressive aspect* of the verb, indicate an ongoing or continuing action.

Present Progressive

I am opening	We are opening
You are opening	You are opening
She is opening	They are opening

Present progressive is formed with the present tense of *be* (*am*) plus the present participle (ending in *-ing*). Present progressive describes an event in progress at the current time: *We are opening the garage door right now.*

Past Progressive

I was opening	We were opening
You were opening	You were opening
He was opening	They were opening

Past progressive refers to what was happening at a given point in the past: *When the alarm went off, he was opening the vault.* Use the past tense of *be* (*was*) with the present participle.

Future Progressive

I shall be opening	We shall be opening
You will be opening	You will be opening
She will be opening	They will be opening

Future progressive describes what will be going on at a given point in the future: *On this day next year, we will be opening our new restaurant in Nashville.* Form future progressive by combining the future tense of *be* (*will be*) plus the present participle, *opening.*

Present Perfect Progressive

I have been opening	We have been opening
You have been opening	You have been opening
Thomas has been opening	They have been opening

Present Perfect Progressive describes an ongoing action begun in the past and continuing into the future: *You have been opening that package for ten minutes.* Present perfect tense of *have* plus the present participle of *open, opening,* yields the perfect progressive.

Past Perfect Progressive

I had been opening	We had been opening
You had been opening	You had been opening
Francie had been opening	The children had been opening

Past Perfect Progressive refers to an action entirely in the past; the action was at one time ongoing but then at one point stopped: *The children had been opening their holiday gifts before the bomb exploded.* Note the past perfect tense of *have* plus the present participle.

Future Perfect Progressive

I shall have been opening	We shall have been opening
You will have been opening	You will have been opening
She will have been opening	They will have been opening

The Future Perfect Progressive refers to an action begun some time in the past and enduring to a definite point in the future: *By tomorrow morning, the coroner's deputies will have been opening graves for 24 hours.* Combine the future perfect tense of *be* plus the present participle of *open.*

Besides this conjugation in active voice, you can also make a conjugation to illustrate subjunctive or conditional mood (used to express an action that is contrary to fact, imagined, or hypothetical). You can also create a conjugation in passive voice (more about passive voice later). For now, though, here's a conjugation of *tell* in active voice with all the basic tenses, all in one chart without explanatory notes.

Conjugation of *Tell*, Active Voice

Tense	Singular forms	Plural Forms
Simple Present Tense	I tell You tell James tells	We tell You tell They tell
Simple Past Tense	I told You told Eleanor told	We told You told All the boys told
Simple Future Tense	I shall tell You will tell My sister will tell	We shall tell You will tell They will tell
Present Perfect	I have told You have told She has told	We have told You have told They have told
Past Perfect	I had told You had told Sean had told	We had told You had told The whole class had told
Future Perfect	I shall have told You will have told The punk will have told	We shall have told You will have told They will have told

Present Progressive	I am telling You are telling Sue is telling	We are telling You are telling The children are telling
Past Progressive	I was telling You were telling The general was telling	We were telling You were telling They were telling
Future Progressive	I shall be telling You will be telling Francine will be telling	You shall be telling You will be telling All of them will be telling
Present Perfect Progressive	I have been telling You have been telling The comedian has been telling	We have been telling You have been telling Our teachers have been telling
Past Perfect Progressive	I had been telling You had been telling He had been telling	We had been telling You had been telling They had been telling

Future Perfect Progressive	I shall have been telling You will have been telling The first-grader will have been telling	We shall have been telling You will have been telling All the children will have been telling

FOR WRITING—CONJUGATING VERBS

Conjugate three of these verbs through all the simple, perfect, and progressive tenses in indicative mood: *catch, comfort, continue, care, come, count, cause, confuse.* Then choose one of the verbs and write a sentence using one example of each tense appropriately.

Remember that not all grammarians think about verbs in the same way or describe verbs with similar language. Most grammarians consider that English actually has only two tenses, present and past, and that what we have in a conjugation and sometimes call a variety of tenses are actually variations in mood and aspect of the verb.

Verbs' Position in the Sentence. Verbs and verb clusters pair with and follow nouns in sentences. A typical English sentence (but don't forget: many sentences are not typical) begins with a noun cluster, which is then followed by a verb cluster; this is the case in the following sentences, where verb clusters (underlined) follow the noun subjects.

1. The coyotes **are howling.**
2. The western Oklahoma sky **seems vast and endless.**
3. Frederick **sighed loudly.**
4. Two dogs **slept in the stream of sunlight.**

In other kinds of sentences, verbs or verb clusters occupy a middle slot between two nouns or noun clusters and express a relationship between the nouns:

1. Janet **put** a log on the fire.
2. Nathan **answered** the phone.
3. The electrician **will clip** the wires.
4. These teachers always **grade** many examinations.

Verb Suffixes. Another way to recognize verbs is by their characteristic suffixes. A few endings besides the *-ed, -en,* and *-ing* tense endings may affix themselves to verbs: *-ify,* as in *typify; -en,* as in *whiten* or *lighten; -ate,* as in *agitate;* and *-ize,* as in *womanize* and *legalize.* In fact, many nouns and adjectives are transformed into verbs in just this way. Add *-ize* to the noun *computer,* for instance, and you get *computerize: The consulting firm can computerize all the records for you.* Some language purists do not like these new word formations or **neologisms** (*neo* = new and *logos*= word). Most linguists recognize, however, that languages change and adapt to fit the needs of native speakers to express themselves; linguists understand these new words and changes in word forms as natural and healthy in the life of a language.

Test Pattern for Verbs. Another way you can test a word to determine its *verbness* is to see if you can fit it into one of these test patterns for verbs by Paul Roberts:

Let's _____. (or) Let's _____ it. (Let's <u>eat</u>. Let's <u>finish</u> it.)

He might _____. (or) He might _____ it. (He might <u>succeed</u>. He might <u>forget</u> it.)

The Phrasal Verb. A verb may also be phrasal; it may combine a verb plus a particle—*up,* for example, or *out*—which is a preposition without its object. Prepositions have to have objects; particles don't. The meaning of the verb is subtly affected by the particle paired with it. Consider the verb *turn*; if you pair it with *up*, you have *turn up*—as in *turn up the thermostat*. This meaning of *turn* is quite different from *turn + around*: *That new coach will turn around the team's performance within a week.* And it also differs from *turn + down*, as in *turn down the sound* and *turn + over*, as in *turn over a new leaf.* Each meaning of *turn* is unique because of a combination with a different particle.

Some of the most common phrasal verbs are

break in

break out

break through

break up

come forward

give in

made out

made up

make up with

pass around

pass out

pull through

turn around

turn down

turn over

turn up

wear out

Can you think of others?

Verb Clusters. Simple verb clusters are composed of verbs, their auxiliaries and particles, their most common modifiers—adverbs—and the words that modify or pattern with them. Let's take a look at auxiliaries first and then adverbs, a very versatile class of words.

Auxiliaries and Verbs

Auxiliary means secondary, functioning alongside or patterning with the primary word—in this case, a verb. You have probably heard **auxiliary verbs** called *helping verbs*. This class of words is fairly small and composed largely of the forms of *do, be* and *have: Do* you *remember* the answer? I *am* tired, We *had* completed the task, You *will be* bored. Although this class of words is small, it is important: *do* and *did* are critical for asking questions; the *be* verbs are essential for forming progressive tenses and passive voice; and *have* is necessary for perfect tenses or the perfect aspect. Also included in the class of auxiliary verbs are what are also called the **modal verbs** or **modals**. Modals, which express conditions applying to main verbs, are never used as main verbs, only as auxiliaries (except in some sentences where the verb is implied). Auxiliaries can help the main verb express the conditions of possibility, probability, obligation, necessity, anticipation. Here are examples to fit each condition:

can, could (the condition of possibility)

may, might (the condition of probability)

shall, should (the condition of obligation)

must, have to (the condition of necessity)

will, would (the condition of intent or anticipation)

Did you see that the modals have only the two tenses (or the one aspect)? We can't create a present perfect tense with *can* or *shall,* for instance, because these words have no participle. In English we don't say *I have can* or *You are shalling.*

Auxiliaries have two rhetorical purposes and effects. First, they allow you the writer to express different tenses or states of verbs and subtly to differentiate time and duration (take another look at the section on aspects of verbs if you are fuzzy on this). And second, auxiliaries make it possible to express conditionality, to hedge, to equivocate, to qualify. Consider these statements:

1. We may buy a new car this spring. (We're not sure and we're not committing ourselves!)
2. Jim Bob could travel to Paris. (But we're not sure that he is traveling: he's simply capable of doing so.)
3. Ellie should be going to the Rangers games this season. (But there's no absolute certainty that she will.)

Finally, observe how all these sentences with the main verb *frustrate* create subtly different understandings:

1. Aunt Edna *frustrated* the robber's attempt to enter her apartment.

2. The students *have been frustrated* throughout the semester by poor teaching.
3. By refusing to practice, Charles *has been frustrating* his piano teacher.
4. Your teasing *might frustrate* Nana Lou.
5. The child's inability to understand conditionality *can frustrate* the parent's attempt to communicate.
6. The postal strike *will frustrate* our attempt to pay our bills on time.
7. Inability to hear clearly *does frustrate* an appreciation of music.

Adverbs: The Form Class and the Verb Cluster

As a form class, adverbs pattern with verbs to express three main conditions of verbs: **where**, **how**, and **when**. The *where* class of adverbs specifying place or location can be represented by the typical adverb *there*. The *how* class of adverbs and the adverbs of manner are epitomized in *thus*. And the *when* adverbs or the *temporal* (related to time) adverbs can be recalled with the typical adverb *then*. It's easy to remember the **there/thus/then** trio of meanings.

Incidentally, the largest of these adverb groups is the *thus* group—*angrily, beautifully, fully*—the adverbs formed by the addition of *-ly* to adjectives like *angry, beautiful,* and *full.* Regardless of what kind they are, however, adverbs work alongside verbs to limit, define, or extend verbs' meanings. You might remember this by thinking of an *adverb* as a word that *ad*heres to *verbs.* We use adverbs rhetorically to expand verb clusters and to deepen the reader's understanding of the action of the sentence, regardless of the extent of that action (which may not be physical or overt, you will recall).

Understanding Adverbs: Movability. The most definable characteristic of an adverb or adverbial phrase or clause is movability: any word or phrase adverbial is more portable and flexible than that of any other form class. Think of the adverb *quickly,* for instance, and of all the places you can insert it in this sentence:

The students left the room.

Quickly the students left the room.

The students **quickly** left the room.

The students left the room **quickly.**

Try substituting the adverbial phrase *in a rush* in the same slots that quickly occupies: you'll find that the phrase works in exactly the same way as the word. The movability factor also applies to adverbial clauses; you'll find that *when the fire alarm rang* can also fit in the above sentences exactly where *quickly* fits— introducing the sentence, before the verb, after the verb phrase.

Understanding Adverbs: Sentence Position. Finally, adverbs tend to pattern in the blank slots in sentences like the following: "She walked _____" or "She had _____done it" (again, Paul Roberts' suggested test sentences). You can check whether a word is an adverb because it is likely to pattern in one of these sentences: *She walked **slowly** or She had **always done it**.* These slots literally cluster around the verb, right before and right after it.

Other Parts of the Verb Cluster: Intensifiers

Intensifiers are a structure class whose members pattern with adjectives and adverbs to mitigate or affect the impact of the adjective or adverb. Thus you will find intensifiers not only in verb clusters where adverbs are present but also in noun clusters where adjectives are present. **Intensifiers** (also called **qualifiers** by some grammarians) do exactly what their name says they do: they intensify or change the degree of meaning of words with which they pattern. The rhetorical effect of words like *too, very, quite, almost, so,* and *extremely* is to mitigate, increase, or reduce the impact of the words they pattern with or modify. Intensifiers frequently pattern with adverbs in verb clusters. Think about the difference between *The thugs slouched smugly out of the pool hall* and *The thugs slouched very smugly out of the pool hall; My sister smiled slyly* and *My sister smiled **quite** slyly* or even *My sister smiled **somewhat** slyly.* In traditional grammar, you know these words as a class of adverbs modifying adjectives and other adverbs. They are different from regular adverbs because they don't pattern with verbs; they pattern only with adverbs and adjectives.

Other examples of intensifiers are *very* and *pretty* (as in *Maggie's coconut pie was **very** good* and *The women's team was **pretty** exhausted*) —as well as a host of other words like *extremely, remarkably, mostly, noticeably, generally.* Many intensifiers ending in *–ly* can be multifunction words: *fairly,* for instance, can function as either intensifier (*The price was **fairly** high for this neighborhood*) or adverb (*The judge dealt with both parties **fairly***).

~~~~~~~~~~~~~~~~~~~~~~~~~~~~~~~~~~~~~

FOR DISCUSSION: THE IMPACT OF INTENSIFIERS

Find the intensifiers in the following sentences and discuss how they work to alter the meaning of the sentence. How, for example, would the sentence mean differently without the intensifier?

1. The dancers were rather late to rehearsal.
2. The peasants swilled ale quite heartily from an oaken tankard.
3. He had rarely prayed so hard.

4. Last weekend, Uncle Sean was really broke.
5. Tamika was noticeably embarrassed by Bobby's loud and obnoxious conversation.
6. Sarah was very quietly reading from an ancient volume.
7. Jamal was pretty sure about what he saw.
8. The jurors were mostly cordial to the prosecuting attorney.
9. Sammy's new car was way cool.
10. The apple pie was too hot to taste.

~~~~~~

Other Parts of the Verb Cluster: Prepositional Phrases

A prepositional phrase is built with a preposition plus its object, which is a noun or a noun cluster. If the object has words patterning with it or modifiers of its own, the string of modifiers is considered part of the prepositional phrase.

Just as prepositional phrases may serve in noun clusters, they may also serve verbs. This is called *patterning with* or *modifying* verbs. Prepositional phrases that pattern with verbs are usually functioning as adverbs that tell *where, when,* or *how: The poodles ate the steak **in dainty bites** (tells *how*); **After sunset,** the playground is empty (tells *when); Many squirrels live **in the woods** (tells *where*). Remember from our discussion of prepositions in noun clusters that there are many prepositions in English and that they are very important in the scheme of the sentence, for they express relationships between words and ideas. In verb clusters, this relationship conveyed by the prepositional phrase is frequently physical or spatial. At other times the relationship is temporal (having to do with time) or causal or analytical (having to do with how or why). Some common prepositions, you will recall, are *around, at, beneath, beside, between, by, down, during, from, for, in, of, on, through, to, toward, with, within, without.*

Just as verbs sometimes occur in phrases, thus creating phrasal verbs, so too with prepositions. Many prepositions pattern together and act as a unit to create variations on the original meaning of the preposition. Consider this partial list of phrasal prepositions:

according to

along with

as for

because of

except for

instead of

next to

thanks to

by means of

in back of

in charge of

in spite of

on behalf of

FOR WRITING—CREATING PREPOSITIONAL PHRASES IN VERB CLUSTERS

Make a list of 20 verbs that begin with the letter *P*. Then, using the list of prepositions (both single and phrasal prepositions) above and others that you can find or recall, create a prepositional phrase to accompany each verb—thus creating a verb cluster that includes a prepositional phrase. You may also add objects for the verbs as well as adverbs and intensifiers. Here are a few examples:

pose coyly (for the camera)

has praised her pot roast (to the heavens)

is pushing the cart (over the hill)

Other Function or Structure Words

We have studied the form classes and along with those, noun and verb clusters. Besides the **form class** words that carry the freight of the sentence's meaning, sentences have **structure** or **function** words—words that delineate the relationships among the form class words. In the discussion of verb clusters, we looked at a few structure words (like prepositions, for instance). Now let's examine the structure words classes more carefully. These include determiners, noun adjuncts, pronouns, conjunctions, auxiliaries, particles, intensifiers, and interrogatives. Some structure words—*preposition, noun adjunct,* auxiliary, intensifier, and *particle*—have already been discussed extensively elsewhere in this book, so I omit them here.

Determiners

You can find **determiners** before nouns. Their function is to *determine* or limit the noun, to help the reader or listener ferret out or specify some quality of the noun. Although determiners pattern in some of the places where you also can find adjectives, determiners are fundamentally different from adjectives. Determiners, unlike adjectives, cannot be headwords or accumulate modifiers; they are strictly words that serve nouns. These are the most common determiners:

- a, an, the (in traditional grammar, called article adjectives)

- no, few, some, several, many, most, all (in traditional grammar, indefinite pronominal adjectives—or pronoun adjectives)

- my, your, its, his, her, their (in traditional grammar, the personal pronominal adjectives)

- first, second, third, and so on (in traditional grammar, ordinal adjectives)

- this, that, these, those (in traditional grammar, demonstrative adjectives)

- each, every, either, neither

The students ate many cookies means something totally different than *The students ate few cookies*. The difference lies in the determiner *few*, which limits our concept of *cookies* in this sentence. In the same way, *Dad gave me **a** dollar* is different from *Dad gave me **the** dollar*. *The dollar* refers to a specific dollar, one mentioned specifically in a previous utterance. *A dollar* is a non-specific, indefinite dollar not referred to previously.

For Discussion: The Importance of Determiners

In your writer's group, read the following paragraph aloud, taking care to consider the boldface determiners. Then try substituting other determiners for the boldface ones: what is the effect? How would you explain the significance of determiners to the clear communication of the ideas in this passage from *The Bean Trees* by Barbara Kingsolver? Be prepared to explain your responses to the class as a whole.

"**A** fig grew by **the** back door, **an** old, stubborn tree, slow to leaf out. **The** moon threw shadows of fig branches across Estevan's face and **his** chest. Something inside **this** man was turning inside out." (132)

Pronouns

Pronouns are noun substitutes, common function words whose duty is to stand in for nouns. Pronouns can assume any sentence role that nouns can assume; rhetorically, they help you vary the sound of a sentence and prevent redundancy and repetition. So if you are writing a paragraph about Izzy, the black poodle, and you would ordinarily refer to Izzy throughout eight sentences and 92 words, you can occasionally refer to Izzy as *she* or *her* instead of repeating her name. You can allude to *Izzy's special qualities* by writing *her special qualities* without having to bore your reader.

Pronouns that function in the subject position (typically before verbs and in subject slots) are *he, she, it, I, we, they*. Pronouns that function in the object position (typically after verbs or prepositions and in the complement slots) are *him, her, it, me, us, them*. Many pronouns also have a determiner form: *her, his, its, my, our, their*—as in *her* brown eyes, *his* faded t-shirt, *its* lovely melody, *my* favorite music, *our* neighbors, *their* weak hearts. The following chart may help you sort out the pronouns.

Pronouns and Determiners

Subject Pronouns	Object Pronouns	Determiner Form
I	me	my
we	us	our
you	you	you
she	her	her
he	him	his
it	it	its
they	them	their

You probably noticed that some words are on both the pronoun and the determiner list. These overlapping lists illustrate the principle of **multi-function words**; many English words can indeed have multiple functions. In the sentence *He lost his wallet, his* is a determiner patterning with the noun *wallet*. In the sentence *He lost his, his* can be considered a pronoun substituting for the noun (perhaps *wallet*, in this context) referred to earlier in the discourse.

Conjunctions

Conjunctions are joining words. They join words, phrases, and/or clauses to create meaning. The root *-junct* (as in *junction, juncture*) refers to the joining function of conjunctions, and the prefix *con-* means *together, with,* or *joint*. Different kinds of conjunctions signal differing relationships among elements being joined; we'll explore these concepts further in the chapters that examine phrases and clauses. For now, though, here are the major categories of conjunctions and the most common conjunctions in each category:

Coordinating conjunctions or **coordinators** are conjunctions that join items of equal grammatical importance. *Co-* means *with* or *jointly,* and the Latin root *ordo* means *order;* thus *coordinate* means *to order with* or *to order together.* The coordinators are *and, or, but, for, nor, so, yet.* These words are small, compact, and light. Here are some sentences containing coordinators:

1. Georgie and Passie raced across the yard and down the fence line.
2. We were early, so the doors were still locked.
3. It was Emma or Caribou outside the door.

Correlative conjunctions are coordinating conjunctions that come in pairs, two coordinators that *correlate* or *relate with* one another: *either* and or; *neither* and nor; *both* and *and; not only* and *but also.* Correlative coordinators join compound elements. When you use correlative coordinators, you call special attention to the items they join. When you see the first coordinator of the pair, you automatically anticipate the second one to follow—and pay attention to the text immediately around it. Look at these sentences, identical except for the coordinators.

*The homicide detectives checked for blood spatters **and** tissue flecks.*

To see the parallelism, look at the sentence this way:

> *blood spatters*
> *The homicide detectives checked for*   *and*
> *tissue flecks*

The compound objects of the preposition *for, blood spatters* and *tissue flecks,* are joined by the coordinator *and.* Here's another version of the sentence with correlative coordinators:

*The homicide detectives checked for **not only** blood spatters **but also** tissue flecks.*

Do you see how much more emphatic the *blood* and *tissue* become once they are linked by the correlatives? The correlatives emphasize the parallelism of the compound objects:

	not only	blood spatters
The homicide detectives checked for		
	but also	tissue flecks.

Subordinating conjunctions or **subordinators** are conjunctions that join items, particularly clauses, of *unequal* grammatical importance—these conjunctions typically signal the power in relationship between the elements. *Sub-* means *below, beneath,* or *under;* thus *subordinate* means *to order some things below others.* Some common subordinators are *while, if, though, although, because, before, when.* The subordinating conjunctions also include what traditional grammarians call the **relative pronouns**: *who, whom, what, that, which.* These pronoun-conjunctions introduce a particular kind of clause, a **relative** or **adjective clause.** They are called relative pronouns because they clearly *relate* the clause to the noun with which it patterns; the relationship between the noun and its relative pronoun (and relative clause) is clear. Here are a few sentences illustrating all kinds of subordinators:

1. **Although** we were young, we knew what we wanted.
2. No one cashed the lottery ticket **because** it had been washed and dried in the laundry.
3. We were too tired to recognize the soldier **who** was approaching.

Conjunctive adverbs are adverbs that literally *join* one item *with* another, that have a connecting quality—note their frequently compounded structure— *however, therefore, nevertheless, henceforth, moreover, consequently.* Conjunctive adverbs typically appear as conjunctions in compound sentences. Some examples appear in the following sentences:

1. We were young; **nevertheless**, we knew what we wanted.
2. It is too late to study for the exam; **moreover**, you haven't even done your homework yet!
3. Paul took the keys; **consequently,** the rest of us could go nowhere.

Some of these conjunctions also appear on the list of prepositions. This is another example of the principle of multifunction words. When, for instance, *before* functions as a preposition, it patterns before a noun or noun cluster in a prepositional phrase, linking the object of the preposition to the rest of the sentence, as in version *A:*

*Version A: We will reach the finish line **before you.***

When *before* functions as a conjunction, though, it links a whole pattern or clause to the rest of the sentence, as in version *B:*

*Version B: **Before you even get started,** we will reach the finish line.*

We decide how to label a word depending primarily on how that word functions in a given sentence. In version A, *before* is a preposition; in version B, *before* is a conjunction because it patterns with a clause or a complete pattern (subject plus finite verb). (You will hear more about clauses later.) The rhetorical impact of a phrase differs from that of a clause. A clause, because it has a complete pattern including a subject and a verb, signals more grammatical importance. Thus if the idea is an important one worth emphasizing, put it in a clause.

Interrogatives

Interrogatives are used to form questions in English. Words like *who, what, when, where, how,* and *why* begin utterances and signal questions—*Why* is the fireplace painted pink? *Who* knocks on my door? *How* am I supposed to do this problem? *Where* is the secret treasure? Generally these interrogatives are also multifunction words; that is, besides signaling a question, they also function or work within the sentence, frequently as adverbs. In *Why is the fireplace painted pink?*, Why is a *thus* adverb. In *How am I supposed to do this problem?*, how is also a *thus* adverb. But in *Who knocks on my door?* who functions as a pronoun **and** the subject of the sentence.

Compound Sentence Elements within Patterns

Sometimes sentence elements get lonely and long for more of their kind. Thus we have **compound sentence elements**—compound subjects, compound verbs, compound objects of prepositions, compound adverbs—all within a pattern. This compounding enables you the writer to enrich your sentence and cram in more information for your reader without adding an extra sentence. Take a look at the sentences with compounded sentence elements below and see if you can identify the element that is compounded. Also notice the kinds of words joining the compound elements.

1. Columbus did not find India or Japan.
2. Fujicolor freezes the action and gives you vibrant color.
3. Soviet leaders left office in a coffin or in disgrace.
4. That car was designed and built in North America.
5. Dirigibles and Zeppelins evolved from balloons.
6. She and her sister could remember dates, faces, and places.
7. The robbers were frantically screaming and gesturing at the people in the bank.

8. She drove the Bugati to the market and the hairdresser.
9. Frances and Oliver longed to see beyond their dark burrow.
10. Friday or Saturday would be a good day for a picnic.

Notice that the compounded items do not change the basic sentence patterns; they merely expand one or more elements of the pattern.

Subject	Verb	Direct Object
She		dates
	could remember	faces
her sister		places

The above sentence has compound subjects (*She* and *her sister*), a single verb (*could remember*) and compound direct objects, three of them (*dates, faces, places*), but it is still one pattern because both subjects and all three direct objects are tied to the single verb.

Nominal versus Verbal: A Rhetorical Observation

You may write in a style predominantly nominal—one dominated by nouns and noun clusters—or a style predominantly verbal—one dominated by verbs and verb clusters. This is a significant stylistic difference that can affect the pace and readability of your prose. Text heavy with nouns slogs more slowly along than text peppered with lively verbs. This is one reason why readers complain that long passages of description bore them. The reality is that the preponderance of noun clusters necessary for describing keeps the text from seeming to move. Text dominated by verb clusters, on the other hand, is tolerated better by restless readers. See for yourself. Look at the two passages below and discuss with your writer's group which one moves with more alacrity and ease. Which passage is more nominal than the other?

Passage A

Birds make adaptations to changes in seasons through migration. Migration is the movement of some species from one location to another. Age, sex, weather, breeding habits and the availability of food, water, and shelter seem to be the major influences in migratory behavior. Many birds will migrate to areas where the food supply is plentiful and the weather is not as severe.

Passage B

Birds adapt to seasonal changes by migrating. When birds migrate, they move from one location to another. A bird's age, sex, and breeding habits as well as the weather where it lives all influence its inclination to move. Birds also migrate to search for more readily available food, water, and shelter, relocating for a season to areas where food is plentiful and weather temperate. —Anonymous. From *Bird Tracks*.

As you can see, Passage A is much more nominal than Passage B. Although the two passages are approximately the same length, Passage B uses more verbs (*migrating* rather than *migration*, for instance). Passage B moves more smoothly and seems to read more quickly, all because of the verbs.

Here are two ways to make your writing more verb-centered and lively:

1. Change the vague *verb* + *noun* combination to a verb (usually the verb form is buried in the noun)—from

The trooper issued us a warning about black ice

to

The trooper warned us about black ice.

Change

Vespucci Amerigo made the discovery of America

to

Vespucci Amerigo discovered America.

2. Delete the expletives *There is* or *It is* (only if you have no rhetorical purpose for using the expletive) and change a key noun
to a verb.

There was a mark on the edge of the page from the scribe's erasure

to

The scribe's erasure marked the edge of the page.

Instead of

There was a serious delay in going to the dentist on Jerry's part,

try this:

Jerry seriously delayed going to the dentist.

Summing Up

Let's review what this chapter has been about. English has four large
word classes called **form classes**—noun, verb, adjective, and adverb—
that carry most of the meaning of the sentence. English has several
smaller word classes called **function words**. So far, we've examined
prepositions, particles, auxiliaries, determiners, pronouns, intensifiers,
and interrogatives—words that make clear the relationships among

the form classes and that pattern together to form noun clusters and verb clusters.

What we call or label a word depends on its function in the sentence, and many words are capable of multiple functions. What makes it possible to glean meaning from a sentence are the cues we get from the structure of the sentence (the arrangement of its words or its **syntax**) and from the form of those words. What makes it possible to extract clear understanding from a sentence is also that English has many syntactical and structural signals to prevent *ambiguity* (something that is *ambiguous* can be read with more than one meaning). Let's now explore further how form classes and structure words work together in English sentences.

Chapter 3. Patterns Transformed

So far, we've examined the basic patterns of English and the form classes and structure words composing the patterns. Let us now think about how those patterns frequently get transformed in everyday speech and writing. To *transform* something means to change its form or appearance: water can be transformed into ice with the application of cold; an actor can be transformed from a young woman into an aged crone with makeup, a wig, padding, and clothes; a junked car can be transformed into a street rod with time, labor, parts, and paint. Notice that the young woman doesn't really become a crone. Rather her external form changes so that she appears to be one. Also note that ice can return to its original form of water and that a restored car can become again a junked car. So too can basic sentence patterns be transformed; that is, they can take different shapes, but underneath the basic structure remains. Many of our most common English sentences and expressions are transformations of basic patterns. In this chapter we'll examine some of the most common changes you can make to the six basic patterns. We'll work with

- negative transformations

- question transformations

- passive transformations

- emphatic transformations

Remember, though, that at the heart of each transformation lies one of the basic sentence patterns and clusters that you worked with in earlier chapters. A transformation does not change the substance of the sentence; it changes only its form and the way that the reader perceives the sentence. And the transformations have different rhetorical purposes and effects from the original patterns. Let's see how they work.

Negative Transformations

Perhaps the first transformation that every English-speaking child learns is the negative transformation: how to negate the meaning of a specific statement.

1. You did not give me a cookie.
2. The water is not hot.
3. I never saw the money.
4. She is not my mother.
5. No book is in this box.

All these statements controvert or turn over an original, positive statement—*You gave me a cookie, The water is hot, I saw the money, She is my mother, A book is in this box.* The rhetorical purpose of the negative transformation is to negate, deny, correct, or clarify an incorrect or previously held impression. We use it to counteract what is said or heard or expected, to call into question someone else's positive or affirming statement. Thus you may find quite a few negative transformations in argumentative or persuasive pieces. You can transform any of the sentence patterns to a negative meaning by adding one of these negative words: *not, no, none,* or *never,* which we will call the **absolute negatives**.

Other words that have negative implications or that question the verity or positive nature of a statement are words like

barely

hardly

rarely

scarcely

To say *The water is barely hot* casts doubt on the temperature of the water and in effect negates the statement that the water *is* hot. Look at the cartoon caption in "It Don't Mean a Thing" and find the negative transformations (*You aren't* . . . . in addition to *It doesn't mean* . . . . plus *It hasn't got* . . . . And *I'm not* . . . .)

It Don't Mean a Thing

All these transformations play on the real song titles (which have non-standard verb usages): "You Ain't Nothin' But a Hound Dog," "It Don't Mean a Thing if It Ain't Got That Swing," and "I Ain't Misbehavin.'"

Strictly speaking, however, all you have to do to create a negative transformation is to add *no* or *not* to a pattern. With many sentences, however, you must add a tense of the verb *do* to the sentence to make it sound natural. And if the verb of a sentence is not *be* and you wish to transform it to its negative form, you must add *do* to the sentence. You must match the tense and aspect of *do* to match the tense and aspect of the original sentence. Thus to transform the sentence *The snowstorm blew in from the West Coast* to its negative form, we first have to change the sentence to its equivalent with *do* in the past tense: *The snow storm did blow in from the west coast*. Now that we have a verb with an auxiliary, we can make the sentence negative by adding *not*: *The snowstorm did not blow in from the West Coast*. Now consider the sentence

Fran's cat seems ill.

To transform this sentence into its negative form, you can write, *Fran's cat seems not ill*, but that sentence sounds like something out of a different time or place. Today speakers are more likely to say *Fran's cat does not seem ill* or—to use the contracted form of *does* + *not* or *doesn't*—

Fran's cat doesn't seem ill.

Now you create some negative transformations.

~~~~~~

FOR WRITING AND DISCUSSION

For each of the basic patterns below, produce a negative transformation, either absolute or implied. Write out the full transformation. Then compare your sentences with the sentences produced by members of your writing group. Did you use more absolute or more implied negatives? What problems did you find in creating these negative transformations? In your discussion, consider these questions: What are the basic patterns of these sentences? Does the negative transformation change the meaning or the physical pattern of these sentences? Can you make a generalization about when you seem required to use *do* to make the transformation sound natural? What is the relationship between auxiliary verbs and the negative transformation?

1. She exposed her husband's adultery.
2. The cat is lying on the desk near her.
3. Eric's telephone rings fifty times a day.
4. Emily's sister sent her an electronic greeting card for her birthday.
5. Leather shoes stretch.
6. In New York, the sun shines often in the winter months.
7. Poetry is a powerful social force.
8. Hamburgers grow on trees.
9. The social climate at her university is hostile.
10. Textbook prices are high.
11. The Federal Reserve Chairman deems the economy stable.
12. Owls look wise.
13. Jordan addressed the customer's complaint crisply yet kindly.
14. *Butch Cassidy and the Sundance Kid* is one of the best American movies ever.
15. Elementary children love fountain pens.
16. Mrs. Antos finds *The Odyssey* irresistible.
17. Jack slowly explained the directions to his house.
18. The road meanders through the county and across the township.
19. Black ink rubs off the newspaper onto my damp hands.

20. Mr. Jacques considers French studies a natural accompaniment to English studies.
21. The pine logs burn hot.
22. Jobs are plentiful in this country.
23. Taxes are probably too high everywhere.
24. Friends fly free on certain airlines.
25. Caramel candy is good for your teeth.

Question Transformations

So far in this book, we have examined only statements or **indicative** utterances, patterns, and sentences. Americans don't, however, speak and write in the indicative mode exclusively. American speakers and writers ask questions too: in fact, we ask a good many questions. Questioning is part of the American way of life! All questions are transformations of basic patterns. But not all questions are alike, nor are their rhetorical effects alike. You probably already know several ways to create questions from basic patterns. Let's take a formal look at these ways.

Creating Yes/No Question Transformations

One of the most common kinds of questions is the **yes/no question,** one that can be answered with *yes* or *no*. An easy way to effect the question transformation is simply to reverse the order of subject and verb. Notice that only the *be* verb reverses simply. You can easily transform the statement

This rose is pink

to

Is this rose pink?

by reversing the order of subject and verb. The same applies to sentences like *Oakes is a professor (Is Oakes a professor?)* and *Esther's cookies are delicious (Are Esther's cookies delicious?).*

With verbs other than *be*, the question transformation requires the addition of an auxiliary verb, usually *do* or a form of *do* appropriate to the tense of the sentence being transformed. Look at these question transformations:

1. *George photographs lions* becomes
   George does photograph lions becomes
   Does George photograph lions?

2. *Cats meow noisily* becomes
   Cats do meow noisily becomes
   Do cats meow noisily?

3. *Janice painted the barn red* becomes
   Janice did paint the barn red becomes
   Did Janice paint the barn red?

4. *Fran will buy us a soda* becomes
   Will Fran buy us a soda?

Because the verb in this sentence includes an auxiliary form already, we do not need to add *do* to create a question.

5. *The rain is coming down hard* becomes
   Is the rain coming down hard?

Notice that when you use an auxiliary to form a question, the auxiliary and the main verb split, and the subject slips in between them, with the auxiliary verb beginning the sentence.

Creating Interrogative Question Transformations

To ask questions that demand answers of more content and substance, speakers and writers use interrogative words and phrases: *who, where, what, when, why, how,* and *how much.* These words and phrases allow you to pinpoint exactly the kind of information you need. Consider, for instance the sentence above, *Cats meow noisily.* To transform that into a question demanding a substantive answer, you may focus on either the subject *(What meows noisily?)*; the verb *(What do cats do noisily?)*; or the adverb *(How do cats meow?)*. You can also ask *why cats meow noisily, which cats meow noisily, when cats meow noisily,* and *where cats meow noisily.* The interrogatives generate considerably fuller responses than do the yes/no questions.

Tag Questions

Another common way that English speakers form sentences is to make a declarative statement, then add on a **tag** or a short question formed from *be* or the auxiliary to the end of the statement. These are called **tag questions.** For example, consider these:

1. Sam closed the garage door, didn't he?
2. You will be at the meeting on Friday, won't you? (will you not?)
3. That tree is dreadfully ugly, isn't it?
4. You have your passport, don't you?

Although tag questions are used frequently in speech, you will likely not use many in formal writing. Also consider limiting tag questions in your speech. You can understand why these sentences can make the speaker sound somewhat insecure: every tag question ventures a statement or opinion then requests an affirmation from the hearer. This structure can also be part of a passive-aggressive dialogue, where one speaker seeks consensus from the other without venturing a direct opinion.

Questions by Intonation

There is another way to create the question transformation, and that is simply to change the intonation of a declaration so that the voice rises at the end of the sentence. On the written page, this kind of question is signaled merely by using a question mark after the sentence. Thus the statement *You want cream cheese on your bagel* becomes the question *You want cream cheese on your bagel?* This transformation is used most frequently in conversation and very informal writing.

The Indirect or Reported Question

Sometimes writing about questions can be tricky. If you are writing about someone else's asking a question, you can report the question directly:

Dad asked, "Where is the screwdriver?"

Notice the punctuation: the speaker is introduced along with the verb (in this case, *asked,* but it could be *shouted* or *whispered* or *complained);* then the speaker's exact words are repeated and enclosed in quotation marks. The question mark at the end of the sentence goes inside the quotation marks because it pertains to what Dad said, not to what the speaker or writer is reporting.

But if you are reporting what Dad said without using his exact words, you might say or write this: *Dad asked where the screwdriver was.*

Note how what Dad asked is changed into a statement; it is now merely reported—and it loses its interrogative force. Notice that there are no quotation marks because Dad's exact words as he articulated them have been reported, not quoted.

~~~~~~

FOR WRITING AND DISCUSSION

Transform the following declarative sentences or statement patterns, also called sentences in the **indicative mode,** into questions. You may generate yes/no questions, substantive questions (by using interrogative words), or tag questions. Afterward, compare your questions with the ones your writing group members produced and discuss how the transformations occurred. Note that a single sentence may contain both a negative transformation and a question transformation.

1. You are not paying attention to me.
2. The groceries are still in the car.
3. The drummer's rhythmic sense is keen.
4. Natalie appears tense.
5. The assembly elected Professor Smugly chairperson.
6. Textbooks have become quite expensive.
7. A dental checkup is an ordeal for some people.
8. The recruit polished dozens of shoes to a sparkling shine.
9. Fatigue and boredom set in.
10. There was a loud, sudden pop from outside.
11. No laundry has been done tonight.
12. A new computer is necessary.
13. The French tapestry in the museum is quite valuable.
14. Students will choose new courses this semester.
15. Many people like unusual fonts.
16. Lemons typically taste sour.
17. Electricity is inexpensive in our town.

18. We are all attending the commencement ceremonies in the gym.
19. Ellen turned on the lamp for her brother.
20. The dinner at the club was delicious but cold.
21. State government is inefficient.
22. Her son is lighting a fire.
23. No one will admit wrongdoing.
24. This circus no longer has freaks.
25. The attic felt dusty, dark, and cold.

~~~~~~

Passive Transformations

You have probably heard about passive voice. Perhaps you have even been warned not to write sentences in passive voice. Some writing specialists dislike passive voice and caution other writers against it. But as you will see as we think together about the passive transformation, certain rhetorical occasions call for passive voice—and the passive transformation is not a structure to be avoided, but one to be used wisely.

Exactly what is passive voice? *Passive voice refers to the verb specifically* although the passive transformation affects the structure of the entire sentence. Look at the following sentence: *The angry student slammed the door.*

This is a transitive verb and an S-V-O sentence. The subject (also called the **agent**) did something to something or someone; the student slammed the door. When we transform the sentence into passive voice, the sentence becomes *The door was slammed by the angry student.*

The nature of the sentence changes, particularly the nature of what is happening to whom and who caused it. Now the emphasis in the sentence is on the object, the thing to which something happens: the door is slammed. The door doesn't do anything; rather, someone (here the agent, the angry student) does something to the door. Here is another active/passive sentence pair alongside one another:

The poodle chased the nimble squirrel.—active

The nimble squirrel was chased by the poodle.—passive

Which sentence is longer? Which sentence emphasizes the poodle? Which sentence emphasizes the squirrel? What operations did the writer perform on the active, transitive verb to turn it into the passive sentence?

Three things happen when an active verb is transformed into a passive verb:

1. First, the object of the active voice sentence moves to the subject position for the passive sentence.

2. Second, the subject or agent of the active voice sentence moves into a "by" phrase at the end of the passive sentence. This agent phrase or "by" phrase is optional and is in fact often left out of the sentence. A passive voice sentence may or may not have an agent, depending on the importance of the agent to the meaning of the sentence. Many passive sentences have no "by" phrase. More about this in a minute.

3. Finally, an appropriate form and tense of *be* is added to the verb, and the verb assumes its **past participial form.** Thus *chased* in the active voice sentence becomes *was chased* in the passive sentence. *Chased* is past tense in the active voice sentence; its past participle happens to look exactly the same, *chased*. (This similarity is not the case with all verbs, remember.) So we simply add the appropriate tense of *be* to the past participle *chased*. Because the active sentence is past tense, we use the past tense of *be*, *was*.

This verb form is always the hallmark of passive voice, whose tense is easily recognizable as a form of *be* **plus the past participle.** You may sometimes also see *get* substituted for *be* in the passive transformation (Chad *got passed over* for the nomination; The toddlers *got tired* from playing at Chuck E. Cheese; The dirty sweaters *got sent* to the cleaners). This kind of structure is called a **get passive**. Study these pairs of active sentences and their passive transformations to see the process (the passive verb forms are italicized):

1. Active: The angry fourth-grader dropped the spaghetti dramatically and purposefully.
2. Passive: The spaghetti was dropped by the angry fourth-grader dramatically and purposefully.
1. Active: The wind overturned the flamingos on the lawn.
2. Passive: The flamingos on the lawn were overturned by the wind.
1. Active: You are eating the whole box of Cheezits!
2. Passive: The whole box of Cheezits is being eaten by you!
1. Active: The artist will draw sketches of suspects.
2. Passive: Sketches of suspects will be drawn by the artist.
1. Active: The professor graded eighty-seven examinations.
2. Passive: Eighty-seven examinations were graded by the professor.

In effect, the subjects and objects switch places, the subject of the active sentence moving to the end of the passive sentence in an agent phrase, the object of the active sentence moving to the front of the passive sentence as its new subject.

Look at how transforming an active voice sentence into passive voice shifts the rhetorical emphasis. Putting a noun in the subject slot gives it the most importance, so if you want to emphasize what overturned the flamingoes on the lawn (sentence 2 above), make the agent—*the wind*—the subject in an active voice sentence. If you want to emphasize what was overturned, put the original direct object—*flamingos*—in the subject slot and use the passive transformation. Finally, notice that in many cases, the passive sentences could make just as much sense without the agent phrase; if what overturned the flamingoes on the lawn is not important, for instance, the passive version of sentence 2 could read simply *The flamingos on the lawn were overturned.* This agent phrase or "by phrase" (in sentence 2, *by the wind*) is frequently omitted when the agent is unimportant or irrelevant.

William Ziegler humorously and astutely notes an interesting use of passive voice, what he calls the "passive-aggressive voice," where passive voice is used as a warning against some unnamed force or watcher. Signs reading

This property protected by Smith & Wesson

or

Unauthorized vehicles will be towed

suggest, for instance, that the sign reader is being observed and will be liable for overstepping some unarticulated boundary—and consider the slightly sinister tone of

The revolution will not be televised.

In the first example, Smith & Wesson—a weapon, wielded by a person, we infer—would protect the property, and in the second example, some unnamed agent would tow away the unauthorized vehicle. In the final sentence, some malignant power will sever communications and the revolution will proceed under cover (at least temporarily!).

Now it's your turn to transform some active voice sentences into passive voice.

FOR WRITING AND DISCUSSION

Change the active voice sentences below to passive voice ones. Be sure to use comparable tenses. Compare your results with those of your writing group partners; then observe whether there are other transformations in any of these sentences and discuss any unusual modifying words (like noun adjuncts) or phrases. Be prepared to report to the class at large.

1. You should not push those buttons.
2. Three patrol cars circled the block.
3. The apartment house had a buzzer system for entry.
4. John saw the pimple on Harriet's chin.
5. That class asks too many questions.
6. I will change my mind before sundown.
7. No one liked the idea of a qualifying examination.
8. Mother is protecting Aaron.
9. Most guests drank coffee or tea.
10. The maids drew the curtains and turned on the lights.
11. The ship reached the equator before midsummer.
12. The wolves circled their prey.
13. After the wedding, Christy and Jack sent notes of appreciation to more than 200 guests.
14. The ten-year-olds happily gobbled up the pizza and ice cream.
15. The arborist trimmed the stately oak tree by the back porch.
16. Myra ripped the ransom note to shreds.
17. Every morning, the chickadee family raids the bird feeder.
18. Frank examined the hammer carefully for blood spatter.
19. We put the *Madame Butterfly* disc in the CD player.
20. Aunt Frieda will clean your room thoroughly.
21. The workmen installed a second telephone line.

22. Few people fear rabbits.
23. The friends exchanged looks.
24. We turned off all the appliances quickly.
25. They were shredding the evidence in haste.

~~~~~~

All the sentences you transformed in the writing exercise above were S-V-O sentences, sentences with subjects, transitive verbs, and direct objects. Yet we know that there are other transitive patterns than those with simple direct objects; there are transitive patterns with indirect objects and objective complements as well. What happens when we transform those patterns into passive voice? Here's an example of an indirect object pattern, an S-V-IO-DO sentence: *The friendly Golden Retriever gave all the guests kisses.*

When you transform this indirect object sentence into a passive voice sentence, you'll get one of these options:

All the guests were given kisses by the friendly Golden Retriever.

or

Kisses were given all the guests by the friendly Golden Retriever.

The first example, *All the guests were given kisses,* contains a **retained object** because the direct object is retained or kept as a direct object in the transformation. In the second option, *Kisses were given all the guests,* the former direct object becomes the subject. You have the rhetorical option of choosing what you want to emphasize by making it the subject of the passive sentence.

Now what happens when you transform an S-V-DO-OC pattern, one with an objective complement, into passive voice? Here's the original S-V-DO-OC sentence:

The scholarship committee considered Sarah deserving of the award.

And here's the transformation:

Sarah was considered deserving of the award by the scholarship committee.

Only the direct object can serve as the subject of the transformed objective complement sentence. Let that sink in a moment. It makes sense because forming any passive means vaulting the direct object to the front of the sentence, where the subject lives. The same is true when the objective complement is a noun:

Our neighbors call their horse Dusty.

And the transformation . . .

Their horse is called Dusty (by our neighbors).

Although these verbs resemble linking verbs because of the presence of *be*, you'll recognize that they have the trademark passive combination of *be* + past participle: *was considered* and *is called*.

~~~~~~

FOR WRITING AND DISCUSSION

Now try transforming these transitive sentences with more than one object or with an objective complement and see what happens. (Not everything will go smoothly!) Talk about the results with your writers' group. What kinds of problems emerge?

1. One student passed another the answers to the hardest questions.
2. No one considered the president blameless.
3. Anthony bought Jennifer a huge diamond.
4. The clerk did not give me enough change.

5. In the morning, the mail carrier brings us our bills, catalogs, and renewal notices.
6. The fashion police thought Rihanna's outfit outrageous.
7. Tom Sawyer painted the tall fence white.
8. That teacher will give Kip a hard time about his tardies.
9. The residents of Hinman have elected Stephanie floor monitor.
10. Film critics have always believed Ingrid Bergman beautiful.
11. A charitable spirit makes one a pleasant person.
12. Titus's great-uncle left him cash for college.
13. The local press considered the firefighters heroes of the first degree.
14. The partygoers took the host a bottle of fumé blanc.
15. Nancy named her mother guardian of her baby son.
16. Parenthood has brought us happiness.
17. The set designer made the backdrop bold and bright.
18. Frances has called me a liar too many times.
19. Bonnie Raitt gave Bruce Springsteen a kiss onstage.
20. The groundhog determinedly made the hole bigger.
21. Billy wrote the family a poem in honor of his birthday.
22. We made the edges of the death announcement a ribbon of black.
23. The students consider the dean important to their school.
24. Everyone considered Dede a fool.
25. Her editor made the book deal irresistible.

~~~~~~

Remember that, rhetorically speaking, the passive transformation is not an indicator of bad writing. In fact, for many occasions passive voice is appropriate and even more effective than active voice. Sometimes, for instance, it is not important for the reader to know who the agent is. In a sentence like *Binghamton's roads were resurfaced last summer,* the agent (that is, *who* paved or resurfaced the roads) is so unimportant that it is omitted entirely from the sentence. What is emphasized in this sentence is what got paved, the subject: *Binghamton's roads.* In many cases too, the agent wishes not to be known. If, for instance, you must write a letter of denial to an applicant for a loan or to a student who applied for a scholarship, you may not want to take the responsibility or the heat of being the agent of that denial. You may prefer to write something like

Regrettably, your application for a loan has not been approved.

instead of

Regrettably, I did not approve your application for a loan.

Notice that when the agent needs to be anonymous, it is simply omitted from the sentence.

In other instances, you may use passive voice for logistical purposes, simply because you need a certain word at the head of a sentence or phrase. Perhaps you are writing about Sarah's new cashmere scarf. You write something like

Yesterday Sarah wore a cashmere scarf.

You can follow this sentence with something like

Artisans in Kurdistan wove the scarf.

But notice how much smoother your text sounds like this: *Yesterday Sarah wore a colorful cashmere scarf, which **was woven by artisans in Kurdistan**.*

In this case, passive voice makes a more liquid link between patterns because it allows the writer to link a descriptive clause to the direct object at the end of a previous sentence. Notice that the pattern in the clause is passive so that the direct object *scarf* becomes the subject, that the *which* substitutes for the noun *scarf,* and that the words *scarf* and *which* abut one another in the sentence smoothly. The key to working with passive voice is to know where you want the emphasis placed in the sentence; then you can decide if passive voice is an appropriate rhetorical choice.

Emphatic Transformations

We have just been thinking together about how passive voice can change the emphasis in a sentence. Good writers need to know how to get readers to attend to the important ideas, and while passive voice is one way to shift the reader's attention, you can also use other rhetorical strategies.

Shifting Emphasis with Inversion

Creating emphasis is partly about knowing the usual, psychologically expected structures and then occasionally altering them in a way to alert the reader that, in a particular sentence, something different is happening. We saw how passive voice can create emphasis by inverting the subject and the object of a transitive sentence. Any time you shift word order significantly in a pattern, you almost certainly draw attention to the word, phrase, sentence, or idea affected by the shift. Consider the difference in, for example, these sentences: one, a typical S-LV-PA pattern; the other, an inversion of that pattern:

S-LV-PA: *She was pretty and shy at the same time.*

S-LV-PA inversion: *Pretty she was, and shy at the same time.*

See how *pretty* leaps to the fore of the inverted sentence and how important the idea becomes? It receives additional emphasis because of the unusual order of the sentence. It's just not what readers expect, so the ear perks up and pays attention. Here's another example:

"Next come density tests."

The usual order of this S-V (adv) sentence would be *Density tests come next*, but in this sentence the sequence of events, signaled by *next*, is emphasized. The author, Janice Paskey, is writing about snowpacks and avalanches in "Mysteries of the Snowpack: Predicting the Unpredictable." And here's another:

"Past Spithead and the Isle of Wight the Titanic steamed."

Here the geographical locations at the front of the sentence are emphasized. Hanson Baldwin in "R.M.S. Titanic" emphasizes that the ship had been at sea by noting places the *Titanic* passed. He inverts the usual word order of the sentence and puts the prepositional phrase at the head of the sentence. Key points of emphasis in any rhetorical structure are first, the front of the sentence and then at the end of the sentence. Words the reader sees first and last are most memorable; what falls in the middle of the structure can be more easily forgotten. This is one reason why, for instance, business writers buffer "bad news" (you didn't get the job or your loan was not approved) with pleasantries at the beginning of a letter and a good will statement at its end. With this strategy of burying bad news in the middle, they hope to diminish its impact. When you want to emphasize a word or idea that is currently buried in a sentence, move the word or phrase to be emphasized to the beginning of the sentence—or alternately, to its end. You may be moving major sentence elements (shifting subjects, verbs, complements) or words or phrases (adjectives, adverbs, prepositional phrases, for instance) that pattern with these major elements. This is a rhetorical device called **anastrophe**: read more examples in Chapter 6.

FOR WRITING

Choose a word or phrase you want to emphasize in the sentences below, then try inverting the word order to see what happens. Do not add any words to these sentences; just rearrange what's already here. There may be more than one appropriate inversion of each sentence, so discuss your transformations with the members of your writing group. Are there any particular sentence patterns that don't invert well? Did you notice that there are no transitive sentences here?

1. The departmental staff is certainly not friendly.
2. The snow is blowing in hard from the west.
3. These moments are precious and few.
4. Birds sit in the trees at dusk.
5. Bats fly out of belfries about that time too.
6. Sixteen cars are ahead of us at the tollbooth.
7. All those brooms whisk across the floor noiselessly.
8. The teacher is snoozing during her planning hour.
9. Foreign language movies with sub-titles can be exquisitely boring.
10. Many students are returning to class today.
11. Her books are open on the library table.
12. Grandpa Crum groans in his sleep.
13. Margaret's mother is an emergency room nurse.
14. The sky is green.
15. Planets revolve around the sun.
16. This northeast wind is oddly vicious.
17. An advertisement for a used wedding dress appeared in the local paper.
18. All my pencils are sharp.
19. The study of particle physics is demanding.
20. All the bells in town peal plaintively into the unreceptive night.

21. This wizard is neither shrewd nor cunning.
22. The old suits hang in the tiny, musty closet.
23. Books are fine companions for a stormy day.
24. Too many tapes are in that cabinet.
25. Francis went shopping alone, with $54.65 in his tattered wallet.

~~~~~~~~~~~~~~~~~~~~~~~~~~~~~~~~~~~~~~

Creating Emphasis with the Cleft Sentence

Another way to create emphasis is the **cleft sentence**. Among the meanings of *to cleave* is the idea of *to cut;* thus a cleft sentence is one that is cut in two, then rearranged with expletives to create emphasis. Expletives are place-holding words. They have little meaning in themselves, and typically they have no function in a sentence other than to fill a spot so that you can shift the placement of other words. Typical expletives are *it, what, there, here.* To follow are some examples of sentences transformed into cleft sentences; notice that each plain sentence is cut in the middle and that an expletive is inserted to rename and emphasize the subject.

Plain: *The dripping water from the bathtub is making the noise.*

Cleft: *It is the dripping water from the bathtub that is making the noise.*

The plain sentence is cut midway through, between the subject and predicate. Then the expletive *it* is added to the first part and the second part is made into a *that* clause or pattern. Here are some others:

Plain: *We want Coca-Cola for the party.*

Cleft: *It is Coca-Cola that we want for the party.* (Emphasizes the Coca-Cola we want.)

or

It is for the party that we want Coca-Cola. (Emphasizes why we want the Coca-Cola)

or

It is we who want the Coca-Cola for the party. (Emphasizes who wants the Coca-Cola).

Plain: *The rain flooded the garden, drowning the vegetable seedlings.*

Cleft: *It was the rain that flooded the garden, drowning the vegetable seedlings.*

It was the vegetable seedlings that were drowned when the rain flooded the garden.

It was the garden that the rain flooded, drowning the vegetable seedlings.

What was flooded was the garden in the rain, and the vegetable seedlings were drowned.

What were drowned were the vegetable seedlings in the garden, flooded by the rain.

Notice that the cleft need not always begin with the expletive *it*; the cleft frequently begins with a *what, how,* or *that* introducing a pattern. Note also that changing the nature of the cleft or creating it to emphasize different parts of the sentence can force you to rewrite the sentence significantly. The meaning of the sentence is not really changed by the rewriting, but its emphasis is altered considerably and the reader's perception of the sentence is changed. So keep these rhetorical possibilities in mind as you revise and rewrite sentences.

FOR WRITING

Rewrite all the following sentences to create cleft sentences. Remember that you'll first cut the sentence, then insert an expletive structure or create an internal pattern where you want emphasis. You'll have to make up the expletive structures.

1. Maurice was sick.
2. I received my formal education in Spanish at the local market.
3. Gran had a round childlike face and big eyes.
4. The hotel lobby buzzes with Polish and Yiddish.
5. My mother came from Tucson.
6. For years, I was too busy for the kitchen.
7. My brother put up his dukes and started yelling.
8. The memory of those chocolate cream puffs always makes Miriam happy.
9. The red-tailed hawks have built a nest high in the gigantic lights on a Cornell athletic field.
10. In this town soccer is a Saturday morning sport.
11. My father hoisted the baggage.
12. I took my paints to the Louvre each day and copied famous paintings.
13. Rivke always lived with her in-laws after the war.
14. The bridegroom is asking for a story.
15. In restaurants, we ate the vegetarian fare.
16. Life was complex during the 1950s.
17. We sat at Aunt Frieda's dining room table in mahogany chairs with needlepoint cushions.
18. I remember the kitchen in my grandmother's Illinois farmhouse.
19. We invited the family.
20. A vicious tornado touched down in an affluent suburban neighborhood south of the city.

21. Dorothea married Uncle George.
22. I grow zucchini, tomatoes, lettuce, and cilantro in my backyard garden.
23. We went out to dinner on Saturday night.
24. Rugs were rolled up and floors were polished every spring.
25. In our neighborhood, the immigrant population dwindled, then vanished.

Creating Emphasis by Varying Diction or Word Choice

You can also create emphasis by varying diction and levels of usage; that is, by shifting from more to less formal expressions or using what linguists call different *registers* of expression. Diction refers to the writer's word choices. Linguist Martin Joos, in his classic *The Five Clocks*, identifies kinds of style among native English speakers. Let's consider how you can use some of the styles Joos described to create a specific tone or effect. The most common of these styles, perhaps the most centered or average or most-used of them, is the **consultative style**.

Consultative Style. We use this style when we communicate with strangers who speak our language but whose personal contexts differ widely from ours. Explicit giving of information, background, and explanation—these qualities mark consultative style. Someone writing in consultative style does not assume that she or he will be understood automatically and as a result offers context and definition of what might not be clearly comprehended. Indeed, consultative style presents information as fast as it is needed and sometimes anticipates the need for it. If two speakers are having a conversation and all the public information needed for their conversation has been exhausted, a consultative discussion will end because presenting the information is the purpose for the conversation. An example of consultative style is a sentence like this: *Because the bank closes at three, we should leave now to get there before closing.*

Casual Style. We find casual style written and spoken among friends, acquaintances, insiders. In casual style, there is frequently an absence of background information; the writer assumes that the reader/listener does not need the background and takes public knowledge and information for granted. If information is exhausted in a **casual** conversation, in contrast to a consultative conversation, the conversation shifts to silence or kidding. Two defining features of casual style are **ellipsis** (omission of words and phrases) and **slang** (in the strictest sense, a widely current but short-lived expression like the recent *way cool,* which is now long passé). In casual speech and writing, words that are commonly understood by all the members of the group are frequently ellipted—or left out or omitted. Instead of writing *We are sure that we are going,* for instance, the casual writer might write *We're sure we're going,* leaving out the *that* that introduces the clause and using contractions with the pronouns. Speakers and writers also use slang to signal that they are among the minority of the population who knows these words. The use of slang is part of the jockeying for position and control in social situations. Casual style is also punctuated by contractions (I'll, you'd, they're) and by simple, straightforward words: *we'll stay at home tonight* versus *we shall remain at our abode this evening.* An example of casual style is a sentence like this: *Let's get to the bank.*

Intimate Style. Intimate style, used between people who know one another extremely well—good friends, family, very close colleagues—is characterized by **extraction** and **jargon**. Jargon means that in a close or intimate relationship certain code words are permanent fixtures; that is, certain words or expressions function like shorthand to refer to a vast set of experiences. Jargon is not slang; slang is used in conversations between insiders and outsiders. Insiders use slang in casual style to confirm their credibility to the group, and outsiders may use it to try to get into the group, to demonstrate that they belong. Between intimates, however, there is no insider/outsider relationship—and therefore no need for slang.

Extraction means that the listener or reader extracts some pattern or meaning from a casual sentence spoken by someone very close to him or her. What the speaker says may not be intelligible to anyone else except the person with whom he or she is intimate. This is not ellipsis, where a portion of the sentence remains. Extraction means deriving some meaning from an expression or utterance that appears to have no relationship at all to ordinary words: your brother says "Hmmph" as he reads the editorial page. Most likely, he has found something that made him indignant. Your style of communicating requires very few words, no background or public information, because each of you knows so much about one another. This style you share requires few to no transitions because you share so much information that only a brief reference will set you to thinking along the same lines. Martin Joos writes that "good intimate style fuses personalities." An example of intimate style along the lines of our earlier sentences about getting to the bank might be *Hey! Time to leave for the bank!*

The speaker and the listener (most intimate language is spoken rather than written) already understand that the bank closes at three and that they have an obligation to get there before that time. All that one speaker needs to do is to offer up a slight reminder of the earlier stored conversation.

Formal Style. This style is designed to inform and to maintain a distance between the writer/speaker and the reader/hearer (the opposite of intimate style). The speaker or writer typically absents her- or himself from the text itself (no first person, usually) and depends on a strict form or shape, logical links among ideas, and explicitness. Formal text, characterized by detachment and cohesion, inserts background information in depth and with ordered precision; it assumes a captive, non-responsive audience. It refrains from using ellipsis and rarely stoops to contractions. Its sentences tend to be long and complex. It is usually characterized by third person and frequently by words of many syllables derived from Latin—here a formal stylist would say "Latinate polysyllabic diction." All these qualities make the careful planning and organizing of such text a necessity. A formal version of our bank sentence might be something like

Waterford National Bank closes at three; we should leave now to arrive before closing time.

Mixing and Shifting Levels of Usage

So what's the point about all these levels or **registers** of style? Simply that you can create emphasis by shifting from one register to the other and then back again simply by altering a word or two. This is particularly noticeable when you make a shift that the reader does not foresee. Of course, this strategy can be used to create humor too, so you have to be careful that you don't make your reader smile when you aren't intending to be funny. Another danger of shifts that are too radical or too unexpected is that you can sound as if you are writing with a thesaurus.

Look at these versions of the same sentence:

1. Savannah put on her Skechers and rushed out the door.
2. Savannah donned her Skechers and hastened out the portal.
3. Savannah slid into her Skechers and ran out the door.

You can readily see the differences among the sentences. You probably wouldn't write number three unless you were writing dialogue or a friendly letter or talking to a friend. Number two sounds really formal, almost as if the writer were trying too hard to impress the reader, perhaps even by using the thesaurus. Number one is the most ordinary-sounding of all the sentences. But if you write *Savannah donned* her *Skechers and rushed out the door*, changing just the more casual verb *put on* to the more formal verb *donned*, then your reader is going to perk up and pay attention. *Donned* is an interesting verb that gives dimension to Savannah's act, making it seem more purposeful.

Most of the time you'll write in a mixture of styles: primarily consultative with a solid dollop of casual and a bit of formal stirred in. This text that you are reading now is just that—a blend of consultative and casual with an occasional formal characteristic for emphasis. I'm not assuming that you know a lot of detail about grammar, so I try to explain everything thoroughly. On the other hand, I want you to feel comfortable as you read and work in this book, so I use second person *you* and an occasional first-person *I* to draw you into the web of my ideas. I also use quite a few contractions. My ideas about grammar and style are, however, highly structured and arranged, and that's where the formal aspect of my style is perhaps most prominent.

~~~~~~

FOR WRITING

Try writing casual, consultative, and formal versions of each sentence below in the chart Levels of Usage and Style. You may have to add or delete words and change word order.

Levels of Usage and Style

Casual Style	Consultative Style	Formal Style
		We regret that we are unable to attend the opening of the opera.
Want some ice cream?		

Casual Style	Consultative Style	Formal Style
	Recent studies of Binghamton's recycling habits show that recycling has saved the city's waste management department over $600,000 in the last fiscal year alone.	
The kids got home from school late today.		

Creating Emphasis by Formatting

There is one additional way to create emphasis on a given part of your text: with formatting. Simply put, you can make the physical text itself stand out by making it bold, italicizing it, writing it in all capital letters, creating a new paragraph (sometimes of a single sentence) or combining these devices. This rhetorical strategy is particularly useful when you are writing dialogue. Here are some examples of how formatting can create emphasis. Discuss how the following examples use formatting to create emphasis, considering the effectiveness of the strategy.

1. We searched everywhere for your car keys!
2. **No one** was willing to join the protest against the administration.
3. Please throw your paper trash HERE.

You may also create emphasis by using different fonts or colors for selected text. And you can create text boxes, make lists, use bullets, and employ borders on the page. All this is relatively easy to do with almost all word processing programs. The important thing to remember about changing the font or the color of text or about making any formatting change is to exercise restraint. If you use fourteen examples of text colored red or changed into a different font on one page, your reader will become inured or accustomed to your attempts to create emphasis—and then there's no emphasis! The reader becomes used to the change and no longer notices your efforts to create difference. Keep in mind, too, that text changes created via your computer may translate differently on-line or when opened by a different program or across a different platform (from Mac to PC, for instance).

~~~~~~

FOR WRITING

Copy each of the following sentences, formatting one word or phrase in each sentence to emphasize it.

1. Jon's piggy friends drank all the Coke.
2. Inside you'll find a special blend of the tastiest fruits under the sun.
3. There are two hundred French travel agents staying at the hotel today.
4. Your own customized program keeps all your information in one convenient place.
5. The spirit of this product is very different.

For Writing

Now put to work everything you have learned about creating emphasis to revise these sentences. Your job is to revise each sentence so that you shift the existing emphasis to a different word or section of the sentence. Keep in mind that you'll have to do more than just rearrange words in many of these sentences. Be prepared to explain the effects of your changes to your class.

1. There's not another car on the planet like this one.
2. A gathering of tourists stood outside the iron gates.
3. I went to Hamilton Farm one afternoon to see the animals.
4. It was a big school of bass just beneath the water's surface.
5. The National Archives in Washington DC now has about five billion documents in storage.
6. In 1992 my parents sold their shop and moved to Louisiana.
7. My uncle was depressed by his sinking financial situation.
8. It was not just symphonies on public radio.
9. The woman did not want to appear confrontational at the news conference.
10. In the early days of my father's illness, he told stories.
11. She must understand something about the conversation.
12. We are discussing our favorite topic, the stupidity of our family.
13. I find Annie, sitting in the windowsill.
14. All this happened at ten o'clock at night.
15. My aunt died in our ancestral home in Edinburgh, Scotland.
16. Synthetic compounds do affect the reproductive capabilities of non-human mammals.
17. At the Elk City Hotel, we sat at the long bar in our stiff new hunting jackets and clean hunting caps.
18. Shopping became important to me.
19. In the hospital I was first introduced to psychiatric medications.
20. I am polite by default.
21. Caroline patches the hole in the soffit.

22. The four-man Fox Sports team is also waiting by the door for Manning.
23. He was always mercurial, mysterious, and confidential.
24. For most people suicide is carefully planned.
25. There is no mechanism here to unseal the tomb.

Summing Up Transformations

Part of the way that English sentences gain variety is through transformation of the basic patterns. The most common transformations allow for changing the meaning of an indicative sentence from positive to negative, for asking questions to elicit a variety of information, and for emphasizing key or important ideas through passive voice, inversion of word order, cleft structures, changes in diction, and formatting. Native speakers create these transformations with such ease that the resulting sentences seem quite normal.

Next we're going to examine how we expand and combine patterns, how we add details to or refine elements of the basic patterns and the transformations. If you're not entirely clear about the basic patterns and transformations, you may find that this is a good time to return to the beginning of this book and refresh your understanding.

Chapter 4. Phrases, Verbals, and Free Modifiers

In earlier chapters you read about how various kinds of words shape themselves into clusters and phrases around nouns and verbs and how patterns can be expanded and combined into compound and complex sentences. In this chapter you'll delve more deeply into the formation of noun and verb clusters and phrases. First we will briefly review compound sentence elements to accustom ourselves to thinking about larger groups of words; then we'll move on to verbals (infinitives, gerunds, and participles) and nominative absolutes. Although these terms may sound intimidating, eventually they'll become familiar. Let's begin with a look at compound sentence elements.

Compound Sentence Elements

Compound sentence elements (like compound subjects, verbs, or objects of any kind) occur when two ideas share the same slot in a sentence pattern and are joined by coordinators or coordinating conjunctions (usually *and, or, but* within a clause). A sentence with a compound subject has at least two subjects, even though it may have just one verb; a sentence with compound objects of the preposition has at least two prepositional objects for a single preposition. Consider, for instance, how a compound subject happens. A writer wants to note, for instance, that he finished his engineering homework. In addition, he observes that Sarah has also finished her engineering homework. He could say

I have finished my engineering homework.

and

Sarah has finished her engineering homework.

Or, because the original grammatical pattern of the two sentences is identical except for the subjects, he could combine them and say

Sarah and I have finished our engineering homework.

He writes Sarah's name first because that is the polite thing to do when you write about someone and about yourself in the same sentence: mention the other person first!

Sentences with the same basic patterns but with compound direct objects would look something like this:

The puppy chewed my dad's slippers.

and

The puppy chewed my sister's yearbook.

And the sentence with the compound direct objects would read like this:

The puppy chewed my dad's slippers and my sister's yearbook.

The basic patterns of these sentences share many words. Creating the compound sentence is a matter of pairing the information that is not shared—if it is structurally the same, of course.

Even objects of prepositions can be compounded. Can you create a sentence containing a prepositional phrase with compound objects from these sentences with the same basic structure?

All the world is tired of lame television commercials.

All the world is tired of game shows.

All the world is tired of reality television.

Combining these sentences would yield

All the world is tired of lame television commercials, game shows, and reality television.

One preposition—*of*—has three objects: *lame television commercials, game shows,* and *reality television.*

~~~~~~

FOR WRITING AND DISCUSSION

To each of the sentences below, add the element specified to create a sentence with compound elements. In at least three sentences, use correlative coordinators (like *either /or* or *neither / nor*). The first few are done for you.

1. Their very footprints are preserved in concrete. [Make the subject compound]
    Possible response: Their very footprints and handprints are preserved in concrete.

2. They are herding their cattle out of the pastures for the night. [Make the direct object compound.]
    Possible response: They are herding their cattle and sheep out of the pastures for the night.

3. Lunch was red beans. [Make the predicate noun compound.]
   Possible response: Lunch was red beans, rice, cornbread, and sweet potatoes.
4. The flavor industry is highly secretive. [Make the predicate adjective compound.]
5. In the last decade, Americans ate an average of about fifty pounds of fresh potatoes. [object of preposition]
6. I smelled black olives. [direct object]
7. The insects are collected. [verb]
8. Smoke flavor is added to barbecue sauces. [subject]
9. Maybe I'll buy myself a beanstalk. [direct object]
10. Rachel could never keep her eyes off my papers. [prepositional phrase]
11. I didn't like his ideas. [verb]
12. You went out for ice cream cones with your Uncle Larry. [object of the preposition]
13. The kitchen was quiet. [subject]
14. There's salt in the North Sea. [subject]
15. After settling in to my hotel room, I called my wife. [direct object]
16. The team of archaeologists unearthed human figurines. [direct object]
17. In Russia, medical care is expensive. [subject]
18. Other people don't seem to notice the bitterness. [direct object]
19. Hutton has read his manuscripts. [subject]
20. I paid her a couple of dollars. [indirect object]

Verbals

A verbal is a verb form that doesn't act or function like a verb. Rather verbals are **hybrid grammatical structures**, partially verb and partially another form class. All the physical characteristics of verbals are those of verbs, but verbals function in a way that is distinctively non-verblike. Grammarians talk about three kinds of verbals: **infinitives**, **gerunds**, and **participles**. All have different physical structures, and all have slightly different functions. And all share many of the verb's qualities; that is, they have verb endings (*-ed* and *–ing*) and they can pattern with modifiers or complements (just as certain kinds of modifiers pattern with verbs). You will find verbals with objects. You will find verbals that have their own clusters (and even their own clauses). You will find that verbals are condensed sentences, mini-sentences if you will, that fit all the sentence patterns except the There-V-S pattern. But you won't find tense in a verbal; this lack of tense makes the verbal **non-finite**. A **finite** or **complete** verb is one that demonstrates tense. It is worth repeating for me to say that **a verbal is not the verb or predicate of a sentence or a pattern** because it will be non-finite—incomplete or missing the tense marker.

So let us now begin with the easiest verbal to recognize: the infinitive.

Infinitives

The infinitive verbal is easy to recognize. It consists of *to* plus a base verb: *to eat, to sleep, to read, to think*. Of course, infinitives may have their own clusters. They may be accompanied by objects and modifiers that typically pattern with verbs: ***to eat** lots of jalapeno peppers early in the morning,* ***to sleep** soundly on a new mattress, always **to read** mystery stories, never **to think** of another's wishes.* Infinitives may function as nouns, adjectives, or adverbs, but they always have the same basic form and look the same way (the *to* plus the base verb are your clues); thus they are easy to identify. When *to* is followed by a noun, it's a preposition, and you have a prepositional phrase; when *to* is followed by a verb, you have an infinitive. (*To* is a multi-function word.)

Functions of Infinitives. Look at the following sentences to see how the same infinitive, ***to play*** *in the state tournament*, can function in a variety of ways, from any variety of noun slots to adjective and adverb positions.

SUBJECT—**To play in the state tennis tournament** was her dream.

DIRECT OBJECT—She hoped **to play in the state tennis tournament.**

PREDICATE NOUN—Her dream was **to play in the state tennis tournament.**

APPOSITIVE (NOUN)—Her dream, **to play in the state tennis tournament**, was a fine dream.

ADJECTIVE—Her time **to play in the state tennis tournament** has not come.

ADVERB—She was afraid **to play in the state tennis tournament.**

The Split Infinitive. The infinitive in the conversation bubble in the cartoon Cast Unceremoniously Adrift, *to unceremoniously cast me adrift*, is an example of a split infinitive.

The crew can no longer tolerate Captain Bligh's ruthless splitting of infinitives.

Cast Unceremoniously Adrift

This means that a word, here *unceremoniously, comes* between the *to* and its verb—*cast,* in this case—effectively splitting the infinitive in two. Some grammarians and teachers consider splitting infinitives a breach of good usage, but split infinitives are often used by mature writers. This now silly rule against splitting the infinitive was first articulated by Robert Lowth in *A Short Introduction to English Grammar* (1762) and is less and less frequently observed. Some quite famous sentences in English have split infinitives, the most popular of which is Captain Kirk's split infinitive, "to boldly go where no man has gone before." Here are some other examples of split infinitives:

1. He hoped to perhaps avoid explanations.
2. The thieves plan to surreptitiously enter the building via the underground utility tunnels.

3. Moses would have to endlessly repeat his story.

If you know that your readers (or listeners) are overly particular, don't split infinitives—or do it for a good rhetorical reason!

~~~~~~

FOR THINKING

Quickly identify the infinitive or the entire infinitive phrase (the infinitive plus all its clusters, all those words that group themselves around the infinitive) in the following sentences. If you have time in your writing group, explain how each infinitive functions (as noun, adjective, adverb). Be prepared to discuss these.

1. It is not difficult to make a glass mirror.
2. Ethan had managed to carve a study out of the little space in the apartment.
3. I was compelled to continue my journey.
4. To really appreciate good pastries is a skill pleasurable to learn.
5. It is exalting to search for the right word.
6. To love one's enemies is a Christian precept.
7. Experts find it hard to make a mistake.
8. I did not want to abandon my old misconceptions.
9. We learned to pay attention to our financial affairs during the downturn of the stock market.
10. Her clutching the handlebar convulsively made it hard to steer the bike.
11. The prisoner was forced to speak.
12. To follow these severe regulations was disheartening as well as time-consuming.
13. To solve the mystery, it was necessary to solve the equations left in the cryptic note.
14. We remain here to watch over our chickens.

15. They gave me a form to fill out.
16. The commandant promised to question all of us later.
17. This word is used to describe the worshiper of images.
18. After the earthquake, it was impossible to identify the ragged and ruined belongings.
19. In the shelter, there is barely enough light to read by.
20. It was easy to identify the infinitives in these sentences!

~~~~~~

Infinitives and Patterns. Because verbals share the characteristics of verbs, verbals also follow all the sentence patterns except the There-V-S pattern. After all, sentence patterns depend on the kind of verb in the sentence. And since any verb can also be part of an infinitive or infinitive phrase, it makes sense that, as verbals, infinitives would also follow the patterns. The infinitive phrases below mimic the basic sentence patterns. Here is an example of a verbal whose pattern is S-V-O (notice that the subject is missing and that you have just the verb here to illustrate the pattern—but also notice that patterns depend entirely on what kind of verb is used):

to read this sentence quickly

A sentence with this infinitive in it might look like this:

Sally is very proud of being able to read this sentence quickly.

Read is a verb form, and *sentence* is its object, answering the question, "What is read?" Here are examples of how infinitives can reproduce the other sentence patterns as well:

S-V-IO-DO—to get me the latest version of the software

S-V-DO-OC—to name my friend winner of the contest

S-LV-PA—to smell fresh and clean

S-LV-PN—to become a public health nurse

S-V—to labor long and hard for a day's pay

~~~~~~

FOR WRITING

Below you will find a list of infinitives or infinitive phrases. Build a sentence around each infinitive phrase, using the phrase in any way you choose. Of course, you may alter the phrase or add to it as you wish. Read your favorite finished sentences to your writing group or to the class. The first one is done for you as an example.

1. to make fritters—The baker tried to **make fritters**. (This is an S-V-O patterned infinitive: V=make-O=fritters.)
2. to dull every spark of talent
3. to use up much of their ammunition
4. to eat the smoked chicken
5. to go and play billiards in the bar downstairs
6. to control myself
7. to be solid and new
8. to earn one's bread
9. to find anything better
10. to reconstruct the accident after all the terror subsided
11. to say with precision
12. to spit on the ground
13. to be afraid of
14. to carry out a sentence
15. to extract a rabbit from a tall silk hat
16. to understand what formulas they were referring to
17. to scrape
18. to protect against death by burning

19. to speak like a sailor
20. to reach far enough to touch the items on the top shelf
21. to fill out
22. to survive
23. to judge from the anonymous, sloppy handwriting
24. to sauté three slices of onion
25. to know as little as possible

~~~~~~

You will probably never need to identify how you are using infinitives, but it is useful to know that they can have many different functions and can occupy many different spaces within a sentence.

Gerunds

Gerunds, like infinitives, are also consistent in form or physical appearance. They are verb forms that always end in the *-ing* suffix, which is the present participial verb ending—*eating, sleeping, reading, thinking.* One difficulty in recognizing gerunds is that other verbals (participles, which you'll read about next) may also end in *-ing.* You can separate gerunds from similar-looking participles, though, by remembering that gerunds function as nouns and only nouns; almost anywhere that a noun can go, a gerund can also fit. Because gerunds are cousins to verbs, they may also have objects and modifiers that pattern with them in verb clusters: ***eating*** *waffles at the corner restaurant, never* ***sleeping*** *past seven o'clock,* ***reading*** *all the Louis L'Amour mysteries, unfortunately* ***thinking*** *about a sex goddess.* So remember: gerunds end in *-ing* and function as nouns.

There's also one grammatical commonplace, a rule that some grammarians now consider outdated, about gerunds that you should know if a situation calls for super-grammar. Because gerunds function as nouns, pronouns that precede them should be in possessive case. This combination of a possessive pronoun (or determiner) with a gerund phrase is called a **gerund-with-genitive** phrase and is a variation on the gerund phrase. For example, you would write

*Mother was not aware of **Jim's** going to the dance.*

rather than

*Mother was not aware of **Jim** going to the dance.*

And according to this rule, you would write

*No one knew about **his** stealing all the money from the trust fund.*

not

*No one knew about **him** stealing all the money from the trust fund.*

Functions of Gerunds. Gerunds always function or work as nouns. Therefore, you will find them in places where nouns are typically found: as subject, direct object, predicate noun, appositive, and object of the preposition. Here are some examples of gerunds in different noun slots:

SUBJECT—**Playing in the state tennis tournament** was her dream.

DIRECT OBJECT—She enjoyed **playing in the state tennis tournament.**

PREDICATE NOUN—Her dream became **playing in the state tennis tournament.**

APPOSITIVE—Her dream, **playing in the state tennis tournament**, was never realized.

OBJECT OF PREPOSITION —She never realized her dream of **playing in the state tennis tournament.**

Rhetorical Impact of Gerunds. Using gerunds pumps up the pace of your writing a notch or two. When you use a gerund, you insert a word that looks like a progressive tense verb—an *-ing* verb that connotes or suggests motion—into a noun slot. Because nouns tend to be stolid and somewhat implacable in sentences, you get to have your cake and eat it too when you use gerunds: you use nouns, but they don't look like nouns. Gerunds name actions, and they can help you maintain a healthy pace for your prose.

~~~~~~

FOR THINKING

Quickly identify the gerund or gerund phrase (the gerund plus all its clusters, all those words that group around the gerund) in the following sentences. If you have time in your writing group, explain in what nominal capacity each gerund functions (or how each gerund functions as a noun).

1.   Watching everyone read out loud was daunting.
2.   You will be in charge of getting clean water.
3.   Cinderella finished her cleaning early.
4.   Organizing the food pantry was hard but rewarding work.
5.   Was Irene interested in remarrying?
6.   She feared running into her old boyfriend.
7.   Joel was personally responsible for instituting Teacher Appreciation Day.
8.   Pretending innocence won't work this time.
9.   Cheating at poker was her specialty.
10. The whining annoyed her greatly.
11. He woke William up with the clacking of his jaw.

12. Fence mending was not her idea of an enjoyable way to spend an afternoon.
13. The doctor warned Mandy about sitting up too soon after surgery.
14. Her belief in changing her life was absolutely fixed.
15. Mrs. Petrocelli likes preparing dinner for her family.
16. Sunbathing is terrible for your skin!
17. Driving the beltway at rush hour is dangerous.
18. Frowning did not become the little princess.
19. Filling out the grant report became our morning's task.
20. Denis was adept at chilling the wine to exactly the right temperature.
21. For being alert and saving the toddler, you win an award.
22. There is the sound of buzzing in this office.
23. Making digital movies is not as hard as it sounds.
24. By the time he was 25, Oliver was already tired of earning his way.
25. Smoking cigarettes is definitely dangerous to your health.

Gerunds and Patterns. Like infinitives, gerunds can also assume the familiar patterns of verbs in sentences. The gerund phrases below mimic the basic sentence patterns except for the There V-S pattern. Here is an example of the S-V-O pattern within a gerund: *reading this sentence quickly*

A sentence with this gerund in it might look like this: *Sally is very proud of **reading this sentence quickly.***

If we think of *reading* as the verb equivalent within the gerund phrase, then *sentence* is its object, answering the question, "What is read?" Here are examples of how gerunds can reproduce the other sentence patterns as well:

S-V-IO-DO—getting me the latest version of the software

S-V-DO-OC—naming my friend winner of the contest

S-LV-PA—smelling fresh and clean

S-LV-PN—becoming a public health nurse

S-V—laboring long and hard for a day's pay

Troubleshooting Gerunds. Be especially mindful that gerunds function only as nouns. In a sentence like *The guards will be noting our arrival*, *noting* is not a gerund. In this sentence, *noting* is the present progressive form of the verb, accompanied by its auxiliaries, *will* and *be*, to indicate the future progressive tense. This is a **finite** or **complete** verb whose direct object is *arrival*; the pattern of the sentence is S (guards)-V (will be noting)-O (our arrival). Gerunds (and infinitives and participles too) are—don't forget—**non-finite verbs**. This means that they are not complete enough to constitute the entire main (or finite) verb in a sentence. If you pair them with an auxiliary, of course you can make them finite: then, however, they are transmuted from gerunds (or infinitives or participles) into main verbs.

Also, do not write as an example of a gerund a sentence like *Noting our arrival, the guard scribbled furiously on his clipboard.*

Observe that in this sentence *noting our arrival* does not function as a noun. *Guard* is the subject of the sentence; *clipboard* is the object of a preposition. These are the only nouns in the sentence. *Noting our arrival* does not occupy a noun slot nor behave like a noun. (It's really a participle, functioning as an adjective. More about this later.) To use the phrase *noting our arrival as a gerund*, use it in a sentence something like this: *The guard was occupied with **noting our arrival**.*

Noting our arrival functions as a noun, the object of the preposition *with*. The gerund phrase, which includes the non-finite progressive tense form, *noting*, thus functions as a noun and together with *with*, constitutes a prepositional phrase.

~~~~~~

FOR WRITING

Below you will find a list of gerunds or gerund phrases. Build a sentence around each gerund phrase, using the phrase in any way you choose as long as it functions as a noun. Of course, you may alter the phrase or add to it as you wish. Read your favorite finished sentences to your writing group or to the class. Observe the pattern of each gerund or gerund phrase as you go along. The first one is done for you as an example. Remember to use each phrase in a NOUN's position.

1. making fritters—***Making fritters*** *was the baker's task for the morning.* (This gerund, *making fritters*, is used as the subject of the sentence; it is an S-V-O -patterned gerund, with *fritters* as the object of the gerund *making*. *Morning* ends in –ing and, as object of the preposition *for*, occupies a noun slot; it is not a gerund because it's not a verb form—it's just a regular noun.)
2. furnishing him with an address
3. arriving from the ends of the earth
4. rationing
5. writing poetry
6. entering air-raid shelters
7. losing myself in the music
8. leaping out of the water
9. healing
10. surprising all the kindergarteners at once
11. accepting all the reports

12. rowing
13. freeing the chained captives
14. sewing the ivory buttons on the sealskin coat
15. watering the delicate African violets
16. adjusting his stock portfolio to meet the market downturn
17. arguing with his girlfriend on the telephone
18. downloading data from the data warehouse
19. singing while you drive
20. monitoring the police channel
21. seeing the sea at Carmel
22. checking your e-mail
23. receiving visitors from his hospital bed
24. noting our arrival
25. watering the livestock

~~~~~~

Participles

Participles are sometimes the most difficult verbals to identify because their appearance is inconsistent; they may have several different endings. But if you remember that they are formed from the past-participial and present-participial forms of verbs, you may find this task easier. Past participles (*eaten, slept, read, thought*) are the forms that pattern with the auxiliary *have* in the perfect tenses. Present participles (*eating, sleeping, reading, and thinking*) pattern with the auxiliary *be* in the progressive tenses. Do present participles look like gerunds? Absolutely. But gerunds and participles function in ways that will allow you to tell them apart.

Functions of Participles. How can you distinguish present participles from gerunds? Participles function as **adjectives**, patterning with nouns or sometimes with whole sentences as sentence modifiers. And, just like infinitives and gerunds, participles may, like finite verbs, have objects and modifiers—the *partially eaten* bananas, a bed *barely slept in*, a book *read by fifty million readers*, an idea *thought ridiculous by many*— these are past participial phrases because they are made with the past participial forms (*eaten, slept, read, thought*). They are also all derived from passive structures: the bananas *were partially eaten*, the bed *was barely slept in*, the book *was read by fifty million readers*, the idea *was thought ridiculous by many*.

In the sentence *We watched the children eating the bananas, eating the bananas* is a participial phrase that patterns with *children*. In the sentence, *The dog quietly moving his paws in his dreams suddenly awoke*, a participial phrase is *quietly moving his paws in his dreams*. In both these phrases with present participles (*eating* and *moving*), participle forms are at the head or center of the phrases.

Where in a sentence do you typically find participles? They usually occur in noun clusters and are found near nouns. This makes sense because they function adjectivally. Sometimes they occur before a noun:

Her *billowing* skirts were lovely and graceful. (*Billowing* patterns before the noun it describes.)

Sometimes they occur after a noun, typically in a phrase: Her skirts, *billowing in the gentle breeze*, were lovely and graceful. (*Billowing in the gentle breeze* is a participial phrase coming after its noun, *skirts*.) Participial phrases can also appear at the head of the sentence. In this position, they sometimes modify the entire idea of the sentence as much as one specific noun:

Billowing in the gentle breeze, her skirts were lovely and graceful. (Here the participial phrase adheres to its noun, *skirts*, strongly.)

Running frantically from the collapsing building, thousands of New Yorkers managed to survive. (This participial phrase relates to more than just the subject noun, *thousands;* many grammarians would call this one a sentence modifier. Did you see the other present participle, *collapsing?* And did you also see the infinitive, to *survive?*)

Participles frequently appear solo, with no clustering words, as in *She lay her head on her **crossed** arms* and *He moved quickly to the **crying** baby*—so they look like ordinary adjectives and function that way too.

And remember: don't confuse participles and predicates. A participle or participial phrase is *not* the verb or predicate of a sentence. Participles are part of noun clusters; although they resemble verbs in form, they are non-finite and they function as adjectives.

Rhetorical Impact of Participles. Participles quicken your text and, when substituted for or used alongside regular adjectives, provide variety. Like gerunds and infinitives, participles provide a verb presence in a sentence; that is, they suggest energy and movement.

For Discussion

See if you can spot the participles and participial phrases in the sentences below. Remember to look for present participles ending in *–ing* and past participles ending in *–ed, -en,* and *–t;* and remember that participles and their clusters function as adjectives and pattern near nouns. Also remember that sometimes you will find a single word; other times you will find an extensive phrase or cluster (the participle with its modifiers). Finally, remember that the participle or participial phrase will exist outside the regular sentence pattern and will not be an element in the pattern. Be prepared to present one or two sentences to your whole class.

1. He looked like a young hawk with plumage ruffled by a storm.
2. The sagging skin of her face was sallow.
3. He is a driver attached to the general staff.
4. A man racked with fever lay on the dirty cot.
5. Hastily throwing their cigarettes away, the students hurried into the building under the disapproving eye of the principal.
6. Glancing at the basket of fruit sitting on the table, she thought regretfully about last night.
7. Shaking hands with all the guests, my father made his way around the crowded room.
8. Framed by a little black beard, Sam's face looked slightly ridiculous.
9. He spat out a few sharp, ugly words.
10. His anger was like a fire, taking life from itself and growing from its own fuel.
11. We ran down the lighted streets.
12. All the living places of the elders have been torn down.
13. The Roman museums were inspiring edifices.
14. Daily he searched the crowded streets.
15. On the day after the crime, he had been home, celebrating the holiday with his family.
16. Recognized by NASA, our sleep technology is raved about world wide!
17. Looking out the window, I can see my garden, covered in snow.
18. Returning from his job as a night watchman, Jan saw the pogrom.
19. Discover newly recorded works by Aaron Copland.
20. Take a hiking and walking trip in Europe.
21. She likes interesting dancers.

22. The small plastic doll baked inside *rosca de reyes* is a symbol of the infant Jesus.
23. Addressing the health concerns of women, this guide gives comprehensive advice on everything from fitness to drugs and alcohol.
24. Eventually, the waiter brought me a small white bowl filled with hot chocolate topped with whipped cream flavored with cinnamon.
25. The witnesses deposed before the tribunal gave false testimony.

~~~~~~

Participles and Patterns. Like gerunds and infinitives, participles can also assume the familiar patterns of verbs in sentences (except for the There V-S pattern). The participial phrases below mimic the basic sentence patterns. Here is an example of the S-V-O pattern within a participle: *reading this sentence quickly.*

A sentence with this participle in it might look like this: *Reading this sentence quickly, Sally felt very proud.*

If we think of *reading* as the verb of the participial pattern, then *sentence* is its object, answering the question, "What is read?" Here are examples of how participles can reproduce the other sentence patterns as well:

S-V-IO-DO—getting me the latest version of the software

S-V-DO-OC—naming my friend winner of the contest

S-LV-PA—smelling fresh and clean

S-LV-PN—becoming a public health nurse

S-V—dressed in an organdy dress

FOR WRITING

Below you will find a list of participles or participial phrases; some of these are identical to the gerunds and gerund phrases from the previous section. Build a sentence around each participial phrase, using the phrase in any way you choose. You may alter the phrase or add to it as you wish. Read your favorite finished sentences to your writing group or to the class. And notice the pattern of each participle or participial phrase as you go along. Remember that because gerunds and participial phrases derived from present participles may look exactly alike, the only difference between some gerunds and their participial doubles will be *how they are used, their functions*. Gerunds are used as nouns, exclusively; participles are used as adjectives, exclusively. You may have to memorize this difference at first.

The first one is done for you as an example. Remember to use each phrase in an *adjectival* position; participles pattern with nouns and act to describe or limit or enhance nouns and noun clusters and sometimes the entire idea of the sentence.

1. furnishing him with an address: Furnishing him with an address, the driver of the other car in the accident cooperated with the police.
2. arriving from the ends of the earth
3. rationed
4. writing poetry
5. entering air-raid shelters
6. lost in the music
7. leaping out of the water
8. healed by the medicinal herbs
9. surprised by all the kindergarteners
10. accepting all the reports
11. slicing

12. freed from a life of abject poverty
13. sewn onto the sealskin coat
14. watering the delicate African violets
15. adjusted to meet the market downturn
16. arguing with his girlfriend on the telephone
17. downloaded from the data warehouse
18. singing while you drive
19. monitored on the police channel
20. seen for the first time at Silver Spring
21. checking your e-mail
22. receiving visitors from his hospital bed
23. noted in the ledger
24. watering the livestock
25. stolen

Reviewing All Verbals

Let's reconsider what you know about verbals now, how they are alike and in what ways they differ. The chart Reviewing All Verbals summarizes this information.

Reviewing All Verbals

Verbals and their clusters remind us of verb clusters. A verbal, however, is a non-finite verb form. It may function singly, just one word by itself, or it may pattern in clusters like a verb—with adverbial modifiers, objects, prepositional phrase modifiers, and even clauses (more about this later) to reproduce the major sentence patterns.

INFINITIVES	GERUNDS	PARTICIPLES
are readily identifiable by form: *to* + verb (*to snore, to tear, to sigh*). They pattern with nouns to function as adjectives and with verbs to function as adverbs. And they can also function anywhere a noun or noun substitute can function— as subject, direct object, predicate noun, object of preposition, appositive.	are also readily identifiable by their form—base verb + -*ing* (*working, cheering, smoothing*). They function only as nouns and so can appear where nouns do—in the subject slot, the direct object, the predicate noun slot. They can also function as object of prepositions and as appositives.	are the most difficult to identify by form because they can have more than one form, either **past participial** form (ends in -*en*, -*ed*, -*t* as in *written, frayed, burnt*) or **present participial** form (ends in –*ing* as in *tearing, weeping, snoozing*). They have, though, only one function: as adjectives and patterning with nouns.

FOR THINKING AND TALKING

Find the verbals in the following sentences. Be prepared to identify each verbal and to explain how it functions or works within the sentence as a whole. Some sentences may have more than one verbal or verbal phrase.

1. "Overnight, the aristocracy would have given anything for the privilege of milking a cow."—The J. Peterman Company. From *Owner's Manual*, No. 136.
2. "He remembered his father's telling of his town in Europe, a common barrel of water, a town idiot, a baron nearby." —Arthur Miller. From "Presence."
3. "In criminal cases, it is common practice to bring relatives of defendants before grand juries." —Jane Mayer. From "The House of Bin Laden."
4. "The marriage broker, a skeleton with haunted eyes, returned that very night." —Bernard Malamud. From "The Magic Barrel."
5. "In order to miss its chilly shadow, our neighbors walked three blocks east to buy a loaf of bread." —Grace Paley. From "The Loudest Voice."
6. "The grain is his hoarded wealth, his greed, his covetousness." —Norman Mailer. From "And the Fire Abated."
7. "The mud, frozen into peaks, was melting." —Cynthia Ozick. From "Envy, Or Yiddish in America."
8. "I bought him a little bone teething ring and a little gilded hat." —Isaac Bashevis Singer. From *Gimpel the Fool*.
9. To keep blood pressure, sugar, and fat levels under control, you should strike the right balance by counting both grams and calories.
10. "He's nervous from working in the factory all day and riding in the crowded El." —Kate Simon. From "Bronx Primitive."

11. "He sometimes played five or six hands of poker in the druggist's back room, trying his luck before getting on the streetcar."—Saul Bellow. From "Something to Remember Me By."
12. "Twilight is also the mind's grazing time." —Alfred Kazin. From *A Walker in the City*.
13. "Reaching toward the sugar bowl, she lifted out the tongs, carefully pinched a cube of sugar, and held it up before his eyes." —Henry Roth. From *Call It Sleep*.
14. "They surround Simha, crouched on her stool." —E.M. Broner. From *A Weave of Women*.
15. "I didn't know quite how to begin on a thing like that." —Daniel Fuchs. From "A Hollywood Diary."
16. "Scattering hat and tissue paper to the floor, he returned downstairs." —Philip Roth. From *Goodbye, Columbus*.
17. "At first, Ricardo wanted to dismiss the query." —Melvin Jules Bukiet. From "The Library of Moloch."
18. "Joshua, sighing, leans back in his chair." —E.L. Doctorow. From "Heist."
19. "She spat like a poisoned cat." —Michael Gold. From *Jews Without Money*.
20. "The morality criterion seems impossible to apply here." —Richard Lanham. From *Style: An Anti-Textbook*, 2nd ed.

Nominative Absolutes

The **nominative absolute** is a curious fellow. It is a phrase, not a sentence, although it seems sentence-like—and it can convey an almost fully realized thought. It evokes the "absolute" essence of a sentence—and looks like a sentence except for one thing: it doesn't have a finite verb. It has a subject or a noun (or nominative) at its head; therefore the *nominative* in its name. So, then, a nominative absolute is a noun-headed phrase that conveys the notion of a sentence absolutely—yet without a finite verb. Absolutes attach to sentences as **free modifiers**; that is, they do not affix themselves to any particular word but to the concept expressed in the sentence. Consider this sentence:

Tires deflated, frame bent, the bike rested against the wall.

You can see two nominative absolutes in this sentence: *tires deflated* and *frame bent*. Each of these phrases is headed by a noun: *tires* and *frame*. Each also has a verb, but not a finite or complete verb. In both instances, the auxiliary, a key part of the complete verb phrase, is missing. In the original deep or basic structure of this sentence, there are actually three sentences:

The bike rested against the wall.

Its tires were deflated.

Its frame was bent.

The sentence resulting when all these sentences are combined contains two nominative absolutes with headwords that are closely related to (but not the same as) the subject of the original or base sentence, *bike*. When we combine the sentences to include a nominative absolute, we leave the base sentence as it is. We shrink the sentences that will become absolutes by removing the auxiliary verbs, *were* and *was*, so that we now have

The bike rested against the wall.

Its tires deflated.

Its frame bent.

In the final iteration of the sentence, we can eliminate *its* because the link between the *bike* and its *tires* and *frame* is clear. Sometimes we leave determiners like *its* in for clarity; in this case we can omit them. See how each absolute clearly retains the meaning of its original sentence and observe how each is really almost a sentence—but not quite.

The bike rested against the wall, tires deflated, frame bent.

Does it matter that we placed the absolutes at the end of this version of the sentence rather than at its beginning (our original version)? No. In this sentence, the link between the noun subjects is so clear that we can move the absolutes to the end of the finished sentence if we so choose. It is not always this clear or this easy, however, so you will have to place the absolutes carefully to maintain the integrity of the sentence.

Rhetorical Impact of Absolutes

The nominative absolute is very powerful. You will find it especially useful when you want to add layers of description to a passage or to fill in a scene with detail. If your professor reminds you to develop your examples or to show details, try writing nominative absolutes. They have the power to magnify the effect of any description. With the absolute, you add absolutely the idea of a new sentence without all its grammatical heaviness because you are not adding complete patterns (of course, the verb is non-finite). With the absolute, you fatten the images and enrich the depth of your writing.

FOR THINKING

See if you can find the nominative absolutes in the sentences that follow. Some sentences have more than one absolute. Underscore the absolute and be prepared to talk in class about what it adds to the sentence where it resides.

1. "Carr sits calmly, his concentration fixed, his hands folded reassuringly across his lap, with the equable, impersonal kindness of a priest or a cop." —Melanie Thernstrom. From "Pain, the Disease."
2. Hips swaying, I sauntered down the street in my platform shoes.
3. Pencil sharpened and paper piled neatly before me, I began to write the exam.
4. The little girls ran through the meadow, hair ribbons cascading behind them.
5. Antlers erect, the deer crossed the creek, eyes focused on the men across the way.
6. Eyes wide open, the cow jumped over the moon.
7. Tail switching slowly back and forth in pleasure, the cat snuggled into the chair.
8. The vampire, fangs dripping with blood, searched for another meal.
9. My insecurities gone, I performed the sonata without hesitation or error.
10. Hands steady, the nurse expertly gave the screaming patient a shot.
11. Here comes Uncle Benny, gift held proudly before him, a full day late for the birthday celebration.
12. "We talked very little during the drive, each of us peering intently into the descending dusk for glimpses of the familiar and the unknown." —Lynda Van Devanter. From *Home Before Morning: The Story of an American Army Nurse in VietNam.*
13. "In a late-summer drizzle, I teeter atop a starting block, my arms swollen as sausages from lactic acid, my head pounding from tension, lack of food, and good old self-loathing." —James Thornton. From *In His Own Words.*

14. On cue, LuLing entered, her petite frame contrasting with GaoLing's sturdier one. —Amy Tan. From *The Bonesetter's Daughter.*

15. "He sat up and put his legs over the side of the bed, his flesh still numb, shivers running up and down his back as if he'd caught an ague." —John Gardner. From *Freddy's Book.*

16. "I sit on the bed at a crooked angle, one foot on the floor, my hip against the tent of Mom's legs, my elbows on the hospital table." —Michael Dorris. From *A Yellow Raft in Blue Water.*

17. "She plodded along beside me solemnly, her rubber boots making deep prints in the snow." —Richard Bradford. From *Red Sky at Morning.*

Did you notice how the absolutes give the reader more information about the central event in the sentence? Did you observe how the noun at the head of the absolute is very closely related to, but not the same as, a noun in the base sentence? This close relationship is critical to the success of your sentences containing nominative absolutes.

FOR WRITING

Now you try creating some sentences with nominative absolutes from the clusters of sentence ingredients below. In each group, you will find from two to four sentences. One will be the base sentence; it will be marked *base sentence.*

1. You should leave the base sentence as it is.
2. Change all the other sentences into absolutes by removing the auxiliary or the *be* verb.
3. Then fold all the absolute phrases (the ones with non-finite verbs) into the base sentences.

4. You'll have to decide where the absolutes should go.

What are the rhetorical implications for their locations in the sentence? If absolutes introduce the sentence, they are likely providing detail that either (a) helps create a scene for the base clause or (b) provides some information necessary for understanding what happens in the base clause. An absolute placed mid-sentence is probably there for clarity—because two noun headwords need to pattern near one another to make the sentence make sense. An absolute placed at the end of the sentence is more likely to be perceived as a comment on what happens in the rest of the sentence or an afterthought. So be careful where you insert absolutes. Now try writing some sentences with absolutes by combining these elements (the first one is done as an example):

1. *The boy was rushed to the doctor.* (base)

His knees were bleeding profusely.

His ankle was twisted grotesquely.

yields

Knees bleeding profusely and ankle twisted grotesquely, the boy was rushed to the doctor.

or

The boy, knees bleeding profusely, ankle twisted grotesquely, was rushed to the doctor.

What is the difference in putting the absolutes after *boy* other than at the beginning of the finished sentence? Which version do you prefer?

2. Icarus splashed down into the cold and salty sea. (base)
3. John clutched the teddy bear. (base)
4. The wedding cake looked perfect. (base)
5. The little girl woke up from a nightmare. (base)
6. Vandals had totally spoiled the car. (base)
7. Natalie picked the perfect pink rose from the garden prematurely. (base)
8. Nathan's dog ran joyously around the yard. (base)
9. Professor White walked into the pouring rain. (base)
10. She sprawled on the couch with ice cream and a movie. (base)

~~~~~~

Distinguishing Nominative Absolutes from Verbals

You *can* tell nominative absolutes and verbals apart although it's also easy to confuse them. The easiest way to distinguish them is to remember that nominative absolutes have **noun headwords** (or they cluster around nouns) and verbal phrases have **verb headwords** (or they cluster around a verb form). Each also springs from a different kind of deep structure. Consider the base sentence

The Corvette tore out of the parking lot.

Now let's add to this base sentence about the Corvette the ideas in these sentences:

The Corvette's tires were spinning.

The Corvette's radio was blaring "Born to be Wild."

The Corvette was running at full throttle in first gear.

Look: in the first two sentences, the subject is not the Corvette itself but two aspects of the Corvette, two items closely related to it: its *tires* and its *radio*. In the third sentence, the subject *Corvette* is identical to the subject of the base sentence, *Corvette*. Because the subject of the third sentence is the same as that of the base sentence, we will fold this sentence into the base sentence as a verbal, retaining only the main form of the verb:

Running at full throttle in first gear, the Corvette tore out of the parking lot.

Because the other two sentences to be incorporated into the base sentence have different subjects than *Corvette*, we must incorporate them into the sentence as nominative absolutes with the related nouns as headwords, *tires spinning* and *radio blaring "Born to be Wild."* Our finished sentence might look something like this:

Running at full throttle in first gear, (introductory participial phrase)

the Corvette tore out of the parking lot, (base clause)

tires spinning and (nominative absolute)

radio blaring "Born to Be Wild." (nominative absolute)

or

Running at full throttle in first gear, the Corvette tore out of the parking lot, tires spinning and radio blaring "Born to Be Wild."

The verbal and the absolutes co-exist nicely in the same sentence, providing a detailed look at just how that Corvette exited the parking lot. The main verb, *tore out of* (a phrasal verb) also contributes to the notion of speed and recklessness surrounding the car's leaving the parking lot.

Looking at Passages for Style

Study the following passages, looking specifically for verbals and nominative absolutes. Be prepared to explain to the class or to your writer's group how the free modifiers work to build the effect of the passage.

Passage 1: "They communicated across Gregor's room. "You'll have to go for the doctor straight away. Gregor is ill. Quick, get the doctor. Did you hear the way Gregor spoke just now?" "That was the voice of an animal," said the chief clerk, with a calmness that was in contrast with his mother's screams. "Anna! Anna!" his father called into the kitchen through the entrance hall, clapping his hands, "get a locksmith here, now!" And the two girls, their skirts swishing, immediately ran out through the hall, wrenching open the front door of the flat as they went. How had his sister managed to get dressed so quickly? There was no sound of the door banging shut again; they must have left it open; people often do in homes where something awful has happened."—Franz Kafka. From "Metamorphosis."

Passage 2: "Over his lavender collar, crushed upon a purple necktie, held by a diamond hoop: over his ammunition belt of tooled leather worked in silver, buckled cruelly around his gasping middle: over the tops of his glossy shoes Braggioni swells with ominous ripeness, his mauve silk hose stretch taut, his ankles bound with the stout leather thongs of his shoes." —Katherine Ann Porter. From "Flowering Judas."

Passage 3: "In he [Ingmar Bergman] came in corduroy pants, green shirt, V-neck sweater, tan windbreaker, his glasses on a string around his neck, his gray hair sticking out over his ears, his smile broad and welcoming. He kissed Dana's hand." —William Kennedy. From "Who Are You Now That You're Not Nobody?"

Passage 4: "Leaning over the balcony railing, I see the waiters, dressed in white jackets, already arranging chairs on the sidewalk. A boy, his face hidden by the ample hood of a burnoose, is bicycling with difficulty toward the grocery store next to the café. Hung over the bar handles are two straw baskets overloaded with fat loaves of bread. Bread is the gift of Allah." —Anonymous Student Writer.

Putting It All Together

Here are some quick tips for recalling the different verbals and absolutes:

Infinitives—verb-headed constructions consisting of *to* plus a base verb; can be used in a noun slot, as an adjective, or as an adverb. ***To earn my professor's respect*** *was hard work.*

Gerunds—verb-headed constructions consisting of base verb plus *–ing* suffix; used only in a noun's position as subject, direct object, predicate noun, appositive, object of the preposition. ***Earning my professor's respect*** *was hard work.*

Participles—verb-headed constructions consisting of the past participle (ends in *–ed, -en, -t*) or the present participle (ends in *–ing*); used only as an adjective. ***Earning my professor's respect****, I labored diligently over the homework assignment.*

Nominative Absolutes—noun-headed phrases that consist minimally of a noun and a non-finite verb; used as a free modifier that is absolutely a sentence (but not quite, owing to the non-finite verb). ***Her hair mussed by the wind*** *and* ***her skin tinted pink by the sun****, Rachel emerged from an afternoon at the beach, looking casually beautiful and relaxed.*

Now let's turn to putting patterns together to create compound, complex, and combination sentences. This next chapter will test your understanding of the concepts of patterns.

Chapter 5. Joining and Combining Patterns and Other Elements

Up to now in this book, you have worked primarily with **simple sentences**. This doesn't mean that the sentences you've looked at have been *easy*. It does mean that most every sentence you have worked with in this book so far has consisted of one clause, one sentence pattern. We call a sentence with just one clear pattern or one independent clause and no dependent clauses a **simple sentence**. It is important to shed any grammatical notion of *simple* as *easy:* many simple, one-pattern sentences are quite long and difficult, with phrase piled upon phrase and modifier upon modifier.

With this chapter, you'll clarify your understanding of simple sentences and develop your notion of sentence architecture to include compound sentences, complex sentences, and compound-complex sentences. You'll look at the kinds of clauses in complex sentences (adjective, adverb, and noun clauses), and you'll marvel at the beauty of combination sentences. Let's begin, however, by clarifying terms and by distinguishing between **phrases** and **clauses**. Then we'll go on to talk about the difference between independent and dependent clauses, then categorize the kinds of sentences, all the while thinking about the rhetorical differences among kinds of sentences.

Distinguishing Phrases and Clauses

A **phrase** is a group of related words, a cluster that does **not** include a complete sentence pattern. You will find prepositional phrases, verbal phrases, noun phrases, adjectival phrases. Some examples of phrases follow; notice that in a phrase there are no complete or finite patterns. Frequently a phrase is missing either a finite verb or a subject cluster, either of which would disqualify the phrase from pattern status:

of the four British vacationers (prepositional phrase)

our very favorite places (noun phrase or cluster around *places*, the noun headword)

too perfect to be believed (adjective phrase clustered around the headword *perfect*; the adjective phrase includes an infinitive phrase *to be believed*—a phrase within a phrase)

a brilliant orange robe (noun phrase or cluster around the headword *robe*)

holding up the bags of grass (participial phrase; the headword is *holding up*; the participial phrase also contains a noun phrase, bags of grass—a phrase within a phrase)

~~~~~~

FOR DISCUSSION

In your writers' group, explain what kind of phrase each of the following phrases is; start out by pointing out the headword of each phrase or the word that seems to be the center of the phrase. Several items contain more than one phrase or phrases within phrases. Prepare to present several of your explanations to the whole class.

1. too scantily presented
2. a personal, actual experience
3. their innocent childhood
4. a Star Trek pillow cover
5. smiling oddly at Leroy
6. was sitting on the crest of a hill
7. a professor of humanities at City College
8. to make love in Venice
9. like two pieces of old furniture
10. the faint light coming up the stairwell
11. a very unpleasant faintness
12. the loud groaning of the hydraulic valves
13. crossed the city
14. in the soft dusk
15. to have a large family
16. asleep during breakfast
17. before the monsoon rains
18. hanging precariously from the edge of the precipice
19. all the pretty horses
20. connected by the most fragile understanding

~~~~~~

Just as a phrase is a group of words, so is a clause. The difference is that a clause contains a sentence pattern or a subject and a finite verb—whereas a phrase does not. Some clauses are complete sentences, and some are not (more about this later). If you see a subject plus a finite verb, however, you have found a clause, regardless of whether it sounds like a complete sentence. Incidentally, many grammarians call phrases **p-groups** (for phrase groups) and clauses **s-groups** (for sentence groups).

FOR WRITING

Phrase or clause? Look at the following items below. Determine which are phrases and which are clauses and mark each as *phrase* or *clause*. Don't forget that a clause has a complete pattern, a subject and a finite verb: a phrase lacks some element that would make it a complete pattern. Most capitalization and punctuation marks have been removed from these phrases and clauses.

_____ 1. from early morning

_____ 2. that went untouched

_____ 3. children had died before

_____ 4. by accident

_____ 5. in their midst

_____ 6. when Neeley arose from the seven days of mourning

_____ 7. in lovingly rendered translations

_____ 8. while her husband had lain on his death bed

_____ 9. to be so famous

_____ 10. in 1918

_____ 11. when she had told him

_____ 12. a cosmopolitan man, a teacher, and a reformer

_____ 13. having groaned to himself

_____ 14. since their hearts had already been broken

_____ 15. from faraway little places

_____ 16. there was so much to catch up on

_____ 17. absorbed by their intertwining fantasies

_____ 18. to lavish advantages

_____ 19: the carpenter wrote down the measurements

_____ 20. at twelve years old

_____ 21. to reward you for your kindness

_____ 22. juice fresh from the orange

_____ 23. he writes, too

_____ 24. Aunt Edna had lived here

_____ 25. I forget myself

_____ 26. where the girls were lively and beautiful

_____ 27. you had a good chance of overhearing something

_____ 28. in the middle of this sparkling day

_____ 29. the most miserable time of year

_____ 30. well over six feet

_____ 31. his mouth was quite dry

_____ 32. when she played the harp

_____ 33. they were clumsy things, words

_____ 34. of the condition

_____ 35. had left all that behind

_____ 36. it had been rather pleasant there in the little shop

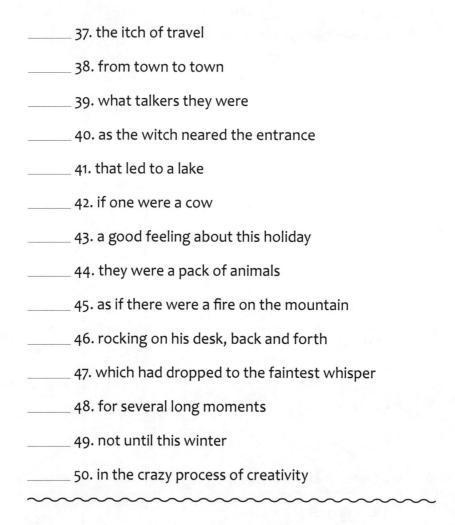

_____ 37. the itch of travel

_____ 38. from town to town

_____ 39. what talkers they were

_____ 40. as the witch neared the entrance

_____ 41. that led to a lake

_____ 42. if one were a cow

_____ 43. a good feeling about this holiday

_____ 44. they were a pack of animals

_____ 45. as if there were a fire on the mountain

_____ 46. rocking on his desk, back and forth

_____ 47. which had dropped to the faintest whisper

_____ 48. for several long moments

_____ 49. not until this winter

_____ 50. in the crazy process of creativity

Distinguishing Independent Clauses and Dependent Clauses

As you worked through the previous exercise on phrases and clauses, you probably identified some clauses that sounded just like (and indeed are) complete sentences: *they were a pack of animals* and *it had been rather pleasant there in the little shop*, for instance. These clauses or complete patterns that sound complete by themselves *are* in fact complete by themselves; they are also called **independent clauses** because they can stand on their own as sentences. You probably also noticed some clauses (complete patterns with finite verbs) that did not sound quite right or complete enough to be sentences. These are called **dependent clauses** or **subordinate clauses.** Examples of dependent clauses are *which had dropped to the faintest whisper* and *as the witch neared the entrance.* In a few pages you'll read more about kinds of dependent clauses (adjective, adverb, and noun clauses). For now, though, let's distinguish between dependent and independent clauses.

FOR WRITING

Mark the clauses below as *independent* or *dependent*, then compare your results with the answers everyone in your writing group got. There is no punctuation here to help you. Ask yourself, "Does this pattern sound complete as it is?"

1. even after you have asked for death
2. no one ever thanked him
3. people were telling each other stories
4. Sarah Sally Smith was born in 1910
5. which I could throw overboard
6. before he heard her
7. forget it [observe the ellipted or shortened subject and imperative mode]
8. she does not want to go with them
9. if I lose ten minutes' sleep
10. when Charles came home
11. a woman is singing to me
12. I walk through the long schoolroom
13. who once before came to Thebes
14. whatever influence I had over the king
15. when he realized the truth about her
16. the woman looked up the road

17. because she caught me smoking
18. I must have seen a rabbit
19. that Mrs. Hinden prayed
20. a bird streaked across the gray sky

~~~~~~

Creating Compound Sentences

Now that you can discern independent clauses, let us consider compound sentences. Put two independent clauses together, and you have a compound sentence. A **compound sentence** is composed of two or more independent clauses. At least two of the clauses must be independent; that is, each independent clause within the compound sentence can be removed and exist as a sentence all by itself. So if you have the independent clause

I listened to the organic chemistry lecture

and the related independent clause

I promptly fell asleep

you can create a compound sentence

I listened to the organic chemistry lecture, and I promptly fell asleep.

Each independent clause is a complete pattern that can exist on its own as a complete sentence.

Use compound sentences to link closely related independent clauses that you consider of equal importance. Rhetorically, the compound sentence yokes grammatically equal ideas. It also lends itself to balancing clauses or ideas and to parallelism because the **coordinator** or **coordinating conjunction** acts like the equal sign in an equation, mediating the two sides that must balance yet are somewhat different in composition and sometimes even subtly different in value.

You have several options for punctuating compound sentences. You can use a coordinator plus a comma; a semicolon alone; a semicolon plus a conjunctive adverb; and, in some special cases where the clauses are very closely related, a colon. Let's take a look at the rhetorical implications of each punctuation choice.

Creating Compound Sentences with Coordinators and Commas. The coordinator-comma combination is the most common way that independent clauses are put together in compound sentences. This combination sounds casual and comfortable, it moves quickly, and it allows you to express a great many shades of meaning with the most popular coordinators:

and (meaning *addition*)

but (meaning *contrast*)

for (meaning *because*)

so (meaning *therefore*)

yet (meaning *contrast*)

or, nor (meaning *alternative*)

The comma goes *after the first pattern* (and then after each subsequent pattern if there are more than two). The comma and the coordinator are of equal importance in this punctuation scheme; consider the two of them a unit linking one independent clause to the next. Some of you may have been taught to insert a comma routinely before each *and* in a sentence: this is **not** a good idea. If you have been taught this as a tenet of punctuation, work hard to disabuse yourself of this notion. What this practice can lead to is misplaced commas between elements of compound subjects, compound verbs, or other compounded sentence elements. Just because there's an *and* in the sentence doesn't mean there should be a comma. Here are some correct examples of the comma-co-ordinator combination:

1. "In shadow, the fields and woods were black, and in the light they were brown, purplish, and dark red." —Ursula Le Guin. From "The Eye Altering."
2. "He made no secret of this, yet people did not believe him." —Franz Kafka. From "A Hunger Artist."
3. "The husband went out to smoke in the first interval, and she was left alone in her seat." —Anton Chekhov. From "The Lady with the Little Dog."

Do you see each pattern? For sentence 1, the patterns are *fields and woods / were / black* (S-LV-PA) plus *they / were / brown, purplish, and dark red* (S-LV-PA); observe the comma after the first clause, then the coordinator *and*. The two independent clauses are related by the device of the same scene in contrasting light. Sentence 2 contains two S-V-O patterns, *he / made / secret* and *people / did believe / him*. These two patterns experience the negative transformation, then are linked by *yet*, which emphasizes contrast and difference. Now you analyze how sentence three above functions as a compound sentence.

Creating Compound Sentences with a Semicolon Joining Patterns. When you join two (or more) independent clauses with only a semi-colon between them, you send a rhetorical message to the reader that the reader needs to slow down and read deliberately. Here are some examples of the compound sentence where independent clauses are joined with only semicolons:

1. "It was true, too; she really did not have time." —Alice Munro. From "Boys and Girls."

2. "And the earth is shallow; there is not a great deal of it there."
   —William Faulkner. From *Go Down, Moses*.
3. "He was all out of breath with whispering; I could hear him
   pant slightly." —Joseph Conrad. From *The Secret Sharer and
   Other Stories*.

Emphasis falls on *too, shallow,* and *whispering,* the pivotal words in
the sentences, respectively. A complete pattern occupies the space before and after the semicolons in each sentence. You'll see in all these
sentences that a semicolon brings the reader up almost as short as a
period does, yet it's not quite a full stop. Rather it's a good long healthy
mid-sentence pause. This makes the last part of the first clause and the
first part of the last clause particularly powerful because they come at a
very important juncture. Imagine the reader's slowing down to attend
to the semicolon; this reader will therefore be dwelling longer on the
material nearest the semicolon. This makes this physical place in the
compound sentence a place of great rhetorical importance that you
may exploit as a writer. Because the semicolon brings the reader up a
bit shorter than does the comma and creates a longer pause, it also has
a more formal personality; it is hard to sound breezy when your page is
peppered with semicolons.

**Creating Compound Sentences with Semicolon and Conjunctive
Adverb Joining Patterns.** When you add a conjunctive adverb to
a semicolon, you heighten the formality of the prose considerably.
Conjunctive adverbs are, literally, adverbs that join. They are frequently
heavy compound words that are fairly easy to recognize: *moreover, furthermore, consequently, nevertheless, henceforth, therefore, rather.*

If the semicolon joining two independent clauses is more formal than
the comma plus coordinator method, then the semicolon and conjunctive adverb device is more formal still. Examine the sentences with conjunctive adverbs below and explain how the conjunctive adverb works.

1. "In spite of the prohibition, clandestine readings still took place for a time in some form or another; however, by 1870 they had virtually disappeared." —Alberto Manguel. From *A History of Reading.*
2. "Little emphasis was given to manufacturing and railroads at these meetings; rather, the stress was on marketing, banking, and credit reform in the South." —Harold Woodman. From *King Cotton and His Retainers: Financing and Marketing the Cotton Crop of the South, 1800-1925.*
3. We missed the deadline for filing our income taxes; therefore, we had to pay a fine.

Conjunctive adverbs will accomplish two goals: first, they will ask your reader to slow down (they are usually set off with commas); second, they will overtly demonstrate the relationship between clauses. For instance, *furthermore* has a meaning similar to *in addition. Consequently* is close in meaning to *because. Nevertheless* means *in spite of this. Rather* signals a contrast. And *henceforth* means *from that time forward.* So if you want to create the rhetorical effect of solemnity, if you want to emphasize one point greatly, if you want to slow the text so that you can govern it better, use a conjunctive adverb.

Creating Compound Sentences with a Colon Joining Patterns. On rare occasions when two clauses are extremely closely related, you may use a colon after the first clause to announce the second or to telegraph to the reader the interrelatedness of the two clauses. Remember that a compound sentence has a set of two complete patterns or independent clauses; you absolutely need a complete pattern **before** the colon—and one after as well—if you're crafting a compound sentence.

1. "She explained the stir: Mr. Hubber was coming at seven to take their photograph for the Christmas card." —John Cheever. From "The Country Husband."

The first independent clause sets up the second one and prepares the reader for the information. Observe also how much more emphasis this information receives than if it had been tucked away without the first clause.

2. "The word *sweetness* denoted a reality commensurate with human desire: it stood for fulfillment." —Michael Pollan. From *The Botany of Desire*
3. "Across the room Catherine was supervising the placing of the lectern: he heard it scrape through the increasing voices." — Cynthia Ozick. From "The Suitcase."

Sometimes—and this is only sometimes—writers join two very short independent clauses with only a comma or only a coordinator. This is done to create a sense of rapid movement through the sentence and to insist on the rhetorical linkage between the clauses. Here are some examples of each:

With only *and* and no comma:

1. "Marion's not well and she can't stand shocks." —F. Scott Fitzgerald. From "Babylon Revisited."
2. "Then they all gathered around Sonny and Sonny played." — James Baldwin. From "Sonny's Blues."
3. "The wine sparkled in his eyes and the bells jingled." —Edgar Allan Poe. From "The Casque of Amontillado."
4. "A breeze was blowing toward them and the grass rippled gently in the wind." —Ernest Hemingway. From "The Short Happy Life of Francis Macomber."

With only the comma and no *and*:

1. "His father never looked at it, he never once looked down at the rug." —William Faulkner. From "Barn Burning."

2. "For a brief moment I hesitated, I trembled." —Edgar Allan Poe. From "The Casque of Amontillado."
3. "His time is precious, he has better things to do." —Cynthia Ozick. From "Usurpation."
4. "Her whim is justice, her word is my law." —John Updike. From "A & P."

The caption of the cartoon *I Get Her Heart* illustrates a compound sentence with three independent clauses.

"He gets her heart, you get her brain, and I get to eat the dog."

I Get Her Heart

Each clause has its own pattern. Each is an S-V-O pattern, with the phrase *to eat the dog* functioning as the direct object in the last clause. Observe how commas are used to separate each clause. What is the rhetorical effect of having all three independent clauses together to constitute one sentence? They are united in effect, as in reality: the relationship among them is demonstrably clear as the characters from the Wizard of Oz lay claim to the spoils of their adventure.

~~~~~~~~~~~~~~~~~~~~~~~~~~~~~~~~~~~

FOR WRITING

Now you try your hand at writing some compound sentences. Below you will find a cluster of independent clauses. From these clauses and from some independent clauses that you construct and add, create ten compound sentences, joined and punctuated in a variety of ways. You have choices. Take one independent clause, make up another, and join them together. Or choose two independent clauses from the list and combine them to create one compound sentence. Change tense or pronoun person or whatever you need to create interesting compound sentences. Be prepared to analyze and discuss the sentences that you have written. Here are the independent clauses, not punctuated or capitalized, upon which you should build your compound sentences:

1. I was conscripted into the army
2. we were surprised by this assumption
3. it's terribly unfair
4. everybody blames us
5. they are ready to defend their deep and famous interests
6. they scowled
7. at one point I asked him about his favorite writers
8. we watched our first rodeo
9. I had touched a sensitive nerve
10. the third volume collects statistics
11. our relationship ended with a joke
12. Vivian sent gifts
13. the tone was shrill
14. he has been right about liberalism

15. he has an affair with an unnamed woman
16. we met at an evangelists' camp meeting near Portland, Oregon
17. the noise ceases abruptly
18. I turned off the oven and opened the door
19. she is not a doctor
20. we'll meet you at that address
21. I'm not ever going back to school
22. we can wait for the bus here
23. in late December it began to snow in earnest
24. he's a very lonely man
25. I spent my entire lunch hour in a phone booth, trying to reach Charles
26. many children clamored for food
27. he waved around the gun
28. her presence embarrassed him
29. the psychiatrist in the film had camera fright
30. he had never killed a nurse

Creating Complex Sentences

A complex sentence is not at all like a compound sentence. Where the compound sentence is balanced, seesaw-like, on the fulcrum of the co-ordinator/comma, the semicolon/conjunctive adverb, or the semicolon alone, there is no such balance in the complex sentence. A complex sentence expresses explicit and usually *unequal* relationships between two or more clauses or patterns. One of the clauses clearly expresses the dominant or main idea, and the other clause or clauses express related but subsidiary ideas or relationships. Thus a complex sentence has one main or base clauses (an independent clause) plus one or more dependent or subordinate clauses. Complex sentences are also rhetorically complicated; in their structures as well as in their words, they demonstrate the ways that ideas relate to one another.

Within complex sentences, the dependent clauses may be of three types: **adjective clauses**, **adverbial clauses**, or **noun clauses**. In any complex sentence, you will find at least one of these kinds of dependent clauses yoked to a related independent clause. Use complex sentences to express relationships among ideas, to note cause and effect, to link events to time, to explain conditions contrary to fact, to express all manners of contingency.

Complex Sentences: The Adjective Clause

Like form class adjectives, adjective clauses cluster around nouns and function as adjectives to describe or elaborate the noun. You can recognize an adjective clause by its position near a noun or within a noun cluster and by the subordinator that introduces the clause. The subordinators most identified with adjective clauses are what traditional grammarians call the **relative pronouns** (perhaps because they articulate and define *relation*ships):

that

who

whom

whose

which

what

But you may also find these words used to introduce adjective clauses:

where

when (on rare occasions)

why (following the phrase *the reason*)

So when you see one of these words, be alert for the possibility of an adjective clause. Here are some examples of sentences with adjective clauses:

1. "My friend Adam, *who had some anxiety problems of his own and was a real pooh-pooher of "talk therapy,"* found me a behaviorist at McLean."—Lauren Slater. From "Black Swans: The Answer to Illness Is Not Necessarily a Cure."
2. "It is precisely this conception of movies *that must be defeated.*" —Susan Sontag. From "Against Interpretation."
3. "Castro slaps a hand against his own midsection, *which is relatively flat.*" —Gay Talese. From "Ali in Havana."
4. "For in reality this is a brutally impolite world *where bad intentions frequently prevail.*" —Verlyn Klinkenborg. From "We Are Still Only Human."
5. "Our mythic prototype of a creature from another planet has round luminous eyes on a face *whose other features seem atrophied.*" —Gordon Grice. From *The Red Hourglass: Lives of the Predators.*

Take a look at the clauses themselves. Each is a complete pattern, with subject and finite verb, but each clause is incomplete if it stands alone. The adjective clauses don't *sound* finished or complete. In these adjective or relative clauses, the subordinator usually assumes the role of one of the pattern elements, frequently the subject. Indeed, the relative pronouns *who, which,* and *that* always play a grammatical role in the adjective clauses they introduce, and they always begin the clause no matter which function they perform. The possessive *whose* functions as a determiner in any relative clause it introduces. Consider sentence one's relative clause:

who had some anxiety problems of his own and was a real pooh-pooher of "talk therapy"

In this clause, *who* is the subject of the clause and also the relative pronoun acting as the subordinator, and the verbs are compound: *who had problems* (S-V) and *who was pooh-pooher* (S-LV-PN). In your writing group, identify the patterns of the other adjective clauses.

In some sentences, the subordinator introducing the adjective or relative clause is omitted, so it is more difficult to notice the clause itself. Nevertheless, a pattern is still identified as an adjective clause if it patterns with a noun or noun substitute and if it has a subject and finite verb. Here are a few examples:

1. Here are the apples *we picked yesterday.* [The *that* ordinarily introducing the clause is omitted or ellipted but understood to be there.]
2. All the movies *I saw last year* were nominated for an Academy Award.
3. Today is the day *you have been waiting for!*

   Look at the caption in the cartoon Love of a Good Cat.

"All you really need in life is the love of a good cat."

Love of a Good Cat

There is an adjective clause in this sentence, *All you really need in life is the love of a good cat,* but it may be difficult to find because the relative pronoun or subordinator has been withdrawn or ellipted; it is merely understood. The adjective clause is *you really need,* ellipted from *that you really need,* patterning after *all* and articulating and qualifying how much of *all* is under discussion. The skeletal base sentence is *All is love,* S-LV-PN.

Restrictive and Non-Restrictive/ Essential and Non-Essential Adjective Clauses. You should pay attention to one other feature of the sentences with adjective clauses: some of those adjective clauses are set off from the rest of the sentence with commas, and some are not. Why are some adjective clauses separated from their sentences and some not? Adjective clauses are of two kinds; they may be *essential* to the understanding of the noun with which they pattern, or they may be *non-essential* to the understanding of that noun. Consider Gay Talese's sentence about Fidel Castro:

Castro slaps a hand against his own midsection, **which is relatively flat.**

This adjective clause, set off from the main clause with a comma, is a non-essential or non-restrictive clause. That it is separated from the main clause means that its information is not required for an under-standing of *midsection* or what happens to the midsection in this sen-tence. In contrast, look at Grice's sentence about extra-terrestrials:

Our mythic prototype of a creature from another planet has round luminous eyes on a face **whose other features seem atrophied.**

No comma exists between the adjective clause and its noun, *face.* The adjective clause is essential to our understanding of *face,* and the ad-jective clause necessarily restricts our understanding of *face;* this is a **restrictive** or **essential** adjective clause.

You can remember the differences in these kind of clauses this way: if the clause must be in the sentence to complete the meaning of the sentence, don't use the comma to fence it out. Leave the gate open to show that the clause is essential. If, however, the clause is not essential to understanding the noun or the sentence, indicate this with a comma to show some degree of separation.

~~~~~~

FOR WRITING

Now it's time for you to create sentences with adjective clauses. Below is a list of adjective clauses. Fold these clauses (or revised but recognizable versions of these clauses) into independent clauses that you create to make complex sentences with adjective or relative clauses. Be conscious of whether you are creating essential or non-essential adjective clauses and punctuate them correctly!

1. which have little defense
2. that were destined to be broken
3. whose name is blessed
4. who was pouring hot water into a teacup
5. which were covered with snow
6. who was dressed entirely in black
7. who had a fear of military service
8. which appeared ragged at the edges
9. that was incredibly exciting
10. which were trembling
11. who lived in the town
12. whose work was on display at the gallery
13. where two girls lived
14. who sees everything and hears everything
15. that were blinking in the moonlight
16. which were covered with heavy shutters
17. who yearns to hear the news from you
18. that will affect her entire life
19. that is covered with gigantic yellow plastic flowers
20. who is crazy in love with Frederick
21. whose daughter was studying at the Sorbonne
22. who was lifting his umbrella and waving it wildly in the air
23. which was a boring, tedious lesson
24. that was made of the finest silk
25. who had been introduced as Janus Man

Adjective Clauses and Participial Phrases: Rhetorical Choices.
Sometimes a clause is just what you need to convey the importance of

an idea. But sometimes a clause is too much or too long and a phrase is more appropriate. You can reduce an adjective clause to a participle or a participial phrase that may function even better than a clause. This assignment asks you first to change some adjectival clauses into participial phrases and next to create some participial phrases of your own to add to base sentences. Look at this sentence that contains an adjective clause:

*The frustrated commuters **who are rushing for the last train** must have stayed late at the office.*

Who are rushing for the last train is an adjectival clause, part of a cluster of words patterning around the noun *commuters*. In this sentence, though, we have some rhetorical and stylistic options. We can, for instance, shrink the adjective clause to a participial phrase. To do this, we eliminate the subject of the clause because it is the same as the subject of the base sentence. Then we eliminate the auxiliary verb to leave only the participial form of the verb. We keep the participle with its cluster, and our transformed sentence reads

*The frustrated commuters **rushing for the last train** must have stayed late at the office.*

Rushing for the last train is a participial phrase functioning as an adjective and patterning with the noun *commuters*; it has been shrunk from the longer adjective clause *who are rushing from the train*.

Here are two other sentences with adjectival clauses transformed into participles and participial phrases:

The setting of the novel is Hiroshima, <u>which was ravaged by war.</u>

becomes

The setting of the novel is Hiroshima, ravaged by war.

Smithson had explained the main mechanisms that regulate sleep.

becomes

Smithson had explained the main mechanisms regulating sleep.

With the last sentence, the form of the verb was changed to the present participle to make sense. The participial form of the verb is the form used with auxiliaries or helping verbs, as in *was torn, have worked, is running, had estimated.* Participles most commonly end in -*ed, -en, -n, -t,* or -*ing.*

Present participles (both one-word and phrasal versions), past participles (one-word and phrasals), infinitive phrases, and gerunds are, then, derived from embedded sentences—the remains of sentences buried within the structure of the base sentence. Rather than insert the entire sentence representing each separate idea and risk repeating words, structures, or ideas, the writer shrinks the sentence to create a verbal, which then functions as a noun, adjective, or adverb within a base sentence. Thus a sentence like

Strolling through the upscale mall, the students gawked at the luxurious items in the well-stocked windows.

has within it the embedded sentences:

The students gawked at the items.

The items were luxurious.

The items were in the windows.

The windows were well-stocked.

The students were strolling through the upscale mall.

The mall was upscale.

~~~~~~

FOR WRITING

Now you rewrite the following sentences, changing adjective clauses into participial or adjectival (see #4) phrases:

1. Sandra, who is wearing large metal earrings and shiny lipstick, is actually quite beautiful as she emerges from the darkness of the other room.
2. Joe, who was refusing a ride, shook hands with me for the first time.
3. Sanders, who is putting his veterinary training to use on the family homestead, has stayed at home in Oklahoma.
4. "The trail ascended through the leafless birch and mountain ash that was ragged, scraggly." —Chip Brown. From "Much About This World."
5. All the noise that was coming from the back yard was annoying me and keeping the baby awake.

Can you find and underline the participles and participial phrases in this sentence?

"The glistening balls mistaken for a snack by Nevada prospectors were later identified as pack rat middens—globs of crystallized pack-rat urine containing sticks, plant fragments, bones, and animal hair."—Leon Jaroff. From "Nature's Time Capsules."

What was the original base clause from which the participial phrase was derived?

~~~~~~

Complex Sentences: The Adverb Clause

Adverb clauses function as adverbs, and like adverbs, they cluster around verbs. That is, adverbs pattern near verbs; they develop ideas by explaining *where, how,* or *when.* You will perhaps remember from the section on adverb form classes that sometimes adverbs are classified as *there* adverbs (adverbs of place, like *where*); *thus* adverbs (adverbs of manner, *like how*); and *then* adverbs (adverbs of time, like when). These three types of adverbs are reflected in the subordinators or words that introduce adverbial clauses, most popularly these:

after

although

as

as if

because

before

even though

if

once

since

until

when

Rhetorically speaking, adverb clauses are perhaps the most flexible of all dependent or subordinate clauses. Not only can they convey information about where, when, how, or why something occurs or exists, but the clauses themselves are quite flexible; they may typically be moved, wholesale, to different sentence locations. For instance, adverbial clauses frequently introduce the sentence or come right at its beginning (here they are called **introductory clauses**). In this role, they sometimes provide important information that the reader needs to know so that the information in the base clause can be accurately understood. Or they sometimes conclude the sentence, providing information that is an afterthought to the information in the base clause or information that comments upon main- or base-clause information. Adverbial clauses may also occur mid-sentence, as interrupters. In this guise, they can slow the pace of the sentence and can help you place information at strategic points for the reader's consumption.

Look at these sentences, all of which contain adverb clauses, with particular attention to the location of the adverb clause and its movability:

1. **When the police arrived at the meeting place,** the gang was all there.

Observe the *when* that begins the clause, then the S-V structure (*police arrived*) within the clause. Note that this clause, which introduces the sentence and is set off by a comma, is called an **introductory clause**. The clause also points to a specific time and fulfills the function of telling *when*. Also observe that the clause is movable; that is, the sentence could also read *The gang was all there when the police arrived at the meeting place* OR *The gang was, when the police arrived at the meeting place, all there.*

2. **As the trial began, the talk around the courthouse intensified.**

Here we have another introductory clause, also a *when* adverb. *As* is the subordinator introducing the clause, which illustrates the S-V pattern (*trial began*).

3. The rebels continued to strafe the plane **until the king was clearly dead.**

Until begins the clause, which is an S-LV-PA pattern—*king was dead*. The adverbial clause concludes the sentence; no comma separates the clause from the sentence because the clause ends the sentence. Most of the time, this is the case.

Use a comma to set off a subordinate clause following the main clause *if the subordinate clause has no effect on the outcome of the main clause*. If the idea in the main clause is so linked to the idea in the subordinate clause that the main clause will not be realized without the subordinate clause, use no comma. You will find that clauses beginning with *although, even though, since,* and *while* are subject to this consideration. So when the adverbial clause begins with *although* or *even though*, a comma is usually necessary:

4. We were late to the Sting concert, even though we left early.

Sometimes a comma is also necessary to prevent misreading, particularly when the adverb clause is an interrupter or comes mid-pattern of the base- or main-clause.

5. It is impossible**, when you are lost in the rain in Juarez**, to find the Jack of Hearts. —Bob Dylan. From "Tom's Thumb Blues."

Here the adverb clause interrupts the main or base clause, as adverbs often do. The adverb clause is set off by commas on both sides. The clause begins with the subordinator *when*, then assumes one of two patterns, depending on how you focus your interpretive lens. *You are lost* can be an S-V pattern if you perceive the verb to be passive, with the *be* (*are*) + past participle (*lost*) form. Many of you will, however, see this as an example of the S-LV-PA pattern, with *lost* functioning as a predicate adjective. Either interpretation offers a clear understanding of how the sentence works.

6. Mitch knew Norm **because Norm had auditioned for a part in a movie.**

The adverb clause concludes the sentence, and no comma precedes it here. The clause has an S-V pattern (*Norm had auditioned*) as well.

Can you find the adverb clause in the caption in the cartoon Coherent Viewing Policy?

"You'll get it back once you articulate a coherent viewing policy."

Coherent Viewing Policy

This clause tells *when* the remote control will be returned. Because the clause concludes the sentence, no comma separates it from the base or main clause. The clause is more effective at the end of the sentence because it contains the punch line and is therefore in a position of emphasis.

For Writing

Now it's time for you to build some sentences with adverb clauses. Below is a list of 25 adverb clauses. To each adverb clause, add a main clause so that the result is a complex sentence with an adverbial clause. You may modify the clauses in any way, just as long as the item remains a clause. Some of the clauses are in subjunctive mode; for a refresher about subjunctive mode, review Chapter 2. As you build these sentences, punctuate correctly.

1. before we reached Mrs. Nix's house
2. when she came in
3. while they all stood in the hallway exchanging pleasantries
4. when he was young
5. as though there were no subject to be avoided (notice the subjunctive form)
6. when you realize the truth about it all
7. if they chose to complain
8. until you are exactly at the corner
9. while two men looked at him in contempt
10. when she pressed her head to my cheek
11. since Paul-William came to live with us
12. while his dinner got cold
13. when Izzy entered the room carrying the knife

14. while the children played, united in their fear of the mother
15. after they had put on their nightdresses
16. as they stumbled up the walk
17. when she had finished
18. if he were killed (notice the subjunctive mode)
19. because he's not even going to look at the essays until Monday
20. because the doctor would like to marry her
21. as they went back to their seats
22. as my aunt's condition worsened
23. because they always wanted to pinch our cheeks
24. when I stepped into the living room
25. when the horse skidded up to the fence

~~~~~~

FOR WRITING

Now you create the adverbial clauses and insert them into the following independent or base clauses. You may insert the adverbial clause at the beginning of the sentence (introductory clause), at the end of the sentence (concluding clause), or in the middle of the sentence (interrupting clause). Be sure to punctuate correctly.

1. The men were squatting there, talking intently.
2. She was the fastest runner in the seventh grade.
3. Elaine takes you down to her place by the river.
4. I was happy.
5. They put arsenic in the king's meat.
6. We must stop seeing each other.
7. The young man smiled urbanely.
8. Miss Rainey was late.
9. The lark sings at heaven's gate.

10. I learned my lesson.
11. A dragon longer than two lances pursued her.
12. A woman is singing to me.
13. Ophelia had a Christian burial.
14. An artist finds reality and satisfaction in work.
15. Sailors have an extra sense that alerts them to danger.
16. I sang the baritone lead in *Pirates of Penzance*.
17. The large poodle sleeps curled up on the blanket.
18. In a refrigerator an apple will keep for weeks.
19. This is a bad map.
20. He dipped the bread into the grease from the meat.
21. He left his pants upon the chair.
22. We sing together.
23. My conscience is active and alert.
24. I had many fine tools.
25. I ask your mercy.

Complex Sentences: The Noun Clause

Noun clauses function exactly as nouns do. You will find noun clauses wherever you find nouns: in the subject slot, the direct object slot, the predicate noun slot, the slots for appositives and objects of the preposition. Noun clauses, like other subordinate or dependent clauses, cannot function on their own; rather, they must link to a base clause. One way that you can identify a noun clause is that when you remove the entire noun clause from the sentence, the sentence loses a big chunk of its important information and the sentence has a gap or hole in it. This loss of information makes sense, though, if you think about it, because the sentence loses a noun when a noun clause is removed. And nouns carry much of the important weight of the sentence as subjects, direct objects, predicate nouns, objects of the preposition, and appositives.

Besides recognizing that a noun clause removed from the sentence leaves a large gap of information, another way you can identify a noun clause is by the subordinator that introduces it. The most common subordinators introducing noun clauses are *who, what, why, how, where*, and *that*. You will notice some overlap with relative pronouns and other words that introduce adjective clauses. The *that* introducing noun clauses is different from the *that* introducing adjective clauses, however. The noun clause *that* functions as an expletive; it plays no grammatical role in the clause. Did you observe that other of these subordinators can also introduce adjective or relative clauses?

Why would you use a noun clause when a simple noun might do? The rhetorical effect of using a noun clause instead of a noun is to give your idea more space, more gravity, and more emphasis. Because a noun clause has its own pattern, it can embody an expanded idea. So use a noun clause if you want to lend more power to a noun or if you just want or need to say more.

When you think about how to punctuate a noun clause, think about how you punctuate nouns in sentences. Like a noun, a noun clause functioning as a subject, direct object, or predicate noun won't be separated from its verb by a comma. Like a noun, a noun clause functioning as the object of a preposition shouldn't be separated from its preposition by a comma either. You may find that you need to separate a noun clause used as an appositive from the rest of the sentence with commas or dashes, just as you will separate some appositives from the rest of the sentence. Most of the time, though, noun clauses require no punctuation. Let's take a look at some and see. Here are some sentences with noun clauses (the clauses are in bold).

1. **What you want** is **what you get at McDonald's today**.

This famous slogan from McDonald's contains two noun clauses. The first functions as the subject of the sentence whose verb is the linking verb *is*. The second noun clause acts as the predicate noun following the linking verb. Together they suggest the absolute unity of the customer's desires and McDonald's products; in this sentence, form follows meaning completely. The subordinator *what* links each noun clause to the sentence and functions as a direct object within each clause. The pattern of each clause is S-V-O: *you see what* and *you get what*.

2. **Why you wore that dress with spaghetti straps in the middle of winter** puzzles me.

If you lifted the bold portion of the above sentence away, you would have this kind of structure: _____ puzzles *me*. What is missing from this sentence is a subject, and this is exactly the precise function of the noun clause in sentence two—as subject of the verb *puzzles*. The noun clause constitutes a pattern all by itself, with the S-V-O structure (*you wore dress*).

3. Jeff couldn't figure out **how he could steal the money from the safe.**

Here the noun clause functions as the direct object of the verb *figure out*. Observe the pattern within the noun clause, S-V-O (*he could steal money*).

4. He noticed **that the cars were white with frost.**

This noun clause also functions as a direct object of the verb *noticed*. Note the pattern of the noun clause: S-LV-PA (*cars were white*).

5. I don't think **she likes the idea.**

The noun clause, with its S-V-O structure (*she likes idea*), functions as the direct object of the verb *do think*. It answers the *what?* question that the verb asks and completes the verb. But this noun clause differs from the other examples because it is not introduced by a subordinator;

the subordinator *that* is implied here but not articulated. This happens quite frequently, especially when the clause is in the direct object slot. The absence of the subordinator or the implied subordinator can make it more difficult for you to spot the clause.

6. "He [Albert Speer] differentiated between what it was known that he knew, what he knew, what he might have been expected to know, what he suspected, what was rumoured, what was kept from him, what was in the archives and what was not." — Jonathan Meades. From "Favourite without Portfolio."

Consider all the noun clauses in this magnificent sentence and notice their parallel structure as well as the rhetorical figures that Meades employs. How would you describe the effect of Meades's piling on of noun clauses?

~~~~~~

For Discussion

Find the noun clauses in the following sentences. Be prepared to talk about how each clause functions and about the pattern or structure of the clauses.

1. He had forgotten who she was.
2. That is what a woman would do!
3. A little change is what she needs.
4. Jeannette maintains she does not want to go with them.
5. This is how it turned out.
6. I want you to know that we were proud of our deeds. [Determine the relationship of the clause to the infinitive *to know*.]
7. Let me explain what we will do.
8. We went to where the land meets the sea.
9. What you have in your apron is a biscuit.
10. Why he is late coming from campus is a mystery.

11. We talked about why the sun goes down in the evening.
12. The main thing we discussed was how we should live to prepare for the concert.
13. I could never believe that he was married.
14. This is how it happened.
15. I told Mother I couldn't talk to her while I was in my decision-making process.

~~~~~~~~~~~~~~~~~~~~~~~~~~~~~~~~

The caption of the cartoon Not a Cult contains three parallel noun clauses, each functioning as the direct object.

"I do what they tell me, I eat what they give me. How do I know they're not a cult?"

What they tell me is the direct object of *do; what they give me* is the direct object of *eat; (that) they're not a cult* is the direct object of *know.* The first two clauses are exactly parallel, and the third is a question transformation of a sentence and parallel to the first two.

Now it's time to write some sentences of your own with noun clauses. Begin by substituting noun clauses within the independent clauses or base sentences below. Remember: you will have to take out a noun and put a noun clause in its place. Here is an example:

*We forgot **the words to the song**.*

Now we're going to substitute a noun clause for the words in the noun phrase *the words of the song.*

We forgot **what the song said.**

The pattern of the clause is S-V-O: *song said what.* Now here's a second example:

The principal gave prizes to the contest **winners.**

Now we'll substitute a noun clause for *winners,* the object of the preposition *to:*

The principal gave prizes to **whoever won the contests.**

Whoever won the contests is also the S-V-O pattern, with *whoever* functioning as both subordinator and subject of the noun clause. The entire clause functions as the object of the preposition *to.*

~~~~~~

FOR WRITING

When you create complex sentences with noun clauses from the base sentences that follow, consider substituting noun clauses for the italicized nouns, just to simplify things. And know that you will have to invent some details to create sensible-sounding clauses.

1. Those events clinched it. [Try a noun clause beginning with *what:* What happened at the playoffs clinched it]
2. He told us a story about his wife and her Israeli folk dancing. [Try a noun clause beginning with *how:* He told us a story about how his wife took up Israeli folk dancing]
3. He showed us *places in the neighborhood.* [Try a noun clause beginning with *where.*]

4. Nobody in the class knew the solutions to *those problems.*
5. That is not the *meaning of education.*
6. I wanted him to see *the truth.*
7. I didn't hear *a word.*
8. *All the participants* were invited to lunch.
9. We wanted to reach *everyone sitting around the seminar table.*
10. He shook his head at *all of us.* [Try *whoever* as the subordinator.]
11. The thing that hurts most is *your words.*
12. Do you know *the answer to my question?*
13. I actually had to remind myself of *the opening date for "South Pacific."*
14. I told him *the truth he wanted to hear.*
15. *Her words* made as much sense as anything.
16. I couldn't help confessing *my doubts.*
17. I had forgotten *the living conditions of others.*
18. *It* was magic to me.
19. From the back of the room I watched *all the events.*
20. We talked about knowledge and about *life.*

Clauses and Comparison

A familiar English construction is the comparative construction, which can be any kind of clause and can pattern with any sentence element— except of course a verb. Let's look at some examples of sentences that contain comparisons and clauses:

1. Jamal is more friendly today than he was yesterday.
   In this sentence, the pattern of the base clause is S-LV-PA (*Jamal–is—friendly*). The comparison centers around *friendly* (an adjective), so the clause functions adverbially. The words

more and *than* signal the comparison and function as subordinating links. *Friendly* is ellipted from the second clause.

2. The SUNY students have higher scores than students in other state schools [do have scores].
    The pattern of the base clause is S-V-O (*students-have-scores*). The ellipted clause, *students in other state schools do have scores*, modifies the direct object *scores;* thus the dependent clause functions adjectivally. The comparison is signaled by *higher* and *than*, which function as subordinators.

3. More consumers shop at Target than [consumers shop] at any other discount department store.
    This S-V base sentence (*consumers-shop*) has an ellipted clause signaled by the conjunctive pair *more* and *than*.

~~~~~~

FOR DISCUSSION

Work with your writing group to analyze the following sentences, all of which have comparative elements and clauses. Most of the clauses are ellipted, so begin by adding back in what you think may have been ellipted. Prepare to present your findings to the class as a whole.

1. Zachary has ridden more winning horses than any other rider.
2. More people like murder mystery than fantasy.
3. That test item has given the fifth-graders more trouble than any other one.
4. Passie is more peaceful than Georgie is.
5. That job was more difficult than the last job.

~~~~~~

Creating Combination or Compound-Complex Sentences

The compound-complex sentence is at once compound *and* complex. That is, it has at least two independent clauses (like a compound sentence) and at least one dependent clause (like a complex sentence). You create compound-complex sentences when you articulate details about a complicated subject because in this kind of sentence, you can show not only parallel or equal grammatical relationships (with compound clauses) but also unequal or hierarchical ones (with complex clauses). Here are some examples and a brief analysis of each example; review them carefully.

1. "I would never again enumerate all that had been taken from me, and I blamed no one for this recurring phenomenon." — William Kennedy. From *Very Old Bones*.

The dependent clause is an adjective clause in passive voice patterning with *all: that had been taken from me*. Remove the dependent clause from the sentence so that you can more easily see the compounded patterns, which are joined by the coordinator *and*. These patterns are S-V-O, *I would enumerate all*, and S-V-O, *I blamed no one*. The sentence also has a prepositional phrase, *for this recurring phenomenon*, within which you can find a present participle, *recurring*.

2. "He cried from the tension, he cried from grief, he cried from the cab ride, from his coke habit, from the piggy insult, from his mother's having to be cramped up in a temporary coffin and then shifted over to a real one when it was ready." —Bruce Jay Friedman. From "Lady (featuring Harry Towns)."

This sentence, which describes a man's breaking down at the end of his mother's funeral, has multiple independent clauses: *he cried from the tension* (S-V); *he cried from grief* (S-V); *he cried from the cab ride, from the piggy insult, from his mother's having to be cramped up in a temporary coffin and then shifted over to a real one when it was ready* (a third S-V). The first three independent clauses are almost identical, the S-V pattern with a concluding prepositional phrase. The last independent clause, though, is most interesting; it has multiple prepositional phrases, all beginning with *from: from the cab ride, from the piggy insult, from his mother's having to be cramped up in a temporary coffin and then shifted over to a real one when it was ready.* The dependent clause occurs at the very end of the last long independent clause: *when it was ready,* an adverbial clause that tells *when* the mother's body was shifted over. Observe also the noun adjunct—*cab* ride. Notice the gerund phrase that acts as the object of the last *from: his mother's having to be cramped up in a temporary coffin and then shifted over to a real one when it was ready.* Finally, note the compound phrasal verbs, *cramped up* and *shifted over,* which are parallel to one another. Fittingly, the sentence winds down with the longest clause; the most important and momentous information is reserved until the end.

3. "When the gold-seekers in their thousands rushed to the north, a very few made great strikes, almost everyone else came up with little or nothing, and the merchants who sold them their pans, grub, and shovels made good solid incomes year after year."—John McPhee. From "Mini-Hydro."

First, let's remove the dependent clauses, which are easy to spot: *when the gold-seekers in their thousands rushed to the north* (an introductory adverbial S-V pattern with *when* as the subordinator); and *who sold them their pans, grub, and shovels* (an adjectival S-V-IO-DO clause patterning with *merchants,* where *who* functions not only as the relative pronoun subordinator but also the subject of the clause's pattern). Then we are left with the three remaining independent clauses: *few made strikes* (S-V-O); *everyone came up with nothing* (S-V-O, with phrasal verb *came up with*); and *merchants made incomes* (S-V-O). One thing that makes the sentence so pleasing is the repetition of this basic direct object or S-V-O structure in the repetition of the patterns.

> 4. The Jews are a remembering people; it is what their religion is about. —Harvey Shapiro. From *A Momentary Glory: Last Poems.*

Here the two independent clauses are readily visible, separated by the semicolon alone. The dependent clause is a noun clause within the second independent clause; this noun clause functions as predicate noun for the verb *is* in the second half of the sentence: *what their religion is about.* This noun clause is introduced by the subordinator *what*, but the *what* also plays a role in the clause's pattern. Let's re-order the clause: *their religion is about what.* You may see two ways of understanding this pattern—first, *is* is an intransitive verb and *about* is a preposition with *what* as its object. But another way to look at the sentence is to consider the verb as phrasal, *to be about:* a person can *be about* his business, for instance. That would make the pattern S-V-O, with *religion* as subject, *is about* as transitive verb, and *what* as direct object. This is a more subtle understanding of the pattern, but the first reading is not incorrect, either.

~~~~~~

FOR DISCUSSION

Now you provide analyses of the following combination or compound-complex sentences. Point out the independent clauses and the dependent clauses and remark interesting features of the sentences: verbals, figures of speech, prepositional phrases, unusual diction or word choice. Discuss your analyses with the members of your writing group.

1. "The street had to be roped off, the policemen had to keep the crowds back, and children had to play hooky

from school when there was a piano moving." —Betty Smith. From *A Tree Grows in Brooklyn*.

2. "I shall make the most frightful noise; I shall do something to make such a scandal that the old affair will seem nothing in comparison." —Edna Ferber. From *Saratoga Trunk*.

3. "It takes about forty-five minutes for the movie [*The Lord of the Rings*] to emerge from Sir Ian McKellen's beard (he plays the garrulous wizard Gandalf), but once it does, this enormous hunk of quasi-medieval myth, based on the work of J.R.R. Tolkien, is consistently beautiful and exciting." —David Denby. From "The Lord of the Rings: The Fellowship of the Rings."

4. "He was never allowed into the mysterious warrens during the workday when he was younger, but at five p.m. he would carry a glass filled with amber fluid, push the swing door with his foot, and enter." —Michael Ondaatje. From *Anil's Ghost*.

5. "I was on the perpendicular part of the cliff, and unless I could get over it soon I would just peel off the wall." —James Dickey. From *Deliverance*.

~~~~~~~~~~~~~~~~~~~~~~~~~~~~~~~~~~~~~~~

FOR WRITING

Try your hand now at writing some compound-complex sentences according to the specifications given below. A word of advice: build the independent clauses first, then fold in the dependent clauses and the other required items.

1. Make one independent clause S-V and a second independent clause S-V-O. Let the dependent clause be an adjective clause. Include one prepositional phrase and one verbal somewhere in the sentence. Use the word *crevice*.

2. Write three independent clauses and two dependent clauses, one of which is an adverbial clause that begins with *because*. Include the word *power*.
3. Make one of the independent clauses S-V-DO-OC. Use a gerund somewhere and find a way to create alliteration.
4. Use a noun clause as one of the dependent clauses. Include three prepositional phrases. Write the word *foliage* some place in the sentence.
5. Create a series of relative dependent clauses, each beginning with *who*.

~~~~~~

Reviewing Patterns and Combinations

Now that you know how to expand individual patterns and combine patterns to create compound and complex sentences, you have enough in your grammar arsenal to understand and to create almost any kind of sentence. Try your hand at analyzing the sentences below. With your writing group, perhaps, discuss whether each of the following sentences is simple, compound, or complex. Look for the presence of verbals, nominative absolutes, and prepositional phrases. Look for compounded elements. Check out the patterns of clauses and verbals. Be on the lookout for figures of speech and unusually appropriate word choices. Be alert even to tenses of verbs and forms of nouns. In short, bring all your grammatical knowledge to bear on an analysis of the following sentences.

1. "Piano, who has a gray beard and never seems entirely comfortable in a business suit, speaks with a mellifluous Italian accent." —Paul Goldberger. From "Spiffing Up the Gray Lady."

2. "Outside it was snowing and very cold, but the room was heated." —Primo Levi. From *Survival in Auschwitz.*

3. "For more than forty years, a bronze statue of Vladimir Vladimirovich Mayakovsky, the Russian Revolution's most celebrated poet, has towered over the square named after him: his massive torso triumphantly arched, an imaginary wind billowing the folds of his baggy pants, he incarnates Soviet man at his most optimistic and confident, striding toward the greatest future ever devised for humankind." —Francine du Plessix Gray. From "Mayakovsky's Last Loves."

4. "On Fridays, driving by, slowing up, I could see six people around the table, could see Sam's curls brazen in the candlelight." —Edith Pearlman. From "Cul-de-Sac."

5. "Some went in the direction of *Weeperstraat;* others made for *Waterlooplein.* —Marga Minco." From *Bitter Herbs: The Vivid Memories of a Fugitive Jewish Girl in Nazi Occupied Holland.*

6. "Choronzicki, well aware of the tortures that awaited him and the dangers of the whole conspiracy, swiftly swallowed a large dose of poison which the conspirators always carried on their person." —Stanislaw Kohn. From *The Treblinka Revolt.*

7. "All across the Earth, there are, of course, traces of climate history—buried in lake sediments, deposited in ancient beetle casings, piled up on the floor of the oceans." —Elizabeth Kolbert. From "Ice Memory."

8. "He dried off with a thin towel, noticing as he often did the twin scars on the backs of his hands." —Chris Bachelder. From "The Throwback Special, Part 3."

9. "She can smell her metallic sweat, the scent of her own panic seeping from her armpits, darkening her blouse." —Myla Goldberg. From *Bee Season.*

10. "We had violent games of football at recess and at noon, bone-jarring rituals where you got your first test in physical courage."—Willie Morris. From "Mississippi."

Looking Ahead

Now that you have a solid understanding of the structure of sentences, it's time to examine some deliberate strategies for enhancing your style. The next chapter introduces you to figures and schemes and gives you a chance to practice writing them.

Chapter 6. From Grammar to Style: Rhetorical Strategies and Figures

If you lived in Shakespeare's day and were lucky enough to attend school, you would have naturally studied the art of rhetoric, then primarily an oral art. You would have learned how to organize your thoughts, your speech, and occasionally even your writing to produce certain effects in an audience—to sway them to your way of thinking, to impress them with your erudition or learning. And you would have learned, as a matter of course, to incorporate the **figures** into your speech and writing to make your thoughts not only clear but lively. You would have been using the figures to study Latin, yes, because English grammar would not be "invented" until the eighteenth century. The figures are associated with an earlier time and originally with another language, but they survive in English in the present.

A **figure of speech** is, writes historical linguist Edward P.J. Corbett in *Classical Rhetoric for the Modern Student,* a generic term for "any artful deviation from the ordinary mode of speaking and writing." Tudor rhetoricians described over 200 different artful deviations or figures in Latin, and the figures were part of every Tudor schoolboy's education (then, most girls didn't receive formal schooling). Today the figures, adapted to English, are taught rarely, partly because you need considerable background knowledge of grammar before you can use the figures well and purposefully—and grammar is not taught so routinely any more. (We have also come to rely less and less on figurative language in everyday discourse.) A sufficient well of grammatical knowledge makes creating the figures easier; indeed, figures are where many grammatical and rhetorical principles converge. Knowing how to produce them and understanding their patterns can make you not only a better writer but a better reader. Now that your grammatical background has deepened, you are ready to use that knowledge as you develop your personal style as a writer and use figures appropriately.

And so you will find in this chapter the most common figures for your study. Renaissance schoolboys learned the figures by copying and imitation, and that is how the figures are presented here—with examples for you to study and then to imitate. This means that the exercises ask you first to copy the model passage exactly, noting its unique structure and punctuation. Then I ask you to create your own sentence or passage, following exactly the form or shape of the model sentence but with your words and meaning, your content. Once the shape of the figure is ingrained in your consciousness, you should be able to reproduce it at the appropriate time and for the appropriate rhetorical occasion. Figures will thus become part of your automatic store of resources for writing. After all, despite the fact that the figures were first devised in Latin an awfully long time ago, they still offer us writers ways to make our writing (and speech) interesting and more graceful. Even if we wish to effect primarily a plain style in our writing, the figures have much to teach us about balance and parallelism and order. To writers concerned with style, the figures, particularly the most common ones explained in this chapter, are well worth learning.

On, then, to the figures and a grammatical consideration of how they work and why they're effective. The general order here is that used by Corbett in *Classical Rhetoric for the Modern Student*, but I have not included all the figures that Corbett presents nor described them in the same manner. First Corbett describes the **figures of balance**: parallelism and antithesis. Thus these first two figures concern themselves with how we balance words along the fulcrum of the sentence and how we create meaningful patterns so that readers can easily follow our ideas. A note—the mostly Greek names of the figures may look exotic to you, so included in the discussion of each figure is a key to its pronunciation. Learn to pronounce these names: you'll enjoy rolling the names around in your mouth. After all, once you get used to them, you'll find them no more strange than other multi-syllabic words like *Connecticut* and *Mississippi*.

Parallelism

Parallelism [par-∂-**lel**-iz-∂m] means that pairs or series of related words, phrases, or clauses have very similar structures. Think of parallel lines, notions of equidistance, and ideas that run in similar directions; parallel structures in sentences are similar in these ways. In a parallel construction, ideas that are equal are presented in equal grammatical structures—nouns balance nouns, prepositional phrases balance prepositional phrases, and introductory clauses balance introductory clauses. Parallel structures help readers organize and remember information. Whether you are writing a quarterly report, directions to the club for your corporation's holiday party, or a speech, you need to understand the notion of parallelism.

Here are some sentences with parallel elements for you to study. Choose one sentence, copy it, and think about its structure as you write. Then construct your own sentence, trying to imitate the model sentence word for word, phrase for phrase, and clause for clause.

1. "She didn't want to be saved; what she wanted was an American holiday, a fresh set of boyfriends, and a leather coat." —Cynthia Ozick. From "Isaac Babel and the Identity Question."

Note the parallelism of articles (*a* or *an*), descriptors, and nouns as the complement of *was*:

an American holiday

a fresh set (of boyfriends)

a leather coat

The subject of this sentence (*She*) desires equally the holiday, fresh set of boyfriends, and leather coat. They are thus presented as grammatical equals with parallel structures.

2. "It is rather for us to be here dedicated to the great task remaining before us—that from those honored dead we take increased devotion to that cause for which they gave the last full measure of devotion; that we here highly resolve that these dead shall not have died in vain; that this nation, under God, shall have a new birth of freedom; and that government of the people, by the people, for the people, shall not perish from the earth." — Abraham Lincoln, "The Gettysburg Address."

This very famous sentence is marked by more than one set of parallel structures. Notice the three parallel clauses beginning with *that*: this common beginning helps orient readers to a new idea and signals that the idea to be presented is on equal footing with the idea just discussed. So we have three equal aspects of the great task before us: *that* we take increased devotion to the cause; *that* we resolve the dead did not die in vain; and *that* this nation shall have a new birth of freedom. Then within the final *that* clause there is yet another example of parallel structure with the three parallel prepositional phrases *of the people, by the people* and *for the people*. Observe how the repetition of *the people* emphasizes that idea that a democracy does belong to its people. The extensive parallelism in this speech makes the message easy to listen to and easy to remember.

Antithesis

Antithesis [an-**TITH**-i-sis] is the placing of contrasting ideas within physical proximity. These ideas are often (and most effectively) in parallel structure. Antithesis may exist in either the words or the ideas. If you manage antithesis capably, it can lend an air of wit to your prose.

Here are some passages with antithetical elements to study. Choose one passage to work with. Copy the passage, thinking about its structure as you write. Then construct your own passage, trying to imitate the model passage word for word, phrase for phrase, and clause for clause.

1. "Illy also observed that what works in America may not work in Italy. 'You like things big,' he told me. 'Big steaks, big cars, and a big cup of coffee. We use coffee not to drink but to sip. It's like eating a chocolate—a little burst of flavor. It's subtle. There is this overroasting culture in America,' he continued. 'It's by far too dark. This is why they feel the need to cover everything with milk and why they have all those syrups.'" —Michael Specter. From "Postcard From Rome."

What *works in America* is echoed with what will *not work in Italy*, its opposite. The idea of bigness, repeated in *big steaks, big cars*, and a *big cup of coffee*, is contrasted with the *little burst of flavor*, its opposite. *Dark* is yoked with *milk*, its antithesis. Clearly, American and Italian ideas about coffee are very different.

2. "Airmobility, dig it, you weren't going anywhere. It made you feel safe, it made you feel Omni, but it was only a stunt, technology. . . . It was great if you could adapt, you had to try, but it wasn't the same as making a discipline, going into your own reserves and developing a real war metabolism, slow yourself down when your heart tried to punch its way through your chest, get swift when everything went to stop and all you could

feel of your whole life was the entropy whipping through it."—
Michael Herr. From *Dispatches*.

Observe the contrast between the notions of mobility and stasis, the
contrast between feeling safe and being safe, your metabolism's slowing down when your heart beats furiously and becoming swift when
everything else stops, and *entropy* and *whipping through it*. Herr bluntly
introduces the topic, *airmobility*, with the first word, then he uses second person *you* to make the passage immediate and personal.

3. "United there is little we cannot do in a host of cooperative
    ventures. Divided, there is little we can do—for we dare not
    meet a powerful challenge at odds and split asunder." —John
    F. Kennedy. From "Inaugural Address." 20 January 1961.

Antithesis occurs between *united* and *divided*, *little we cannot do* and
little we can do. The em dash that comes just after the antithesis emphatically separates—or splits in two—the ideas of possibility and
impossibility from the reason why we must be united (we dare not meet
a powerful challenge when we are weak and split in two).

Now for the schemes of unusual or inverted (turned around) word order, anastrophe and apposition, and unusual word order (parenthesis).

Anastrophe

Anastrophe [ə-**nas**-trə-fe] is the inversion of the usual or natural word
order. Because this inversion confounds the reader's expectations
of how the sentence goes together, it is an especially effective atten-
tion-getting device and a strategy for emphasizing important ideas.

Here are some sentences containing anastrophe. Study them all
carefully, choose one sentence to work with, and copy the sentence,

thinking about its structure as you write. Then construct your own sentence, trying to imitate the model sentence word for word, phrase for phrase, clause for clause.

1. "From America letters came." —Nessa Rappoport. From "The Woman Who Lost Her Names."

The normal word order of this sentence would be *Letters came from America*. By moving the prepositional phrase to the beginning of the sentence out of its usual place near the verb of the sentence, the writer forces readers to sit up and take notice. "This sentence is different" is clearly the rhetorical signal.

2. "'More bread!' somebody yells." —Charles Simic. From "Dinner at Uncle Boris's."

Somebody yells "More bread" would be the normal word order for this sentence: subject (*somebody*) plus verb (*yells*) plus complement ("*More bread*"—what someone yelled). Both the yells and the "*More bread*" receive more emphasis with this revision.

3. "Among the 562 vials are eighty different cap designs, possibly suggesting eighty different manufacturers, and each cap is usually produced in ten or twelve different colors." —Paul Sheehan. From "My Habit."

This one is a bit harder to spot, but the typical word order for this sentence would be *Eighty different cap designs are among the 562 vials*. What do you think is the effect of revising the sentence to emphasize the number of vials being considered in this sentence?

4. "Inside was a gift shop that sold everything from rubber alligator jaws to t-shirts printed with a picture of a giant mosquito and the words 'I gave blood in the Florida Everglades.'"
—Daisann McLane. From "Into the Wild, Wet World of the Everglades."

The normal order for this sentence would go something like *A gift shop that sold everything from rubber alligator jaws to t-shirts printed with . . . was inside.* Beginning with the word *inside* helps readers picture where the shop is and emphasizes its location.

Apposition

Apposition [ap-ə-**zish**-ən] occurs when you place two coordinate elements (that is, two elements that are grammatically equal) side by side. Typically, the second element (called the *appositive*) then explains or limits the first. We say the two elements are "in apposition." That means that they are positioned together in a special relationship. These appositioned elements are nouns or noun clusters. Apposition is quite common in writing but less frequent in speech. It does not wrench the sentence's natural order as does parenthesis—probably, because it is grammatically *simpatico* with the element paired with it: both are typically nouns. Apposition is useful for defining or explain terms and for repeating key ideas.

Here are some sentences illustrating apposition. Study them all carefully, choose one sentence to work with, and copy the sentence, thinking about its structure as you write. Then construct your own sentence, trying to imitate the model sentence word for word, phrase for phrase, clause for clause.

1. "Meet the first in-dash personal assistant, the E-Office Assistant."

The *personal assistant* equals the *E-OfficeAssistant*; in this sentence they have the same referent. You point out the appositioned elements in the other sentences.

2. "That man—Pearl—had the same thickened French accent as Franklin's." —Alexi Zentner. From *Touch*.
3. "In her mind's eye the old woman could see her niece Virginia as clear as day, all dolled-up in rouge and lipstick, artificial black lashes, the stiff, half-dead looking dyed-blonde hair teased high over her head in a wide bouffant, cigarette between her fingers."—John Gardner. From *October Light*.
4. "Wyoming's first-year coach, Steve McClain, an assistant at TCU from 1994-1998, brought Billy Tubbs's up-tempo style with him to Laramie." —B. J. Schechter. From "The Buzzer."
5. "By the end of the summer of 1861—the first summer of the war—the quality of life had changed."—Robert Penn Warren. From *Band of Angels*.

Parenthesis

Parenthesis [pə-**ren**-thə-sis] occurs when a cluster of words interrupts the normal word order of a sentence. A parenthesis diverts the reader's attention temporarily from the idea at hand; its purpose is sometimes to call attention to the parenthetical matter itself, to provide additional but not vital information, to suggest the writer's opinion or feeling, or to create a mood (often a conspiratorial one where the reader feels in cahoots with the writer). The parenthetical matter may also be a device for controlling the pace of the sentence. Stuck in the middle of a rather long clause, for instance, a parenthesis can dramatically alter the pace or break a monotonous stretch of words.

Because parenthetical material typically occurs mid-sentence, its boundaries need to be marked by punctuation. If the parenthetical material is plunked in the middle of a sentence with the regular sentence flowing before and after it, use the same marks on each side of the parenthetical material: either commas, dashes, or parentheses. Each kind of punctuation creates a different rhetorical effect. Commas set the slightest boundaries and create the least resistance or interruption; dashes are far more dramatic and noticeable. Parentheses may suggest a conspiratorial or *by the way* effect that encourages the reader to draw the chair closer and listen harder.

Of course, if the parenthetical material begins mid-sentence then actually concludes the sentence, you'll put a period at the end of the interruption or at the end of the parenthetical material. Here are some sentences containing the scheme of parenthesis. Study them all carefully, choose one sentence to work with, and copy the sentence, thinking about its structure as you write. Then construct your own sentence, trying to imitate the model sentence word for word, phrase for phrase, clause for clause.

1. "The Park View Pharmacy—the drugstore my parents bought—stood on Colonial Avenue between Continental and Burr." —Cynthia Ozick. From "A Drugstore Eden."

Here the parenthetical material between the dashes, *the drugstore my parent bought,* is in apposition with and defines *the Parkview Pharmacy.* The dashes effectively keep the emphasis on *the drugstore* equal to the emphasis on *Parkview Pharmacy;* the reader can't miss that the two are the same entity. Notice also the repetition of the same idea in *drugstore* and *pharmacy.*

2. "One of the Dabney daughters was a fawn-faced creature of twelve named Edmonia; her fragile beauty (especially when contrasted with ill-favored brothers) and her precocious breasts and bottom had caused me—young as I was—a troubling, unresolved itch." —William Styron. From "Shadrach."

This sentence has two interrupting phrases, perhaps because it is a long sentence. Styron uses the parenthetical material to control the pace of the sentence. The first parenthetical material in parentheses has a kind of *sotto voce* or whispered effect; this material strengthens the notion of *fragile beauty* by contrasting Edmonia with her ordinary if not ugly brothers. The second parenthetical passage, *young as I was*, is set off by dashes to emphasize the writer's youth and provide context for this description.

3. "A nose ring, they might tell you, would be my last choice for a fashion accessory, way down on the list with a sag-enhancing specialty bra or a sign on my butt reading 'Wide Load.'" — Natalie Kusz. From "Ring Leader."

The clause *They might tell you* is here set off with commas; it functions as an aside, primarily to break up the length of the sentence.

4. "Ancient cultures (Greek, Egyptian, Chinese, Indian, and others) used color therapies of many sorts, prescribing colors for various distresses of the body and soul." —Diane Ackerman. From *A Natural History of the Senses*.

Here the material in parentheses defines or explains the noun just before it (*cultures*) by expanding it and naming its aspects. Because Ackerman uses parentheses around the added material rather than commas or dashes, we know that she wants us readers not too linger too long over the list.

Third are the schemes of omission, ellipsis and asyndeton. In each of these figures, something is left out. Also here is polysyndeton, the opposite of asyndeton, to round out this cluster.

Ellipsis

Ellipsis [i-**lip**-sis] is deliberate omission of a word or a cluster of words. If you use ellipsis, you can economize on sentence space—but you must be very careful to ensure that the omitted or understood words are grammatically compatible with the words you leave behind.

One kind of ellipsis, **structural ellipsis**, depends on the writer's knowing grammatical structure, usually knowing that a particular conjunction or preposition ordinarily belongs in a given structure. For instance, in the sentence "I think you are wrong," *that* is ellipted before *you are wrong*. And in a sentence like "We've waited for Godot two days already," *for* is ellipted before *two days already*.

Many headlines, titles, and advertising slogans are ellipted.

Here are some sentences containing ellipsis, many of which are from advertisements. Study them all carefully, choose one sentence to work with, and copy the sentence, thinking about its structure as you write. Then construct your own sentence, trying to imitate the model sentence word for word, phrase for phrase, clause for clause.

1. Introducing the world's smallest 35 mm zoom camera.

Before ellipsis, this sentence was probably something like *We are introducing the world's smallest 35mm zoom camera:* the subject and the auxiliary verb have been ellipted. Removing the subject throws the emphasis on *introducing* and *camera*, the first and last words in the sentence. See if you can imagine what the entire original sentence might have been for each of the ellipted sentences below.

2. Four questions you should ask about a vacuum.
3. Herbal Essences . . . a totally organic experience with style.
4. This doesn't mean missing your 3,000 mile oil change is okay.

5. Time for more milk.
6. We'll fix it right, guaranteed.
7. His eye was open to beauty, and his ear to music. —Ralph Waldo Emerson. From "Thoreau."
8. She spoke of him with respect abroad, and with contempt in her closet. —Royall Tyler. From *The Contrast*.

Verbatim Recoverability. Check the above sentences for recoverability: that is, make sure that the omitted or understood words are grammatically compatible with the part of the sentence actually on the page. For instance, saying that "the mother cat *forgets* her mittens, and her kittens their gloves" creates a non-standard usage. Why? Because the ellipted verb *forget* is slightly different than the articulated or written verb *forgets*. *Cat* is singular; *kittens*, plural. Consequently, different verbs are needed for each subject. The second verb should not, therefore, be ellipted. This principle is called **verbatim recoverability** or the ability to recover the exact word.

Asyndeton

Asyndeton [ə-**sin**-di-ton] is a scheme of omission: it means that you leave out conjunctions between a series of related words, clauses, or phrases. Asyndeton speeds the pace of the sentence, creating either the impression of simultaneity (everything seems to happen at once) or else a sense of deliberateness and firmness. Remember: leave out the conjunctions; just let the punctuation do the work of separating the ideas.

Here are some sentences containing asyndeton. Study them all carefully, choose one sentence to work with, and copy the sentence, thinking about its structure as you write. Then construct your own sentence, trying to imitate the model sentence word for word, phrase for phrase, clause for clause.

1. "Sexism, violence against women, and different, lowered expectations for girls cause them to lose touch of their interests, their confidence, their personhood." —Carol Winkelman. From "Battered Women's Stories about Life in Schools."

The items *interests, confidence, personhood* are much more emphatic because of the determination to push through them to the end of the sentence. There is no break for a conjunction, so the words appear to be part of a package, a group. The lack of a conjunction binds them closely. Also notice how emphatic *personhood,* as the last item in the list, becomes.

2. "In reality, taste buds are exceedingly small. Adults have about 10,000, grouped by theme (salt, sour, sweet, bitter), at various sites in the mouth." —Diane Ackerman. From *A Natural History of the Senses.*

The parenthetical list is an example of asyndeton because there is no conjunction separating the taste "themes," especially between *sweet* and *bitter,* where we would expect an *and.* One of the effects of no conjunction in this list is that the list seems as if it could go on for quite a long time.

3. "To outsiders, they look tough, scruffy, poor, wild." —Donna Gaines. From "Introduction." *Teenage Wasteland: Suburbia's Deadend Kids.*

Gaines writes about high school students called "burnouts," students near the bottom academically, economically, and socially.

4. "After Hegelstead left and the night was still, Jack tottered into the concrete-walled bathroom, pissed, rinsed his mouth with ice-cold iron-tasting water, drank a great draft, swallowed, spat,

gulped down three aspirin he found in a truck's glove compartment." —Louise Erdrich. From *Tales of Burning Love.*

5. "A rising sheet of water curved over him, fell down upon him, blinded him, strangled him!" —Ambrose Bierce. From "An Occurrence at Owl Creek Bridge."

Polysyndeton

Polysyndeton [**pol**-e-**sin**-di-ton], the opposite of asyndeton, means a generous use of conjunctions in a series of phrases or clauses. Polysyndeton has the opposite effect of asyndeton: it tends to separate the elements, to make each one important and individual, and to slow the pace. It can often create a solemn effect, and the conjunctions separating the elements seem to say about each: "Look at me!"

Here are some passages containing polysyndeton. Study them all carefully, choose one passage to work with, and copy it, thinking about its structure as you write. Then construct your own passage, trying to imitate the model passage word for word, phrase for phrase, clause for clause.

1. "He was two years old and at first he cried for the shack and the familiar smell of the wood stove and his mother's lean, hard hands." —Annie Proulx. From *Accordion Crimes.*

The repetition of *and* imitates the way that young children tell stories— by piling detail upon detail and connecting each one with *and.* This is an appropriate style to describe a two-year-old's response to being without his mother.

2. "Which of the four is not only the right man for the job but a "real" man (which is the subtle subtext of every presidential election)? By some definitions (war hero or great athlete or

Texan or responsible family man), all of them. By other definitions (compassionate and honest and responsible and self-aware and sober and high-minded and battle-tested), none of them." —Jane Smiley. From an unknown source.

In this passage, Smiley repeats *or* and *and* to delineate the separateness of each item, as if to tote them up in some sort of reckoning—which is what she is doing: reckoning or figuring who is the right man for the job.

3. "I will put my law in their inward parts, and write it in their hearts, and will be their God, and they shall be my people." — Jeremiah 31:33. King James Version of *The Bible*.

How would you say the *and's* function in this sentence? Consider how the sentence would sound without the *and's*.

Now here are the figures of repetition: assonance, alliteration, anaphora, epistrophe, epanalepsis, anadiplosis, and antimetabole.

Assonance and Alliteration

Assonance [as-ə-nəns] is the repetition of similar vowel sounds in words that are next to or near one another. Although assonance is used primarily in poetry, a prose writer may also use assonance to knit sentences together by repeating sounds. Depending on the repeated sound, other effects may be created: repeated long *O* sounds may emphasize a mournful effect, for instance, and repeated *E's* may create a bright textual atmosphere.

Here are some sentences containing assonance. Study them carefully, choose one to work with, and copy it, thinking about its structure as you write. Then construct your own sentence, trying to imitate the model closely.

1. "Susskind glanced down at his shabby, baggy knickers." — Bernard Malamud. From "The Last Mohican."

Listen to the effect of the short *a* sound in *shabby* and *baggy*. Because the two words sound alike, their effect is increased.

2. "When I'm up to my knees in honeysuckle, I beat a retreat and visit the duck pond." —Annie Dillard. From *Pilgrim at Tinker Creek*.

How do you describe the effect of the *e* sounds? What do the *e* sounds do for the pace of the sentence?

Alliteration [ə-lit-ə-**ra**-shən] is the repetition of initial consonant sounds—that is, consonant sounds occurring at the beginning of adjacent words or words that are next to one another. Like assonance, alliteration occurs frequently in poetry to emphasize particular words or to create a tonal effect. You will also find it often in advertising.

For both assonance and alliteration, moderation is the key. Using either device excessively can create an unintentionally humorous effect. Here are some sentences containing alliteration. Study them, choose one to work with, and copy it, thinking about its structure as you write. Then construct your own sentence, trying to imitate the model sentence closely.

1. "The tide shoves and sucks through the islands and makes the current curl in odd patterns." —John Hersey. From *Of Men and War*.

What is the effect of the alliterated *s*'s (*shoves, sucks*) and *c*'s (*current, curl*)?

2. "From its tip grew two thin slips of green tissue shaped like two tears; they enclosed, like cupped palms sheltering a flame,

a tiny tulip leaf that was curled upon itself and bowed nearly in the middle." —Annie Dillard. From *Pilgrim at Tinker Creek.*

Observe how the repetition of the *t* sound through this sentence knits it together. Underline all the words beginning with *t*. Then read the sentence again, savoring its sounds. What is the effect of the alliteration?

Anaphora

Anaphora [ə-**naf**-ə-rə] is a repetition scheme where a word or group of words occurs at the beginning or front of successive clauses or phrases, phrases or clauses that come one right after the other. Sometimes you find *incremental anaphora,* where the repeated words or phrases change ever so slightly or incrementally with each repetition. Anaphora is quite deliberate, creates a distinct rhythm in the text, and emphasizes a key point or evokes an emotional effect. As more and more words are repeated, the intensity of the passage increases.

Here are some passages containing anaphora. Study them all carefully, choose one passage to work with, and copy the passage, thinking about its structure as you write. Then construct your own passage, trying to imitate the model sentence word for word, phrase for phrase, clause for clause.

1. "All that is left upon me is the scent of her perfume and I find, even once I hang the phone up, that I can't get rid of the smell. I can't get it off me. I can't stop thinking of her and I see things. I see her in my deepest thoughts." —Louise Erdrich. From *The Antelope Wife.*

See how *I can't* is repeated at the beginning of three successive sentences. The reader is unable to miss the writer's inability to stop thinking of "her" because the phrase *I can't* is placed repeatedly at a place of emphasis, the front of the sentence.

2. "When I need to relax, I dream of lazy walks along palm-shaded paths, I dream of black swans gliding over tranquil lagoons, I dream of thatched-roof days without telephones, televisions or radios. I dream of Kona Village." —Advertisement for Kona Village Resort.

How do you characterize the effect of the repeated phrase *I dream*?

3. "The reason why I object to Dr. Johnson's style is that there is no discrimination, no selection, no variety in it." —William Hazlitt. From "On Familiar Style."

The repeated *no's* emphasize the lack of discrimination, selection, and variety.

4. "The first door lets out drivers. The second door lets out passengers. The third door lets out convention." —Saturn advertisement. Print.

This is an example of incremental repetition; *door* is repeated in each sentence, but with each repetition, the determiner before *door* changes from *first* to *second* to *third*. The final object is especially emphatic not only because it is the last object but also because it is not a physical thing like *drivers* or *passengers* and suggests the uniqueness of the Saturn, which was a General Motors product sold in the United States from 1985 to 2010.

Epistrophe

Epistrophe [i-**pis**-trǝ-fee] is a repetition scheme where a word or group of words occurs at the end of successive clauses or phrases. Sometimes you find *incremental epistrophe,* where the repeated words or phrases change ever so slightly or incrementally with each repetition. Thus, like anaphora, epistrophe is quite deliberate, creating a distinct rhythm in the text, emphasizing a key point, or evoking an emotional effect.

Here are some passages containing epistrophe. Study them carefully, choose one to work with, and copy it, thinking about its structure as you write. Then construct your own example, trying to imitate the model word for word, phrase for phrase, clause for clause.

1. "The lobbyists don't like you. The voters don't like you. The majority doesn't like you. (Our judges will love you.)" —advertisement for The John F. Kennedy Library Foundation Profile in Courage Award.

The phrase *don't like you* is repeated so many times that when the readers come across the last phrase, *will love you,* they are pleasantly surprised. This sentence also illustrates antithesis in the contrast between *don't like you* and *love you.*

2. "Wherever there is a needy child, there is a great cause. Wherever there is ignorance or want, there is a great cause. Wherever there is violence and hate, there is a great cause."— John McCain. From "Commit to Causes Higher Than Yourself."

Besides being an example of epistrophe by virtue of the repeated noun cluster at the end of each sentence, *a great cause,* this passage is also an example of anaphora (*Wherever there is* is repeated at the beginning of each sentence. When both epistrophe and anaphora are present in the same sentence (as they are here), this figure is called *symploce.*

3. "One cannot think well, love well, sleep well, if one has not dined well." —Virginia Woolf. From "A Room of One's Own."

The repetition of *well* at the conclusion of the verb phrases links all the verbs together and emphasizes the importance of doing all these things *well*.

Epanalepsis

Epanalepsis [e-pan-ǝh-**lep**-sis] is a repetition scheme where a word or group of words from the beginning of a clause or sentence is repeated at the end of that same clause, sentence, or sometimes passage. This scheme lends an air of finality to a sentence, bringing it to a close at near the same place where it began. It has a nice round "feel" to it that satisfies a reader's need for closure. Yet it is an extremely rare scheme because it is so powerful. To overuse it seems extremely self-conscious, so be very discreet with it.

Here are some passages containing epanalepsis. Study them carefully, choose one passage to work with, and copy it, thinking about its structure as you write. Then construct your own sentence, trying to imitate the model sentence word for word, phrase for phrase, clause for clause.

1. "That a famous library has been cursed by a woman is a matter of complete indifference to a famous library." —Virginia Woolf. From "A Room of One's Own."

Famous library is introduced at the beginning of the sentence and reiterated at its end.

2. "Erotic pleasure, derived from the most physical contact, thrives on the paradox that only by keeping alive the strangeness of

that other person can eroticism last."—Siri Hustvedt. From "A Plea for Eros."

Erotic, the first word in the sentence, is repeated in its nominal (or noun) form, *eroticism*, at the end of the sentence. Thus this key word is both the first thing the reader "hears" in the sentence as well as its closing note.

3. "The most incomprehensible thing about the world is that it is comprehensible." —Albert Einstein. From "Physics and Reality."

Notice that *incomprehensible* at the beginning of the sentence is repeated in its opposite form, *comprehensible*, at the close of the sentence. This is a variation of epanalepsis employing contrast via a variant form of the repeated word. Thus, the sentence employs not only epanalepsis but contrast and balance as well.

Anadiplosis

Anadiplosis [an-∂-d∂-**plo**-sis] is a repetition scheme where a word or group of words is repeated at the *end* of one clause or sentence and then subsequently at the *beginning* of the next clause or sentence. This scheme neatly links sentences or clauses and at the same time repeats important ideas or phrases for emphasis.

Here are some passages containing anadiplosis. Study them carefully, choose one to work with, and copy it, thinking about its structure as you write. Then construct your own passage, trying to imitate the model word for word, phrase for phrase, clause for clause.

1. "For Chrysler, it's about creating extraordinary cars. Cars born from breakthrough design and brought to life through innovative engineering."—Chrysler advertisement.

Notice how *cars* ends the first sentence and begins the second. This strategy emphasizes *cars* and underscores the identification of *cars* with *Chrysler*.

2. "But Moses is dead, dead without the preparations and failures of old age, dead in the midst of his strength." —Max Apple. From "Joshua."

Here *dead* ends the first part of this compound predicate adjective phrase and begins the second. Look how *dead* is repeated anaphorically for a third time in yet another predicate adjective phrase.

3. "If David has had Uriah killed with the sword, the sword will rampage among his sons." —Lore Segal, "II Samuel."

Do you see the anadiplosis? Point it out in this sentence and in the examples that follow.

4. "Reading is an activity that makes a difference, and this difference cannot be minimized or foreshortened . . .." —David Shapiro, "Proverbs."
5. "How then can higher education escape dogmatism, narrowness, the invasion of academic freedom, and failure in its proper intellectual task and still do its duty by morals and religion? A possible answer lies in the Great Conversation. The Great Conversation began with the Greeks, the Hebrews, the Hindus, and the Chinese and has continued to the present day." — Robert Maynard Hutchins. From *Morals, Religion, and Higher Education*

Antimetabole and Chiasmus

Antimetabole [**an**-te-mƏ-**TAB**-Ə-le] is a scheme of balance involving two repeated series. A phrase at the beginning of a passage (usually a sentence) is repeated at the end of the passage—but with its elements reversed. This reversal combined with the elements of balance and repetition creates a very powerful epigrammatic sentence or passage. Use it wisely to drive home a very important point or to make your words especially memorable. When the phrases or clauses are parallel in structure, the figure exemplifies **chiasmus** [ky-AZ-mus].

Here are some passages containing antimetabole. Study them carefully, choose one to work with, and copy it, thinking about its structure as you write. Then construct your own sentence or passage, trying to imitate the model word for word, phrase for phrase, clause for clause.

1. "In fact, Daniel suggests that ideas do not make history but history makes ideas . . . ." —Lore Segal. From "Daniel."

In this complex sentence with compound noun clauses, you can see the reversal and repetition of the noun clauses' subjects and direct objects, *ideas* and *history*. These are the key ideas in the sentence, and Segal emphasizes them deftly at the end of the sentence so that the reader is left with this epigrammatic twist at the end.

2. "But though I could not with a crayon get the best out of the landscape, it does not follow that the landscape was not getting the best out of me." —G. K. Chesterton. From "A Piece of Chalk."

Here we have a complex sentence with an introductory adverb clause. The two words that are repeated and reversed in the antimetabole/chiasmus are *I*, subject of the introductory clause (which becomes object of the preposition me in the base clause) and *landscape*, the object of the preposition in the introductory clause and the subject in the base clause.

3. *Open your door to the census and the census will open doors for you.*

You can readily identify this pattern because it's "marked with an X." If you put the parallel clauses above one another, you can draw an X between them:

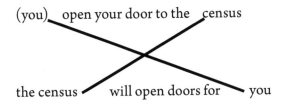

(you)   open your door to the   census

the census   will open doors for   you

In this compound sentence the understood *you* as the subject at the beginning of the first independent clause (*you open your door*) is balanced with the *you* as the object of the preposition at the end of the clause. In the second clause, *you* and *census* switch places: *census* becomes the subject of the independent clause and *you* becomes the object of the preposition.

All these sentences are also examples of *chiasmus*. Why? Because in each example of reversal, the clauses are parallel in structure. If the phrases or clauses are not parallel, the structure is simply antimetabole.

And finally, here are two other noteworthy devices of style, onomatopoeia and the virtual sentence.

Onomatopoeia: A Device of Sound

Onomatopoeia [on-ə-mat-ə-**pe**-ə] **is** a figurative strategy where the sound of words echoes their sense or meaning. Its effect is therefore to create an immediacy, an intimacy, between the reader and the text.

Onomatopoeia also makes a passage more memorable, easier to remember because of the musicality of the passage.

Here are some passages with examples of onomatopoeia. Study them carefully and copy one of them, thinking about its structure as you write. Then construct your own example, trying to imitate the model as closely as you can. Can you hear the onomatopoeia in *lapped, scraped, roaring, slap, clink, clack, creak, thudding*?

1. "An apron of sound lapped out of each dive. Inside, chairs scraped on the floor, loud music and talk tangled with roaring laughter, there was endless traffic toward and from the back where little rooms lined the hall and young black girls took customers until their flesh was raw, the rap of matches, the slap of cards and the clink of bottles on glass, the clack of glasses on tables, the creak of table legs on the floor, the thudding feet of dancers doing the slow drag, the itch, the squat, the grind." —Annie Proulx. From *Accordion Crimes*.

This noisy passage lives up to the forecast of an *apron of sound* in the opening sentence. Listen to the sounds: *lapped, scraped, tangled, laughter, rap, slap, clink, clack, creak, thudding, grind*. The many broad *a* sounds and the *g* and *p* sounds create the effect of knocking and clapping throughout so that the passage resounds with cacophony.

2. "The Ultra-Blast Key Chain consolidates three tools into one: a compact key chain, a high-intensity flashlight with a 180-degree radius of bright light, and a built-in, shockingly loud whistle." —from *Levenger: Tools for Serious Readers* catalog.

This passage sounds shrill, with its assonance of repeated *e* and *i* sounds. *Whistle* is a good example of onomatopoeia; the word *whistle* itself sounds like a whistle.

3. The raindrops plopped and blobbed on the windowsill, pooling in a shimmering circle of water.

Plopped and *blobbed* evoke the sound of soft objects landing noisily; in addition, there is considerable assonance in the repeated broad *o* sounds. In addition, the shimmer sounds like a motion of soft undulation.

4. "'What!' Mrs. Holley screeched." —Alice Walker. From "The Revenge of Hannah Kemhuff."

Screeched is an excellent imitation and evocation of a high-pitched, scratchy, and altogether unpleasant yell. Thus we get a fine sense of what Mrs. Holley's voice sounded like.

The Virtual Sentence

The **virtual sentence** is a purposeful reduction of any basic sentence pattern. It is not a sentence fragment or an incomplete sentence, for it is used by a writer who is entirely in control and wishes to create a certain effect. Use the virtual sentence to introduce a topic, to describe a scene, to represent conversation, to provide a succinct (even sometimes terse) conclusion, or to emphasize a point or an idea. Most virtual sentences depend a great deal on the reader's understanding the context of the sentence. Be sure, then, to use the virtual sentence when there is a purpose as well as a clear context available to your readers.

Here are some passages with virtual sentences. Study them carefully, choose one passage to work with, and copy it, thinking about its structure as you write. Then construct your own passage, trying to imitate the model one word for word, phrase for phrase, clause for clause.

1. "Early, grainy half-light in an old apartment by the frozen river. Gerry slips into the brown-aired entryway and jiggles the key

in the lock, pulling outward the way Dot told him, closing the door after and treading softly up the cat-grey carpeted stairs." —Louise Erdrich. From *Tales of Burning Love.*

The first sentence, a virtual one, sets the scene for the action that occurs in the second sentence. The virtual sentence sketches an image for the reader and helps him/her think about the coming action. Because there is no verb in the virtual sentence, the effect of timelessness is created, an effect reinforced by the present tense and present participles of the second (and complete) sentence.

2. "Still, in years to come, I tried to practice all I'd learned, always made the inward cut, took the step forward, always looked where I was hitting. These, I considered, were the crucial aspects of the science. Insider's Knowledge. A Part of Who I Was." —Richard Ford. From "In the Face."

Here the virtual sentences repeat and underscore those crucial aspects referred to in the second sentence: *insider's knowledge* and *a part of who I was.* Because each idea is in its own virtual sentence, it has more weight and is grammatically more important. Did you notice the compound verbs and the asyndeton in the first part of the passage (*tried to practice, made the cut, took the step forward,* and *always looked*)? The lack of conjunctions is actually echoed in the two short virtual sentences at the end of the passage.

3. "He had been expecting something more definite—chest pains, a stroke, arthritis—but it was only weakness that put a finish to his living alone. A numbness in his head, an airy feeling when he walked. A wateriness in his bones that made it an effort to pick up his coffee cup in the morning." —Anne Tyler. From "With All Flags Flying."

The virtual sentences articulate the weakness, enumerate examples of it, show us readers what the writer means by *weakness*. The writer sketches the feeling for the reader with strokes of virtual sentences, a different weakness for each virtual sentence. Did you also notice the alliteration of *weakness, when* and *walked*? This repetition helps to link the sentences and lend coherence to the passage. There is further coherence with the alliterative *coffee cup*—and a noun adjunct/noun pattern as well.

4. "The next three years I was probably the happiest I'd ever been outside of Tonic or Molokai. No more frustrations with the ladies at the temple." —Allegra Goodman. From *Paradise Park*.

The virtual sentence at the end of this passage explains why the writer was happy in the next three years: no more frustrations. As the first word in the virtual sentence that has no verb, *no* is especially emphatic.

Periodic and Loose Sentences

Finally, let us consider two basically different approaches to the sentence: the **periodic sentence** versus the **loose or cumulative sentence**. A *periodic sentence* delays its main idea until the end (near the period) and presents the subordinate ideas or modifiers first. In contrast, the *loose or cumulative sentence* begins with the main idea and finishes with the subordinate one(s). The main idea appears first with the subordinate ideas loosely following behind. Here are some examples of each kind by Hilary Mantel from "How to Be Tudor."

Loose sentence: *Her French income would cease once the arrears were collected.* Notice that the main idea, *the income would cease*, appears straight on at the first of the sentence with details about when the income would cease trailing behind.

Periodic sentence: *A few months after the death of Mary Rose, Charles married an heiress of 14.* Here Mantel prepares us for the surprise of Charles Brandon's marriage to such a young girl by alerting us that he waited "a few months" after his wife died.

In a periodic sentence, the main idea comes near the period or the end of the sentence, and its position reinforces its power and slight shock. So keep in mind the effect you want to have on your reader and position your main ideas accordingly. Incidentally, the longer a sentence is, the more pronounced the effect becomes. Consider this periodic sentence, for instance, by Edmund Burke, edited slightly for readability, and notice how the accumulation of infinitive phrases at the beginning of the sentence provides a spectacular lead-in to the main idea of how Burke describes the circumstances from which can arise a natural aristocracy:

"To be bred in a place of estimation; to see nothing low and sordid from one's infancy; to be taught to respect one's self; to have leisure to read, to reflect, to converse; to be led to a guarded and regulated conduct from a sense that you are considered as an instructor of your fellow-citizens in their highest concerns and that you act as a reconciler between God and man—these are the circumstances of men that form what I should call a natural aristocracy without which there is no nation."— Edmund Burke. *An Appeal from the New to the Old Whigs.*

Four lengthy infinitive phrases, the last of which includes two adjective clauses, leads us readers to the *these,* emphatically separated from the introductory elements with an em dash. Burke makes us wait and builds his definition of the circumstances from which arise a natural aristocracy to a crescendo before he articulates exactly what he is defining, a natural aristocracy.

After you have written many sentences imitating these figures and stylistic turns, you will have acquired them in your repertoire of stylistic devices, ready to be called up by your mind when your subject matter demands them. It is good to maintain a habit of trying your hand at reproducing the sentence structure of other writers because doing so forces you into another way of seeing and thinking about the writing: it opens your style up to the interesting aspects of others' styles.

In the next chapter, you'll find longer passages for your reading and grammatical analysis. You might try copying some of those too.

Chapter 7. Thinking about Usage

You are an undergraduate English major or a high-school English teacher or a even a college professor of English, and you're at a party. Someone you don't know engages you in a friendly chat and very early in the conversation that person is almost fated to pose the question, "What do you do?" or, if you're a student, "What is your major?" When the questioner hears you respond "English major" or "English teacher" or "English professor," the typical response is "Oh, I'd better watch my grammar!"

But it's not grammar that anyone should watch: it's **usage**. To understand usage more clearly, consider what you already know about what grammar is. You have already read in the first chapter of this book that grammar is a way of organizing what we know about language so that we can talk about and manipulate linguistic knowledge. Grammar is an invisible framework for understanding sentences and explaining how they work; we use the language of grammar to articulate what and how we think about language and its structures. You'll also remember that much of our adult knowledge of grammar is intuitive and unconscious, acquired as we learned language as children; that is, native speakers display their excellent knowledge of grammar merely by being able to converse intelligibly: to put subject before verb before object, for example, or to raise the tone of their voice at the end of an utterance to signal a question. Thus by merely formulating the question "What do you do?" the speaker has already demonstrated an understanding of the grammar of forming questions in English.

Usage, on the other hand, is concerned with correctness and social approbation or approval. Usage refers to a writer's or speaker's ability to choose and use the most socially acceptable forms of words and to frame linguistic constructions in ways that educated people understand, appreciate, and approve. The self-deprecating statement "Well, I'd better watch my grammar" reflects the fear of being incorrect in the presence of someone who may know a lot about language, the reluctance to be judged for one's use of language. This statement belies the speaker's insecurity with the socially acceptable forms of language and lack of confidence in his or her ability to manipulate the language. Speakers who think they should "watch their grammar" care about how they are perceived through their speech; usage matters to them.

Does, however, usage really matter? This simple question lies at the heart of one of the most vitriolic debates among linguists. One group of linguists, the **Descriptivists**, focuses on describing usages that occur in the population and understanding how these usages were formed— not on correctness in writing and in speech. Descriptivists tend to be academics who note and study language as it is actually used. Thus their opinions about usage tend to be accepting and in terms of language politics, very liberal in the most academic sense.

The chasm between the Descriptivists and their linguistic counterparts of the opposite approach to usage, the **Prescriptivists,** is deep. Prescriptivists believe in precise diction, correct usage, succinct prose; they advocate for linguistic tradition. David Foster Wallace (yes: the famous American author of *Infinite Jest*, perhaps the most erudite writer of our time, now dead by suicide) argues at length *for* Prescriptivist principles and *against* Descriptivist principles in *Harper's Magazine*. Wallace calls himself a S.N.O.O.T—his family's nickname for a "really extreme usage fanatic" with the "big historical family joke being that S.N.O.O.T. stood for 'Sprachegfühl Necessitates Our Ongoing Tendance' or 'Syntax Nudniks of Our Time.'" That is, Wallace is the epitome of a **Prescriptivist**—someone who believes in linguistic tradition, correct usage, precise syntax, someone who believes, like Bryan A. Garner, that "English usage is so challenging that even experienced writers need guidance now and then."

Prescriptivists *prescribe* linguistic practice; they set standards about what the majority of educated speakers consider correct or appropriate. Are these standards sometimes arcane, complicated, and subject to dispute? Yes. But your speech and your writing reveal you. Your usage is, whether this situation is fair or accurate or neither, a gauge of your intellectual acumen, your sophistication with language, and sometimes your position in society. Being educated about language and language usage levels the playing field, so to speak; knowing grammar and, yes, knowing the principles of best usage give you power and control over language. Yes, usage matters: unfortunately, people really do judge you by your use of language.

This reference chapter contains a list of prescriptions for use in **Standard Written English**, also called SWE. Notice the *Written* in this label; Standard Spoken English, a name I just made up, would be impossible to define because in American English there are so many discourse communities or audiences or groups that speak regional or cultural dialects—for example, African American Vernacular English, Latino English, Rural Southern, Urban Southern, Standard Upper-Midwest, Maine Yankee, East-Texas Bayou, Boston Blue-Collar—and there I stop, despairing of being able to identify them all. The point is that you need to know when to use *your* regional or cultural dialect in speech and in writing and when to use SWE—that is, you need to know when to code-shift, to shift to a language "code" that matches the expectations of your audience. When you are with your friends or family, you probably speak in your regional or cultural "code," but when you are in a school or work or professional situation, you should know how to shift codes to SWE. Here is how Wallace puts it: "In this country, SWE is perceived as the dialect of education and intelligence and power and prestige, and anybody of any race, ethnicity, religion, or gender who wants to succeed in American culture has got to be able to use SWE. This is How It Is." (54)

So let's get on with it! The list of usage conundrums in this chapter is not complete; there are many specialized dictionaries recording the niceties of thousands of best practices in usage. Here, though, I'll mention the usage items I find most interesting, and you can begin the refinement of your linguistic education regarding usage here.

Tired Phrases and Clichés

Clichés are trite, predictable phrases used repeatedly and often without much thought; they come to mind when we are too tired or too careless to be original in writing. *Cliché* comes into English as the past participle of the French word *clicher,* variant of *cliquer, to click.* Originally, it referred to the process of printing and the clicking sound of a cast or 'dab' striking a metal stereotype, a thin plate where the metal type in each page is soldered together to form a metal sheet. Hence the close relationship in contemporary English between *cliché* and *stereotype,* both of which originate in the printing process and have evolved to meanings associated with words.

Here are a few of the most common clichés and their meanings. Because clichés mark you as intellectually lazy, don't use them—or use them with purpose or with a twist to make a point! And remember that just because a phrase sounds new to you, that doesn't mean that it hasn't been used for hundreds of years and you are just becoming acquainted with it.

- at the end of the day—after a certain period of time has elapsed and an activity or event is finished. Unnecessarily used as a transitional evaluative phrase as in *At the end of the day, Robert turned out to be a decent fellow.*

- bated breath—literally breath that is slowed, subdued, or restrained in awe or terror, it has come to mean nearly a holding of the breath. Someone is always eagerly awaiting a lover with *bated breath!* And *bated* is frequently misspelled as *baited* in this phrase, which presents an entirely different mental picture to the reader.

- big time—a slang cliché for *very much* or *a great amount: I owe you big time for that favor.*

- blissful ignorance—ignorance that doesn't know it is ignorance and therefore cannot be troubled by what it does not know. In truth, ignorance is never bliss because what you don't know *can* hurt you.

- bottom line—the final total of a financial statement, literally the line at the bottom. Used to mean "when it comes down to it."

- comparing apples and oranges—trying to compare two items that are superficially different.

- cut to the chase—originally from film editing, meaning to edit close to the chase scene to focus on the exciting part of the story.

- dead as a doornail; also dead as a doorknob—in the 17th century, carpenters secured vertical and horizontal door panels together so that they would not pull apart by using nails long enough to go through all layers of wood and stick out on the other side. The nail was then pounded over and down into the wood so that the layers of wood could not come apart without some effort. This kind of nail was known as a "dead" nail or one that could not be used in any other way because of the way it was permanently bent. *Dead as a doorknob* is a confusion of *dead as a doornail.* These expressions have been used for centuries.

- deer-in-the-headlights—dazed or momentarily panicked.

- fierce competition—an example of over-emphasis. Do you ever hear of any competition that isn't fierce?

- going forward—a relatively recent usage, meaning "in the future" or "as our relationship progresses." No one wants to go backward, but this usage has become very prevalent—and boring: listen for it in public discourse.

- going postal—going berserk and perhaps violent in attacking coworkers or schoolmates, as in the 1990s events involving postal workers.

- Herculean efforts—labors requiring the strength of Hercules or Heracles (Greek name), who had to perform twelve extraordinarily difficult superhuman tasks in the service of King Eurystheus as a penance. This phrase has been used in English since 1594 and is fairly worn by now!

- heavy lifting—to do more than one's share of the work on a group task or project; slang for *hard work.*

- his own worst enemy—used to describe someone who sabotages him- or herself involuntarily.

- keeping it real—maintaining an air of honesty and openness; not being fake. Slang.

- moment of truth—an instant of realization or decision, typically during a crisis.

- nip in the bud—stop a situation before it blooms or becomes larger and/or more serious.

- on the same page—thinking alike, sharing an understanding of a situation.

- sea change—originally a change caused by the sea, a radical change. Now often used to reflect a major change in circumstances or situation.

- taking one for the team—sacrificing one's interest for the good of a group.

- that is so over—overly emphatic; the *so* is unnecessary, but some people think that it makes the speaker sound current and hip.

- throw the baby out with the bathwater—this expression is typically used by someone who is trying to improve something and has the intention of dumping everything and starting over from scratch—in the process, unnecessarily getting rid of the good aspects of the situation simultaneous with ridding it of its bad aspects.

- value added—in everyday usage, adding features to an item or product but not charging for them; adding value without increasing cost.

- win-win—describes a situation for which there are positive outcomes for both parties.

Tautologies or Redundancies

A tautology repeats something that has already been said without adding anything new; we can also say that tautologies are redundancies or repetitions. These expressions tend to be verbal tics that writers or speakers don't recognize as such because they are often used as stock phrases. Add ones you can think of to this list!

- absolute necessity—if something is a necessity, it is absolute already.

- aggregate together—*aggregate* means *to form into a group or cluster.* You don't need *together.*

- answer back—to *answer* means to speak back to a query; you don't need *back.*

- associate together—if you are *associating* with someone, you are together, if not physically, at least in a communicative sense.

- but nevertheless—*nevertheless* means *but;* both express contrast.

- conspire together—to *conspire,* you must have another person present, so you are automatically together with someone.

- congregate together—*congregate* means to assemble or come together; you don't need *together.*

- consensus of opinion—*consensus* means general agreement or shared opinions on an issue or issues; *opinion* is unnecessary.

General consensus is also a tautology because consensus implies some level of agreement among everyone.

- dash quickly—*dash* means to move quickly.

- due to the fact that—*because* will suffice for this wordy construction.

- each and every—*each* includes *every* in its meaning, so you don't need to write both words.

- each separate incident—*each* includes *separate* because it means everyone or everything.

- early beginnings—all *beginnings* are by definition *early.*

- exceed more than—*exceed* means to go beyond or to be greater in number than something. You don't need *more than.*

- far distance—a *distance* is implicitly *far,* and *far* means *over a great distance.*

- final outcome, final result, final upshot—*outcome, result,* and *upshot* all imply finality.

- free gift—a gift is given freely; if you are receiving a gift, you don't pay for it.

- future forecast—*forecast* means to look into the future, to predict or estimate. Several television stations now call their weather prognostications *futurecasts!*

- for the reason that—just use *because.*

- former veteran—being a *veteran* of some experience means that you went through it in the past; you can never be a former veteran unless you have died.

- I personally—you don't need *personally*; if you say *I*, of course you are being personal.

- in the amount of—just say or write *for: I wrote a check for $2,500.*

- in point of fact—verbose: just say *fact* or *actually.*

- in order to, in order that—just omit *in order:* not *we changed our names **in order to** protect ourselves from the assassins*, but *we changed our names to protect ourselves from the assassins.*

- increasingly more—to increase means to make more of something; omit *more* in most cases.

- joint cooperation—*cooperation* requires more than one person, so it is always *joint*. Don't use both together.

- kill dead—if something is killed, it's quite dead.

- mingle or mix together—both mingle and mix mean to be *put together* or combined with other things, items, or people.

- on a regular basis—*regularly* works nicely and saves three words.

- on the grounds that—long way of saying *because.*

- reason is because—*because* implies a reason, so don't use both together. Say *We broke up because we were always arguing* or *The reason we broke up is that we were always arguing.* Most of the time, *because* works most efficiently in sentences like this.

- regress back—*regress* means to go *backward,* so if you are regressing, you don't need *back* for emphasis.

- respond back—*respond* means to answer back, so you don't need *back.*

- so therefore—they both mean the same thing, so choose one. *We have no money, so we can't go shopping* or *We have no money; therefore, we can't go shopping.* (Notice the difference in punctuation and level of formality.)

- surrounded on all sides—*surrounded* means that something is all around you, on all sides. You don't need both.

- 10 a.m. in the morning—*a.m.* means *ante meridiem* or before noon, which is in the morning. Choose one or the other.

- true facts—*facts* are supposedly always true or empirically provable.

- unfilled vacancy—if something is *vacant,* it is empty or not filled. You don't need both words.

- various different—like saying *different different* because *various* means *different from one another.*

- very unique—something unique is unlike anything else, one of a kind, so it has no degree or comparison. Omit *very.*

- visible to the eye—*visible* is something you can see (with your eyes).

- with the exception of—for *except, except for, aside from*, or *apart from*—in most of these cases, *except* will work just fine. Everyone went to the party *except* me. Use the prepositional structure.

- whether or not—*whether* is conditional, so it already includes the possibility of *not: We don't know whether to take our umbrellas!*

Unhappy Usages: Stay Away from These!

The expressions in this section should simply be avoided if you want to conform to the strictest usage requirements.

- ain't—considered ignorant and unlettered, except in certain dialects or songs. Short for *am not* or *are not*.

- bring vs. take—you *take* something to a place away from where you are: *I will take Prosecco to the party; take* moves from *close* to *far*. Someone *brings* something from somewhere to where you are, a *far to close* move: *Gabriel is bringing Prosecco to me, and he is also taking it to the party.*

- can't hardly—in traditional grammar, a double negative; just say *can hardly: I can hardly bear the scent of freesia.*

- have went—very unacceptable use of the past tense of *go; should be have gone: We have gone to the river to take photos.*

- if I'd of been there—the *of* is superfluous; just write *If I'd been there . . . .* or *If I had been there . . . .* This is a result of mishearing *of* for *have* or *had.*

- irregardless—just *regardless; irregardless* is considered uninformed.

- laundrymat—no: it's *laundromat,* even if you do take your *laundry* there.

- none—*none* has two meanings (*not one*) or (*not any*); it can be either singular or plural, despite what strictly traditional grammarians say. To decide whether to use a singular or plural verb, substitute the phrases in the sentence and choose accordingly.

Singular: Many people have tried to swim across that river, but none [*not one,* singular] has succeeded.

Plural: Although many books have been taken out of the library, none (not any) have been returned.

- not hardly—another double negative involving *hardly,* which is itself a semi-negative word; omit *not.*

- orientated—just *oriented: As soon as Savannah was **oriented** in her new surroundings, she adopted a cat. Orientated* is a back formation, the creation of a verb, *orientate,* working backward from *orientation,* the noun originally formed from *orient.*

- publicly, not publically—*publicly* is the correct spelling.

- sacreligious for sacrilegious—the adjective is formed from *sacrilege,* meaning a misuse of the sacred, not from *religious,* meaning *believing in a religion.*

- Segway for segue—*Segway* is a brand name for an electric scooter that you stand on with both feet. *Segue* means to move from one thing to another (especially in film or music) without interruption.

- should of—*should have. Of* is never part of a verb structure.

- Web—short for the *World Wide Web,* which is not synonymous with the Internet. The Web is one aspect of the Internet, which also includes email, news, etc.

- wreck havoc—should be *wreak havoc,* meaning *to inflict or cause.* Because *havoc* can imply *wreckage,* this is how the mis-spelling probably originated.

Pronoun and Preposition Confusions

This section describes some ways that we can get tangled up with pro-nouns and prepositions in our writing.

- between you and I—after the preposition *between,* you need a pronoun that can be an object for the preposition; you need *me: The secret must remain between you and me.*

- due to—This is what is called a **skunked** term—and when it comes to skunked terms, it's safer to avoid them. A skunked term is one whose meaning and use changes significantly over an indefinite time, and in the middle of this time of change, some people will embrace the change, others will tolerate it, and some will hate it. Bryan Garner quotes Lucille Payne, who in 1965 advised that *due to* was a "graceless phrase, even when used correctly" and it should be avoided altogether. Today it is commonly used as a preposition or a conjunctive adverb mean-ing *because of, owing to,* or *caused by: George left the party early due to a migraine.* Another phrase is almost always, however, better or more specific than *due to: George left the party early because of a migraine,* for instance.

- Me and Paul are going now—This short sentence brings up two usage issues: first, the sentence needs a subject pronoun, *I*, rather than *me*; second, when the speaker articulates him- or herself as part of a compound subject, the other part of the compound, the other person, should always be mentioned first: *Paul and I are going now.*

- We have as much money as them—This is actually an ellipted sentence: *We have as much money as they have money,* so the proper pronoun should be *they,* the subject pronoun: *We have as much money as **they**.* As functions as a conjunction in this comparative sentence.

- *which,* applied to people—*Which* is more appropriately assigned to things or ideas rather than people. Use *who* when you need a relative pronoun to represent something human. **Not** *We wanted to meet all the Saulmon sisters, which were gathered downstairs in the garden* **but** *We wanted to meet all the Saulmon sisters, who were gathered downstairs in the garden.*

Homonyms, Misspellings, Idioms, and Misprisions

Some of the usage problems below result from hearing a word but not seeing it in print; some are just plain misspellings; others are idioms that are twisted; and some are phrases that are misheard or misunderstood. Here's what *to* say (or write).

- *accidentally* is the adverbial form of *accidental; accidently* is the unfortunate marriage of a noun, *accident,* plus the adverbial suffix *-ly.* Use *accidentally.*

- *barbecue* rather than *bar-b-cue, bar-b-que,* or *BBQ* because it is closest to the Spanish word from which English borrowed it, *barbacoa.*

- *a breach [or transgression] of conduct* not a *breech of conduct*.

- a person in a coma is *comatose*, not *coma toast*.

- *deep-seated* feelings [ones that are seated or rooted deep within], not *deepseeded* ones.

- *duct tape* holds ducts or other items together—not *duck tape*.

- an actress may be in her *heyday* [her state of highest feeling and exaltation], not her *hayday*.

- we see our friends *every once in a while*, not *ever once in a while*.

- *everyday*—an adjective; *your everyday chores. Every day* is adverbial; *we mop the floor every day in our everyday clothes.*

- *first annual* is an expression of hope that the event will recur yearly. For the first year, however, the event is just the *first: Join us for the first Bridge Run!* not *Join us for the first annual Bridge Run!* It can't be an annual event until it has happened more than once.

- *like*—traditionally a preposition: *Oded looked like his mother.* However, it is becoming increasingly common as a conjunction: *We did our homework like good students always do.* A usage purist will blanch if you use *like* as a conjunction, so be aware of your audience. Also note that *like* has, like *you know*, become a verbal tic: *We were, like, so happy to, you know, see like the whole gang there!* is much weaker than *We were so happy to see the whole gang there!*

- a *memento*, not a *momento*, is a keepsake to help you remember a special occasion.

- it is a *privilege* to be here, not a *priviledge*.

- *than* is a conjunction used in comparison: *she is thinner than I am thin*. Notice that a clause follows *than*. If the clause is ellipted, then you should write *she is thinner than I*. *Then* is an adverb marking a point in time: *We were **then** ready to board the carriage*.

- *that* and *which* are both relative pronouns, but for strict usage mavens, they have different usages. *That* is a relative pronoun introducing restricted or necessary clauses: *The jewelry **that they wore** marked the corpses as 15ᵗʰ-century*. *Which* typically introduces non-restrictive clauses: *Sue's jewelry, **which she wore casually, almost effortlessly,** was worth a fortune*.

- *their/there/they're*. These words have caused many a writer a good amount of trouble because they sound alike. *Their* is plural, adjectival, and possessive, and it appears before a noun: All the little bears ate *their* porridge. *There* is a place adverb (you can remember this because it contains *here*, also a place). *There* is used to designate a specific spot (*You can put your umbrella there*) or to act as an expletive or placeholder to begin a sentence (*There are three umbrellas in the vase*). *They're* is the contraction of *they + are: They're arriving late tonight*. The apostrophe indicates the removal of the letter *a*, contracting or drawing together the two words *they* and *are*.

- we drove *through* the Holland Tunnel, not *thru* the Holland Tunnel. Don't use *thru*: it makes you look casual and lazy.

- you may have shopped at a *used-book store* (one where the books were used). But you have probably not shopped at a *used book-store* (one where not the books but the store was considered used). Attend to where you place hyphens.

- we *used to* hang out at the carousel, not *use to*. The phrase refers to an action or item from the past.

- you can't *center around* something because the center is the most interior single point. Rather you have to *center on* or *revolve around* something.

- *coleslaw* is a cabbage salad, not *cold slaw*. Coleslaw comes from the Dutch *kool* (cabbage) + *sla* (salad).

- you may see your cousins *once in a while* not *once and a while*.

Sorting Similar Pairs

Some of the pairs below are homonyms; that is they sound the same (or at least almost the same). Some are spelled similarly. But all are frequently mistaken for the other.

- advice and advise: When you *advise* (verb) someone, you are giving *advice* (noun).

- affect and effect: This pair is tricky because both words have two meanings, and both words can function as either nouns or verbs. *Affect* is most commonly a verb, meaning to impact someone in some way: *The sappy movie **affected** her emotions profoundly.* But it also has a meaning in psychology, to describe the particular emotion or feeling that a person is projecting: *My boring sociology professor has so little **affect** that I can't tell if he likes me or even what he's teaching. Effect* is most commonly a noun: *The sappy movie had a profound **effect** on her emotions.* But it can also function as a verb meaning "to bring about," as in *Two weeks of quiet in the mountains **effected** a change of heart.*

- allude and elude—*Allude* means "to refer to": *John* **alluded** *to his uncle's death when he was talking about his increased income. Elude* means to slip away from momentarily: *When I met Cynthia at the party, her name* **eluded** *me* or *The thieves cleverly* **eluded** *the detectives who were hot on their trail.*

- already and all ready—*Already* is an adverb referring to something previously accomplished in time: *The twins had* **already** *raked the leaves. All ready* describes the state of readiness of a group: *We are* **all ready** *to board the train now.*

- amount and number—*Amount* refers to an amorphous quantity, a quantity that can't be empirically measured (or not easily): *At the Thanksgiving dinner, an enormous* **amount** *of food was served.* We can't itemize all the pieces or scoops of food that was served. *Number* refers to something that can, on the other hand, be counted: *A large* **number** *of people showed up for the Thanksgiving dinner.* We could have counted the number of people easily; people are countable.

- anxious and eager—These two adjectives are often misused, with *anxious* being used where *eager* is intended. *Anxious* means having anxiety, being disquieted or mildly worried about something. *Eager* means to look forward to something with pleasure, typically an event, so if you say that you are anxious to meet your best friend's fiancée, you really mean that you are concerned and mildly worried about the meeting. To say *I am eager to meet my best friend's fiancée* is probably a more accurate statement if you are looking forward to the meeting. Here are two more clarifying sentences: *The night before the final exam, all of Professor Mortimer's students were* **anxious** *and fretting about whether they had studied enough. Only the resident genius with a photographic memory was* **eager** *to take the examination and prove his brilliance.*

- attain and obtain—*attain* means to reach some desired achievement; *obtain* means to acquire: *When Paulo **attained** the level of CEO, he **obtained** many perks.*

- ascent and assent—*ascent* means the act of going up; it's a noun: *Fernanda's **ascent** up the corporate ladder was speedy. Assent* can be either a noun or a verb, but in both cases it refers to agreement: *Jane **assented** to the role of maidservant. Her agent got Tobi's **assent** to this role in the movie.*

- bare and bear—*bare* means empty of ornamentation, uncovered, basic and simple: *Tina's little house has **bare** floors and walls. Bear* as a nominal can refer either to the animal (*We ran from the angry grizzly **bear***), or it can be a verb meaning *to carry* or *to endure*: *She will **bear** her sorrow without complaining.*

- brake and break—*brake*, which can be either a noun or a verb, refers to the act of stopping: *Mario **braked** sharply on the tight curve* or *The **brakes** on the semi-trailer truck failed.*

- bridal and bridle—*bridal* is the adjectival form of bride: *She wore a lace **bridal** gown by Vera Wang. A bridle* is a piece of headgear for a horse: *The mare's **bridle** was made of expensive leather.*

- canon and cannon—the *canon* is a body of literature that critics and scholars consider of the highest quality: *William Shakespeare will always be in the **canon.*** On the other hand, a *cannon* is an armament used in warfare: *At Gettysburg, you can see some **cannons** used in the famous battle there.*

- Calvary and cavalry—*Calvary* (also called *Golgotha*) is a physical place, a hill outside Jerusalem where Jesus was crucified: *If you travel to Israel, you can see **Calvary** for yourself. Cavalry* originally referred to soldiers on horseback, but today it refers to soldiers who fight in armored vehicles and helicopters: *The First Air **Cavalry**, also known as the First Cav, fought in Viet Nam.*

- chord and cord—A *chord* is a group of musical notes sounded together, usually harmoniously: *Beethoven's famous Fifth Symphony was written in the key of C minor; the **chord** is composed of notes C, E flat, and G.* A *cord* is a length of string or rope made of several twisted strands: *Instead of a leather belt, she wore a simple rope **cord** around her waist.*

- course and coarse—*course* comes to us from the Latin verb for *run*, so all the several nominal meanings of *course* have to do with movement: a route, progress, a procedure, a path for a race or other movement. As a verb, it means to flow or run unobstructed. Here are two examples: *We followed the **course of treatment** recommended by the doctor* (nominal or noun) and *Anger **coursed** through her body* (verb). On the other hand, *coarse* means ground into rather large chunks or something unrefined, rough, scratchy, not smooth: *The peasants wore tunics made of **coarse** wool.*

- complement and compliment—a *complement* is something that completes or makes another thing whole: *Today the Yankees will have a full **complement** of players* (all players will be healthy and ready to play). A *compliment* is something nice that you say to someone; it can be either a noun or a verb: *Effie received a **compliment** about her lovely hair* (noun). *Amir **complimented** Effie's hair* (verb).

- discrete and discreet—*Discrete* is an adjective meaning separate or distinct: *The students were arranged by **discrete** categories.* *Discreet* means careful and unobtrusive, not bringing attention to oneself: *Peter was **discreet** about his relationship with Heidi.*

- deprecate and depreciate—Only one letter separates these two words! To *deprecate* something means to disapprove of it or to disdain it: *Georgie **deprecated** the accommodations at the inn by the airport.* To depreciate means that something diminishes or goes down in value over time: *Those baseball cards you've been saving have **depreciated,** not gained, value.*

- detract and distract—*detract* means to take away the worth of something so as to deny it: *Her behavior **detracted from** her reputation and made me question whether she would be a good candidate for the job.* Distract means to prevent something from receiving one's full attention: *Texting while you drive **distracts** you from paying attention to the road.*

- device and devise—A *device* (noun) is a thing made for a particular purpose: *The jihadist detonated the bomb with a tiny hand-held **device.*** To *devise* (verb) means to plan or to invent: *Dale **devised** a plan for circumventing the firewall and accessing the university's servers.*

- diffuse and defuse—If you *diffuse* something, you spread it over a wide area: *The strong skunk scent was **diffused** when we opened the garage door.* To *defuse* something means to disarm it or to reduce danger or tension: *The bomb squad specialist **defused** the suitcase bomb cautiously.*

- epithet and epitaph—an *epithet* is a descriptive phrase expressing something about a person (or item) being discussed, as in "a timid librarian" or a "dirty old man"; it can also be used as abuse: *As Zander backed away from the advancing crowd, he screamed **epithets** at them.* An *epitaph* is quite different; that's what's written on your tombstone to evoke your memory, as in *Ella wrote her own **epitaph** about a month before she died and* insisted that her tombstone be carved with it in preparation for her death.

- farther and further—*farther* refers to physical distance: *Nate can throw the discus **farther** than Sidney can* or *You live **farther** from campus than I do. Further* more typically refers to a less literal distance, something more or something in addition to what has already happened: *My mother would not discuss the matter **further***.

- faze and phase—*faze* means unbothered, not disturbed; *We were not **fazed** by the extra work Professor Hinden gave us before the final exam.* The word that sounds just like it, *phase*, means, however, a specific time or stage in a process: *A cocoon is but one **phase** in the development of a butterfly.*

- hangar and hanger—a *hangar* is a very large building, a garage for an airplane: *Mark Zuckerberg parks the Facebook company jet in a private **hangar** at the regional airport.* A *hanger* is a piece of wire, plastic, or wood shaped to hold clothing and prevent wrinkling: *Barbara uses padded **hangers** for her formal satin gowns.*

- hearty and hardy—*hearty* means vigorous, healthy, cheerful: *Santa gave a **hearty** laugh at the elves' mischief. Hardy* has a meaning of similarly robust, but it also means "able to survive or endure difficult conditions": *The natives had **hardy** constitutions; they were capable of surviving extreme cold and wet weather.*

- hew and hue—*hew* means to adhere to or stick to, to be consistent with: *Jonathan **hewed** to the club's rules and eventually was made president.* It can also mean to chop or cut something: *We **hewed** the fallen trees into firewood.* But *hue* has an entirely different meaning: it refers to a color or shade of a color: *Jessica's hair was the **hue** of bright straw.*

- immigrate and emigrate—This pair is tricky. *Immigrate* means to come into a country to live: *Farah **immigrated** to the USA from Turkey in 2003. Emigrate,* however, means the opposite: to leave one country to live in another: *During the war, many families chose to **emigrate** from Somalia, leaving behind their businesses and homes.*

- imminent, eminent, immanent—Again, three words difficult to discern. *Imminent* means that something is about to happen: *When the sirens screamed through the base, we knew an attack was **imminent**. Eminent* refers to something of high stature or importance, famous: *The Swedish royal family is being treated by the **eminent** physician, Dr. Nosalot. Immanent* means that something is inherent or operating within: *The requirements for this course are **immanent** within the syllabus.*

- implicit and explicit—*Implicit* describes something that is implied but not specifically expressed: *A threat was **implicit** in the tone of the principal's message to us. Explicit* means just the opposite— something specifically stated, as in *The commander gave us **explicit** instructions to breach the building.*

- lightning and lightening—*lightning* is the discharge of electricity during a storm: ***Lightning** struck the giant oak tree on the riverbank, slicing off a huge branch. Lightening* means growing brighter or less heavy, becoming lighter: *Gradually, the skies **lightened** as the storm passed.*

- lose and loose—*lose* means not to have something you had before; sometimes it refers to someone killed or lost: *We have **lost** the ability to protest. Loose* is most typically an adjective meaning not tight, not strict, or not conforming: *Vivian has very **loose** guidelines for her curfew.*

- nauseous and nauseated—*Nauseous* is an adjective, referring to something disgusting or repellent or likely to cause nausea: *The details of the crime were lurid and **nauseous.*** *Nauseated*, however, describes the state of having nausea: *The crime scene **nauseated** her.*

- pail and pale—a *pail* is a container or bucket with a handle for carrying liquids: *The farmer lurched out of the barn, a **pail** of warm milk in each hand. Pale* has two distinct meanings: in one sense, it refers to the absence of color, either adjectivally or as a verb: *Her skin **paled** at the mention of the villain's name* or *She was **paler** than a white dress.* In its second meaning, it means to seem less impressive or important: *Janna's intelligence **pales** in comparison to her sister Sue's.*

- passed and past—*passed* is the past tense of *pass: Shemaya **passed** the algebra test easily. Past* refers to something beyond, no longer existing, or gone by in time: *The time for mourning was **past.***

- peers and piers—*peers* are the people within your age, status, or social group (the nominal meaning): *All my **peers** were laughing at me as I stood at the chalkboard. Peer* as a verb can also mean to look carefully or with difficulty: *Because he was short, Kyle stood on tiptoe and **peered** over the edge of the counter.* The noun *pier* sounds just like its homonym *peer*, but it means a structure leading out into the water, a place to tie up a boat, perhaps: *As our boat approached the **pier**, we saw Grandpa standing there waving at us.*

- pique, peak, and peek—As a noun, *pique* means a feeling of irritation or resentment: *When Giovanni wasn't chosen captain, he left the field in a fit of **pique**. Peak* is a pointed top, usually of a mountain, but it can also refer to the highest point of an experience: *As we drove toward the **peak** of the mountain, we noticed that our gas tank was almost empty* or *The **peak** of my high school experience was being the star in the school musical when I was a senior. Peek* is a verb meaning to look surreptitiously or quickly; as a noun it means the act of doing so: *Johannes took a quick **peek** out the window when Annah wasn't looking.*

- pray and prey—*pray* means a solemn hope or request to a deity or other object of worship or a strongly expressed wish: *The principal **is praying** that the sun shines for the school picnic* or *The rabbi **prays** so softly that we can barely hear her. Prey* has a very different meaning. As a noun, it refers to animals that are hunted and killed by other animals for food: *The Cornell red-tailed hawks carry their **prey** to their nests: small birds, squirrels, chipmunks, and snakes.* As a verb, it means to take advantage of, exploit, cause trouble for, or hunt and kill: *Child molesters often **prey** on children who seem vulnerable and alone.*

- principle and principal—*principle* means a fundamental truth or belief in a system of beliefs; it can also refer to a quality of a morally correct person: *The chief **principle** governing the actions of a committee is entropy: after a while, nothing gets done!* or *Zachary operates under strict **principles** in business dealings.* Its homonym, *principal*, means the person of highest importance or the thing of most importance: *The new **principal**, Mr. Burch, has greatly improved the atmosphere of our high school because he is a man of principle and fairness.*

- rein and reign and rain—These words, all pronounced the same, have very different meanings. *Rein* is an instrument used to control a horse, for instance, but the word can be used met- aphorically to mean the power to direct and control: *Ferrari's new CIO has taken the* **reins** *and reinvented the carmaker's public image* or *The new congress has failed to* **rein** *in public spending. Reign* refers to the period of rule of a monarch; as a noun or as a verb, it means to be the best at something or to hold royal office or a special title: *The poodle Izzy* **reigns** *as queen over the back yard, also known as Izzyland* or *During the reign of Elizabeth 1, English life changed dramatically.* Finally, *rain* refers to pre- cipitation, water coming from clouds, but it can also mean a lot of things that are descending or coming down: *During the afternoon, the* **rain** *subsided, and we sent the children out to play in the puddles* or *Troubles* **rained** *down on Calendula: first it was the furnace, then the refrigerator, then his right rear tire—and then his girlfriend left him for good.*

- site and sight—A *site* is a place, physical or metaphorical: *Barsotti drove as fast as he could to the* **site** *of the accident* or *We went to the web* **site** *where the teacher said we could find the in- formation. Sight* refers to seeing, to something that sees or can be seen: *Stevie lost his* **sight** *when he was an infant* or *Carly was* **sighted** *in the motley crowd outside the auditorium.*

- tack and tact—*Tack* has many meanings; it can be a thumbtack used to stick paper into a cork board; *tack* can also refer to a long stitch used to hold two pieces of fabric together tempo- rarily (*She* **tacked** *the two sheets together quickly with embroi- dery thread*); it can refer to the equipment needed for horses (*Go to the* **tack** *shop to get some saddle soap and a new bridle for the pony*); it can also mean (from sailing) to take a different direction, angle, or course of action: *When diplomacy failed to win over her students, the teacher thought she might* **tack** *toward bribery. Tact* means being sensitive to difficult situations or delicate conditions: *Jenna's supervisor told her* **tactfully** *that her skills in filing needed improvement.*

- taut and taught—*taut* means stretched or pulled tight: *The nylon cord used by the kidnappers was* **taut** *around her wrists.* *Taught* is the past participle of *teach*, and it refers to giving instruction or information on a subject: *For thirty-five years, Mrs. Patterson* **taught** *second grade in our small community.*

- track and tract—a *track* is a prepared course, a trail, or a small road (the nominal meaning): *The hounds followed the* **track** *of the escapees through brutal upstate forests.* It can also refer to a recording of one song or piece of music: *The songs are so long that there are only six* **tracks** *on this CD.* As a verb *track* means to follow the course or trail of something: *The hounds* **tracked** *the escapees through brutal upstate forests.* A *tract*, on the other hand, is always a noun. It means an area or a major passage as in *The ITMB corporation bought up several expensive* **tracts** *of land outside Binghamton for its new headquarters.* There is also a less known meaning of tract as a pamphlet, usually religious, philosophical, or political: *The true believers were at the mall, passing out* **tracts** *on bright yellow paper.*

- waist and waste—the *waist* is the part of the human body below the ribs and above the hips: *Ami has a very narrow* **waist**. To *waste* something is not to use it wisely, to spend or use it carelessly for no purpose: *Emma* **wasted** *the money in the trust left to her by her great aunt Shanda, spending it all on travel and clothes within two years.* *Waste* can also mean to deteriorate or shrink away, often from disease or neglect: *Multiple sclerosis* **wasted** *her muscle tissue within three years.*

- waive and wave—*waive* means not to insist on enforcing one's right or a claim: *Falysiti's tuition was* **waived** *by the dean* or

When *Shemika abandoned Freddy, she* **waived** *her rights to visit the children too.* *Wave* means to motion with one's hands to and fro either in greeting or to get attention: *As the ship left the harbor, everyone on board* **was waving** *to someone on shore.*

- wary and weary—if you are *wary*, you are cautious and skeptical: *Paul was* **wary** *of the investing advice, even if it came from Warren Buffett.* But if you are tired, fed up, or extremely bored, you may be *weary: Mae was* **weary** *of cooking fried chicken and biscuits every day.* *Weary* can also be a verb: *Paddy's constant nagging* **wearied** *his wife's patience.*

- *yoke and yolk*—*yoke* is a crosspiece fitting over the neck of animals and sometimes humans, enabling them to pull a cart or carry a balanced load; as a verb, it can also refer to the way that animals or people are joined or bonded in an endeavor (carrying or pulling a load, metaphorically): *The new* **yoke** *fit the oxen more comfortably, enabling them to plow more acreage per day* and *Nick and Amanda are* **yoked** *in marriage.* *Yolk,* pronounced slightly differently because of the letter *l*, is the yellow inside of a bird's egg: Ami likes eggs cooked with soft yolks.

Those Tricky Apostrophes

Apostrophes indicate possession or omission; they have nothing to do with plurals. So if you are making a word plural, don't even think about using an apostrophe. Here are some ways that apostrophes show up when they shouldn't and how you can remember to use them correctly—or not use them!

- *Reader's will be astonished*—should be *Readers will be astonished.* The writer obviously intends to use the plural form of *reader,* and no possessive is needed—nor is an apostrophe.

- *Get your donut's here*—Again, the writer is referring to more than one donut, so there is no need for an apostrophe because the concern is the formation of the plural, not the possessive. The sentence should read *Get your donuts here!*

- *Your kidding*—In this case, the writer is telling someone that she is kidding, so the writer might have originally intended *You are kidding.* Then if the writer wanted to make that sentence more informal, he or she could have used a contraction, removed the noun *a*, and inserted an apostrophe to indicate that a letter had been omitted: *You're kidding.* Remember: *your* is the possessive pronoun or **determiner** patterning with a noun: *your new dress, your Lamborghini, your test scores, your astonishment, your grandfather.*

- *Her's was the last house on the block*—should read *Hers was the last house on the block.* Here *Hers* functions as a pronoun, the subject of *was*, and *hers* is already possessive, so no apostrophe is needed. Don't let *hers* ending in *s* confuse you; you don't automatically have to put an apostrophe before the *s!*

- *Their's was the game to lose*—should be *Theirs was the game to lose.* As in the previous example, *Theirs* is functioning as a noun, the subject of the sentence, and it is possessive in nature already without the apostrophe and superfluous *s*. *Their* is the typical plural possessive form (of *they*), used as a determiner: *Their game was lost early on.*

- *The Nazis' murdered millions of Jews during the Holocaust*—should read *The Nazis murdered millions of Jews during the Holocaust.* Because *Nazis* is plural of *Nazi*, a simple *s* suffices.

- Nazi = singular: *Alain deceived the Nazi who knocked on the door.*

- Nazi's = singular possessive: *The Nazi's uniform was bloodied by the morning's work.*

- Nazis = plural: *Nazis combed the cellar looking for Jews hiding there.*

- Nazis' = plural possessive: *Everyone in the ghetto was terrified of the Nazis' ruthlessness.*

- Whose and who's—These two are easily confused. *Whose* is the possessive form typically used as a relative pronoun or subordinator to connect an adjective clause to a main clause: *We bought our Audi TT convertible from the dealer **whose** service is the best in the valley.* *Who's* is a contraction for *Who is: Who is going to the party tomorrow?* or *Who's going to the party tomorrow?*

Weasel Words

A word or two about *weasel words*. These are the words that pad speech and prose, words that mitigate, reduce the impact of, and undermine lovely, crisp writing. They often indicate the writer's insecurity or reluctance to commit to an idea. Most of the time, they are redundant because their meaning is inherent in the sentence, but writers and speakers use them to fill space and air, to sound important, or to hedge or qualify their words. Here are some weasel words (italicized) and weaselly usages:

- I was *candidly* shocked at the governor's behavior.

- *Clearly,* I believe that Goire was *obviously* the winner of the race.

- The ragamuffins were *duly* grateful for the pennies.

- *Seriously*, you should vote for Miss Tay Kingyu.

- The robins are *perfectly* content in their new nest.

- *Frankly*, we found the service *rather* stupid.

- The room was *virtually* empty, a fact that *quite* surprised us.

- Janice was shocked by the *somewhat* rude behavior of the clerk.

These sentences are not wrong, and your saying or writing them will probably not raise any concerns. But notice how vapid and empty the words tend to be. How many of the italicized words can you omit or replace with a stronger, more specific word, with stronger sentences as a result?

Five Myths and Superstitions about Usage

In the history of the English language, change has been constant: change in vocabulary, change in pronunciation, change in styles, change in usage. Individual words and expressions, especially ones that are popular and frequently used, shift meanings frequently. So some of the myths that we will look at here have been—and may still be—taught in public school and university classrooms. The truth is that writers in the real world, the world of publishing and business and media, contradict these myths every day in their writing; they defy superstitions and break "rules" that many of us have been taught along the way in our education.

Myth #1. *You can't begin a sentence with and, but, or, or however—in other words, a conjunction.* In reality, writers begin sentences with these words all the time, particularly when they want to emphasize either the fact that there is an additional thought (*and*) or a contrasting one (*but*, *or, however, nevertheless*). Beginning the sentence with the conjunction emphasizes the kind of relationship between the two sentences or ideas. Here are some examples:

"I do still find myself pulling all-nighters. **But** I've discovered that the best time for me these days is to start [writing] soon after waking."—Luc Sante. From "The Art of Nonfiction No. 9."

"That was his youth. **And** I remembered someone saying that as a boy he loved to look at the Texas capitol building in Austin—he loved to look at it."—Robert Caro. "The Art of Biography No. 5."

"He would have in fact preferred chatter and merriment and derision to solemnity and isolation, which he found exhausting. **But** the custom reflected the will of the men, for whom the haircut was as private as a urological exam."— Chris Bachelder. From "The Throwback Special: Part 4."

"No association has ever been found between the substance and autism; as a safeguard against infection, thiomersal has undoubtedly saved countless lives. **Nevertheless**, ignorance and paranoia carried the day." — Daniel Smith. From "Call a Kid a Zebra."

Myth #2. *You shouldn't end a sentence with a preposition.* This is nonsense that you shouldn't put up with. Sometimes a sentence becomes awkward when the writer tries to avoid that preposition at the end of the sentence.

"I was about to leave Cairo myself, but since I still had the book, there was someone I thought I should show it **to**."—Raphael Cormack. From "Short Cuts."

"He would have been a glorious teacher to study **under**." —August Kleinzahler. From "Under the Flight Path."

Myth #3. *Passive voice is weak; don't use it*. Passive voice is neither good nor a sign of weakness. There are good reasons for using passive voice. Sometimes you want to write a sentence where the subject is not an agent, particularly when the agent is not important:

"Roughly 25,000 **women will be diagnosed** with [pancreatic cancer] this year, at a median age of 72; by contrast, **almost 10 times that many will be told** they have breast cancer." —Kristen Mascia. From "Six Months to Live."

The unspoken agent, the persons who will do the diagnosing and the telling, are not important in this sentence, but the women who are the subject, the women who will be diagnosed with cancer, are important.

"If [Cotton] Mather went to Disneyland, then, he would undoubtedly have already been vaccinated, assured of the rightness of the procedure and of his health." —Kelly Wisecup. From "If Mather Went to Disneyland."

Again, the agent is irrelevant because who inoculated Cotton Mather against smallpox (he was one of the first to be vaccinated against the "cowpox") is not important. The author wants Mather to assume the importance inherent in the subject position.

Another reason for using passive voice is to position a clause so that you can join sentences: *Lauren was adopted by the Warrens, who live on a thousand acres in Wyoming* instead of *The Warrens adopted Lauren. They live on a thousand acres in Wyoming.*

Myth #4. *Don't split infinitives*. This myth is a remnant of the Latin influence on English, and sticking to this rule strictly can result in difficulty in expressing what you mean with precision. Consider, for instance these variations of a sentence:

She promised to happily go. You see that the infinitive *to go* is split by the adverb *happily.* The placement of the adverb suggests that the going will be done happily, that she will go with gladness.

Happily, she promised to go—if you place the adverb as a sentence modifier as in this version of the sentence, you may be saying that you are happy or even relieved that she promised to go.

She happily promised to go—this version indicates that the promise was made happily. So sometimes, a split infinitive is the most accurate way to say what you mean.

Myth #5. *I.e. and e.g. mean the same thing and can be used interchangeably.* Not so! These abbreviations have different meanings. *I.e.* is from Latin *id est,* meaning *that is:* "For the examination, you will be expected to identify items related to the authors whose works we have read since the last exam, i.e., Hawthorne, Poe, and Cooper." *E.g.* means *exempli gratia* or *for example:* "Goire has many talents, e.g. song-writing."

The Author's Pet Peeves

Just about everyone (or every English teacher or professor at least) is annoyed by certain usage errors. Some errors are simply more grating than others, and here are the ones that are my pet peeves.

- Alot—just do not use this; it is not an acceptable alternative for *a lot: We received* ***a lot*** *of compliments on our new carpet.* And don't confuse it with the verb *allot,* meaning to portion out or to allocate: *The state* ***allotted*** *grants to seventeen school consortiums.*

- Alright—don't use this either; it is not an acceptable alternative for *all right: The kids are* ***all right*** *is correct.*

- *Au jus* as a noun—*au jus* is French for *with juice,* typically meaning a sandwich with meat juice or gravy ladled onto it. So if you say *Do you want that sandwich with au jus?* you are actually saying *Do you want that sandwich with with juice?* Instead, just say *I'd like that sandwich au jus.*

- Being that (instead of *because* or *since*): *Being that we will already be in town, I will pick up some lemons at Wegmans* sounds awful. *Because we will already be in town, I will pick up some lemons at Wegmans* sounds cleaner and smarter—and more succinct.

- *Chaise lounge*—a misprision of the French *chaise longue* or *long chair.* The chair does not necessarily imply lounging.

- *Conferencing*—*Confer* already exists as a perfectly good verb related to participating in a conference, so why do you need a longer word? Use *I am conferring with all my students this week,* not *I am conferencing with all my students this week.*

- *Equally as*—a redundancy. You don't need them both. You can use either *The chairs were equally expensive* or *One chair was as expensive as the other.*

- *Hopefully*—*Hopefully* is one of those skunked terms, meaning that some people think its current and typical usage as a sentence modifier (*Hopefully, we will finish this sanding job before dinner*) is acceptable and some others do not; the term is in a kind of linguistic approval limbo now. Strictly, *hopefully* is an adverb meaning *full of hope* and used correctly in a sentence like this: *Kelli **hopefully** opened the college admissions email message.* In other words, she did it with hope that she would be admitted. Most of the time when *hopefully* is used, the writer or speaker intends to use *I hope,* a phrase that is clearer and more precise: *I hope we will finish this sanding job before dinner.* To a good writer, precision matters—so use *hopefully* cautiously and appropriately, not as a substitute for *I hope.*

- *Hung* and *hanged*—the verb *hang* has two distinct senses: one refers to people, and the other, to objects. *Clothes are **hung** on the line to dry,* but *People are hanged by the neck until dead.*

- *I feel like* instead of *I think* or *I believe* as in *I feel like the conservative candidate will win the election.* The phrase reeks of confused and clichéd thinking and, according to Molly Worthen in the *New York Times,* it says a great deal about "our muddled ideas about reason, emotion and argument — a muddle that has political consequences." So don't leave the impression that you are less than brilliantly articulate: don't write or say *I feel like!*

- *Invite* as a noun—Please don't say that you have sent the *invites* out already! *Invite* is a verb; *invitation,* the noun formed from that verb. *If you **invite** someone to a party, you give them an **invitation.*** But recently *invite* has crept into usage as a noun: *We are getting the **invites** for the alumni banquet ready now.* Be sophisticated and use the perfectly good word that already exists: *invitation: We are getting the invitations to the alumni banquet ready now.*

- *Less and fewer*—Especially annoying is the use of *less* to mean *fewer,* as in *You own less sweaters than anyone* or the sign in the supermarket express line for *7 Items or Less.* The correct usage would be *You own fewer sweaters than anyone* and *7 or Fewer Items.* Why? *Fewer* refers to a countable number of items, so if you can count things, use *fewer: Fewer people in my class have red hair than brown hair*—because *we can count the number of people who have red hair and brown hair.*

- *Loan* for *lend*—*loan* is a noun: *Dad gave us a **loan** for the down payment on the house.* *Lend* is the verb corresponding to the noun: *Dad will **lend** us money for the down payment.* To write or say that *Marco will **loan** me the money for my invention* reveals one's ignorance of the distinction between these two words.

- *Off of* and *off*—to tell the dog to *get off of the couch* is redundant (but the dog won't care!). *Off* suffices nicely by itself: *Get off the couch!*

- *Outside of* and *outside*—*outside of* is also redundant; lose the *of*. Write *The children are outside the house playing*, not *The children are outside of the house playing*.

- *Preplan*—this word has built-in redundancy, for to *plan* means to look ahead. *Preplan* literally means *plan plan* or *plan to plan*. Not so happy a construction: *Sadie and Edward are preplanning their wedding*. Much happier: *Sadie and Edward are planning their wedding*. Usually this is used to emphasize the need to allot sufficient time for planning.

- *At the present time* for *now*—just write or say *now* so as not to sound pretentious. *Marvin K. Mooney, will you please go **now**?* Not *Marvin K. Mooney, will you please go **at the present time**?*

- *Resume* for *résumé*—don't be lazy and omit the accents ague; otherwise you have misspelled the word that refers to the document listing your accomplishments and experience, *résumé*. *Jonathan sent his **résumé** to sixteen different accounting firms.* *Resume* means to begin or start again: *Let us **resume** planting the corn so that we can finish by nightfall.*

- *Snuck*—please don't use this as the past participle of *sneak*, whose principal parts are *sneak, sneaked, sneaked,* and *sneaking*.

Say *The terrorists **sneaked** C4 into the warehouse in their underwear*—not *The terrorists snuck C4 into the warehouse in their underwear*. Or write *We **sneaked** out the window, not making a sound*, not *We **snuck** out the window, not making a sound*.

- *Sort of* and *type of*—avoid these expressions because they add words unnecessarily: Instead of *We were **sort of** tired*, write *We were somewhat tired* or *We were very tired* or *We were tired*. What does *sort of* mean, anyway? *Type of* is also usually unnecessary: *The victim wore a red chemise **type of** dress* is much wordier than the crisp *The victim wore a red chemise dress* or even *The victim wore a red chemise*.

- *Upmost* and *utmost*—*upmost* is sometimes a mishearing of *utmost* and because *utmost* means at the most extreme or the greatest, it seems logical that *up* should be combined with *most*, as in *The children had the **upmost** respect for the nuns*, which should be *The children had the **utmost** respect for the nuns*. *Upmost* is a weak usage of *uppermost*, which has a slightly different meaning than *utmost*; *uppermost* means the highest in place or importance or sometimes rank: *The climber eyed the **uppermost** reaches of the cliff* or *Evaline's welfare was **uppermost** in her uncle's mind*.

This chapter is merely an introduction to the complicated world of English usage. If you are interested in usage or have a usage question, go first to a dictionary and read the usage notes for the words or phrases that you are curious about. For deeper investigations into usage, consult one of many dictionaries of usage.

Chapter 8. A Punctuation Gallery

This chapter presents all the major marks of punctuation, mark by mark, with examples of correct punctuation and discussions of the conventions of best punctuation. We begin with the most commonly used mark, the period.

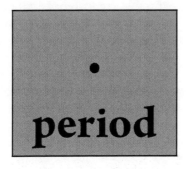

The period is the most elemental and definitive mark of punctuation. It is final. It marks the end of the sentence and the conclusion of the thought. In speech, the period requires a full stop at the end of a sentence and is the equivalent of coming to a complete stop at a traffic stop sign. A period draws the boundary between sentences, and it is probably the first mark of punctuation you learned as a young writer. You will find the period at the end of declarative sentences or sentences that make a statement, at the end of most virtual sentences, after initials and some abbreviations. Periods are important for reading because they help readers construct text by grouping ideas. Instinctively, readers know to process the text between periods as a complete idea; they expect that the territory between periods to be inhabited by something intelligible and finished. Let's look at some examples.

Periods after Declarative Sentences

A period signals the end of a declarative sentence, as in these sentences.

1. "At 40,000 feet Yeager began his speed run." —Tom Wolfe. From "The Limits of the Envelope."
2. "I could see her defeat and helplessness." —Janet Frame. From "You Are Now Entering the Human Heart."
3. "A good many factors contributed to the decline of sport." —E.B. White. From "Preposterous Parables: The Decline of Sport."
4. "Warts are wonderful structures." —Lewis Thomas. From "On Warts."
5. "I loved to pick through trash piles and collect empty bottles, tin cans with pretty labels, and discarded magazines." —Russell Baker. From "Make Something of Yourself."

Periods after Virtual Sentences

Periods also conclude virtual sentences and, because many virtual sentences are short anyway, emphasize their punch. Here are some examples:

1. "Weird. Sleeping in the neuropsych ward at night, I sensed the presence of a very large rabbit under my bunk. A seven-foot rabbit with brown fur and skin sores, who took long, raking breaths." —Thom Jones. From "The Black Lights."

Notice how the one-word virtual sentence *Weird* sets the tone for what follows, prepares your mind to accept the oddity of it. And observe too how the final virtual sentence describing the giant rabbit is given additional importance by existing as its own sentence and by not being attached to the previous sentence as an appositive.

2. "I guess I'd resolved the soul and sin thing by lapsing from my heavy-duty Catholic background, giving up my immortal soul for a blues kind of soul. Funky and low-down, the kind inspired by reading too much Carlos Castaneda and Rilke and Robert Bly and dropping acid with a guy who claimed to be my cosmic mate from a past life." —Julia Alvarez. From "The Rudy Elmenhurst Story."

The virtual sentence, which begins with *Funky and low-down*, draws out what Alvarez means by a *blues kind of soul*. That it has its own sentence elevates it to the status of important information. Did you also notice the repetition of *soul?* And the cluster of words that have a metaphysical connotation—*soul, immortal, cosmic?*

3. "She had ten wigs, ten colors, fifty styles. She looked different, the same, and very good. A human theme in which nothing began anything and was gorgeous. To me she was the world's lesson." —Leonard Michaels. From "Murderers."

A human theme in which nothing began anything and was gorgeous is a virtual sentence because it has no verb cluster. This virtual sentence comments upon the various appearances of the woman, who always looks good regardless of which wig she has on, and interprets the woman's chameleon-like appearance. Did you also notice the asyndeton in the first sentence: *ten wigs, ten colors, fifty styles?* The asyndeton and the virtual sentence create a clipped, slightly terse tone for this passage.

4. "Here ghosts sat as if already in the World-to-Come, explicating Scripture. Or whatever." —Cynthia Ozick. From "Bloodshed."

The *Or whatever* virtual sentence is a blunt, sarcastic comment on the notion of the ghosts in the World-to-Come, explicating scripture. The speaker is not only disbelieving but also dismissive. It is the current equivalent of saying "Not!" after a declarative statement.

5. "Still, Rita suspects, even knowing all there is to know about her, he sees her as his entryway to the land of dreams. His bridge. His American girl." —Lynne Sharon Schwartz. From "The Melting Pot."

The two virtual sentences at the end of this passage are grammatically parallel: *His bridge, His American girl*. They articulate what the writer means by his entryway to the land of dreams. The virtual sentences would be appositives if they were in the base sentence.

6. "I am Dell Enterprise. PowerEdge servers, storage, infrastructure software, and Premier Enterprise Services. And I am backed by thousands of service and support people: on-site, online and on the phone." —Dell advertisement, *Wired*.

At the center of this excerpt is a virtual sentence that defines what Dell Enterprise is by providing a catalogue of its services. Virtual sentences are common in advertisements, where the writer wants to reach the reader with short bits of trenchant information. Notice the other aspects of this selection: the very short opening sentence; the third sentence beginning with the conjunction and as if to remind the reader of the connection to the first sentence; the paired and alliterative *service* and *support*; and the anaphoric structure following the colon: *on-site, online,* and *on the phone.* (The style of this magazine is to not include the comma after the next-to-last item in a series.)

Periods with Abbreviations

Periods also mark abbreviations and initials, as in

M.D. (Medical Doctor)

Ph.D. (Doctor of Philosophy)

etc. (etcetera or *and so on*)

a.m. (ante meridiem—before the meridiem or noon)

Esq. (Esquire)

L.L.C. (limited liability corporation)

Mr. (mister)

Increasingly, however, periods are disappearing in abbreviations. Abbreviations are being written in capital letters and without the periods, particularly acronyms or words created from the initials of each word in a phrase, such as *RAM* (random access memory). This trend may have accelerated with the U.S. Postal Service, which quite a few years ago asked the American public not to put periods after state abbreviations on U.S. mail. Indeed, the Postal Service completely supported the rewriting of state abbreviations so that each was only two letters with no periods, all the better to be read by machines scanning envelopes and sorting mail. (Evidently, at the time periods threw glitches in the scanning procedures.) So the abbreviation for *Illinois* (*Ill.*) became *IL* (two capital letters, unpunctuated); the abbreviation for *Oklahoma* (*Okla.*) became *OK*; and the abbreviation for *Indiana* (*Ind.*) became *IN*. The postal service also created new, easily scanned abbreviations for words like *street* (formerly *st.*; now *ST*); *lane* (*LN*); *road* (*RD*); *court* (*CT*). Interestingly, British, Australian, and Canadian convention is not to use periods in abbreviations.

In most acronyms, the periods have totally disappeared, and in many (like *scuba*, which was originally an acronym representing *self-contained underwater breathing apparatus*) the original meanings have been nearly obscured. Do you know what these acronyms represent?

NATO (North Atlantic Treaty Organization)

GRE (Graduate Record Exams)

YWCA (Young Women's Christian Association)

NAACP (National Association for the Advancement of Colored People)

AMA (American Medical Association)

MLA (Modern Language Association)

APA (American Psychological Association)

Periods Indicating Ellipsis

Periods are also used in threes (generally with intervening spaces) to indicate ellipsis or omitted words or a pause in speech. Four periods indicate an ellipsis plus the period at the end of the ellipted sentence.

1. "She doesn't even answer me. She says . . . you want to know what she says?" —Grace Paley. From "Zagrowsky Tells."

This ellipsis indicates a pause in the speech.

2. "But though I pined away and talked about it, I knew that I couldn't go; there was no money . . . ." —Mary Mebane. From *Mary: An Autobiography*.

Each section of this autobiographical piece concludes with an ellipsis just like this one. Perhaps the ellipsis indicates the omission of certain details or even the passage of time between recorded events.

3. "And there I was, caught up in a mass flight into collective murder, into the fiery furnace . . . . Something had come up from the depths, and it was happening now." —Louis Ferdinand Céline. From *Journey to the End of the Night*.

Something is omitted here between the actual recounted events of fleeing and the reflection or interpretation of those events. The ellipsis functions as a kind of transition between the remembered past and the present.

4. "She tries to speak and then stops and takes a shuddering breath, and the tears pour and pour down her face. 'I'm . . . resting,' she says finally. 'Just resting.'" —Paula Keisler [Paula Huston]. From "The Singing of Angels."

These ellipses indicate a pause in the conversation and mirror *resting*.

5. "It was one in the morning, and I began to count ahead in my mind . . . two, three, four, five . . . sunrise." —Victor Montejo. From *Testimony: Death of a Guatemalan Village*.

Here the ellipsis indicates the omitted numbers intervening between the beginning of the counting and sunrise.

? question mark

The **question mark** indicates a question or posits a condition of tentativeness or uncertainty. Even its shape, curving first one way and then another, suggests an insecurity about which direction it should turn. Use the question mark after any of the question transformations or after a declarative sentence or phrase that you want to transform into a question. You can also use the question mark to show the reader that you are unsure about something you are writing. Like the period, the question mark requires a full stop at the end of an utterance or sentence.

Question Mark as Part of a Question Transformation

In all the sentences below, the question mark comes after a question transformation. You can tell because of the inversion of subject and verb and the insertion of the subject between verb and auxiliary: *Was he? How have you been? Do you take? Has a quarter disappeared?*

1. "Was he deranged, was he a sex maniac?" —Margaret Atwood. From "The Man from Mars."
2. "How have you been this week, sweetheart?" —Ann Beattie. From "The Cinderella Waltz."
3. "When friends dropped over and sat around the kitchen table, my grandma would ask, 'Do you take cream and sugar?'" — Stuart Dybek. From "Pet Milk."
4. "Has a quarter disappeared from Paula Frosty's pocket book?" — William H. Gass. From "In the Heart of the Heart of the Country."

5. "Do you think anybody will come back on Thursday?" —
   Charles Richard Johnson. From *"Kwoon."*

Question Mark Causing a Question Transformation

In these questions, the question mark itself causes the question transformation because the word order is regulation subject-verb. The only
thing that differentiates these questions from their indicative counterparts is, in fact, the question mark.

1. "You don't like the nose?" —Thom Jones. From "The Black
   Lights."
2. "You know what I'm thinking? Of all the people in Cedar Falls,
   you're the one who could understand Vern best." —Bharati
   Mukherjee. From "The Tenant."
3. "You don't know? Typical. Burton's leaving, see?" —Mary
   Robison. From "Coach."
4. "'You live in a Hetrick and Dewitt?' said Doreen." —Michael
   Chabon. From "S Angel."
5. "I must be hungry. And not you?" —Allen Hoffman. From
   "Building Blocks."

Question Mark Indicating Writer's Uncertainty

In these questions, the question transformation occurs after a declarative sentence: there is no internal transformation in the grammatical
structure of the sentence or alteration of syntax. In some of them, a
grammatical tag reinforces the writer's uncertainty, but in others, the
question mark alone accomplishes this purpose.

1. "Julie's place is that way, right?" —Ron Carlson. From "Blazo."
2. "Sometimes it's hard. You know what I'm saying?" —Raymond
   Carver. From "Cathedral."

3. "I gotta ask. You two married, or what?" —Jonathan Penner. From "Emotion Recollected in Tranquility."
4. "You believe what you saw—the crown?" —*Bernard Malamud. From "The Silver Crown."*

A Note About Question Marks

Notice that question marks go with the section of the sentence that actually is the question or the section that actually asks the question. Also observe that question marks may go inside or outside quotation marks, depending on where the question actually concludes. Consider this sentence from Ann Beattie's "That Last Odd Day in L.A.":

"'I've come up against Amy Vanderbilt's timetable for accepting a social invitation at Thanksgiving?' he asked."

In this sentence, the question mark accompanies the actual question— the part about the Thanksgiving invitation timetable—and thus goes inside the quotation marks to identify it as part of what was said. The *he said* is **metalanguage**, language about language, language reporting on the speaker's actions or words.

These sentences illustrate times when you would place the question mark outside the quotation marks:

Do you mean that we're supposed to underline all mentions of "euro"?

and

Who screamed "Fire"?

and

"What rhymes with 'weaponize'?" —Dennis Cass. From "Meter Made."

In all, the quoted material is within the original utterance, a part of it, and the entire utterance is a question. Therefore, the question mark goes after the complete utterance, which includes the quotation mark.

exclamation point

The exclamation point, highly dramatic, wants to jump off the page. It is primed for excitement. Because this mark indicates such intensity, use it sparingly and wisely. One exclamation point is always sufficient. Multiple exclamation points can suggest anything from a writer out of control to one just plain silly or hysterical. Overused, the exclamation point loses its potency, and readers become inured or accustomed to it—therefore rendering it useless. Like the period and the question mark, the exclamation point requires a full stop (although a series of words or short phrases punctuated with exclamation points can create a rush of motion). The exclamation point is a fine indicator of surprise, extreme pleasure, sound effects, threats, or any heightened emotion.

The exclamation point follows a classic exclamation or the **exclamatory transformation,** which denotes surprise or astonishment and requires a transformation of a base sentence. To create an exclamatory transformation of the sentence *You look pretty,*

1. move the complement before the subject: *pretty you look*
2. insert *what* a or *how* at the front of the sentence: *How pretty you look*
3. then finish it off with an exclamation mark: *How pretty you look!*

Other examples of exclamatory transformations are *How green is my valley! How delightful you look today! How dreadful! What a big nose you have!*

The exclamation mark can also have the effect of converting any indicative utterance to an exclamatory one. Here then is the exclamation point in action.

1. "'I can't believe it!' she cries out, aware of triteness, as Thant hands over the bags to her." —Alice Adams. From "Barcelona."

This exclamation point emphasizes disbelief. Notice that there is no other end punctuation for the clause and that the exclamation point goes inside the quotation marks because her words, not the entire sentence, are exclamatory.

2. "How dreadful is the state of those that are daily and hourly in the danger of this great wrath and infinite misery!" —Jonathan Edwards. From "Sinners in the Hands of an Angry God."

This sentence is the result of an exclamatory transformation. Notice the *how* and the inverted syntax.

3. "'You are a shining star!' she says with amazing volume and venom. 'Stick to your plan!'" —C.S. Godshalk. From "The Wizard."

The exclamation points go inside the quotation marks in both these instances because they apply specifically to the material being quoted.

4. "Breaking into somebody's place there's a way your heart beats, like a hummingbird's whirring wings, and a sharp taste in your mouth you don't get anywhere anytime else!" —Joyce Carol Oates. From *Bad Girls*.

Here the exclamation point underscores the extremity of the sensation described in the sentence.

5. "Doctors used to be so confident that severed nerves could not transmit pain—they're severed!—that nerve cutting was commonly prescribed as a treatment for pain." —Melanie Thernstrom. From "Pain, the Disease."

In this sentence, the exclamation point applies to the interrupting clause and has the effect of increasing its emphasis, which is already considerable because of the dashes.

6. "But they let you go free!" —Ursula K. Le Guin. From "The New Atlantis."

This exclamation point seems to express amazement and surprise.

7. "This is a country of six million people, and it can mobilize a million in twenty-four to forty-eight hours!" —David Remnick. From "The Dreamer."

Here the exclamation point seems to reinforce the excitement of the discovery, along with amazement.

8. "Now that's rapid-fire convenience!" —Todd Lappin. From "Eureka! Great Moments in the March of Technolust."

A strong feeling of affirmation is conveyed by this exclamation point.

Passages to Punctuate: Terminal Marks

Copy the passages below, either by hand or by keying them in to your computer. As you copy, find sentence boundaries in the passages below and punctuate each passage with terminal punctuation marks only—that is, punctuation at the ends of sentences. Internal punctuation (commas, semicolons, and colons) is already here, but capitals signaling the beginnings of sentences have been removed. You will find the original passages, punctuated as published, after the exercises.

1. Anthony Bourdain. From *Kitchen Confidential: Adventures in the Kitchen Underbelly.*

The last cook to arrive is our French fry guy this is a full-time job at Les Halles, where we are justifiably famous for our frites Miguel, who looks like a direct descendant of some Aztec king, spends his entire day doing nothing but peeling potatoes, cutting potatoes, blanching potatoes, and then during service dropping them into 375-degree peanut oil, tossing them with salt and stacking the sizzling hot spuds onto plates with his bare hands I've had to do this a few times, and it requires serious calluses

2. Annie Dillard. From *An American Childhood.*

We children lived and breathed our history—our Pittsburgh history, so crucial to the country's story and so typical of it as well—without knowing or believing any of it for how can anyone know or believe stories she dreamed in her sleep, information for which and to which she feels herself to be in no way responsible a child is asleep her private life unwinds inside her skin and skull; only as she sheds childhood, first one decade and then another, can she locate the actual, historical stream, see the setting of her dreaming private life—the nation, the city, the neighborhood, the house where the family lives—as an actual project under way, a project living people willed, and made well or failed, and are still making, herself among them I breathed the air of history all unaware, and walked oblivious through its littered layers

3.   Bobbie Ann Mason. From *Zigzagging Down a Wild Trail.*
Peyton slept beside her, not waking until they crossed the Mississippi River again, at Memphis when he stirred, she turned to peer out the window at plow-scarred fields after Memphis, the delta stretched out flat and blank—old cotton fields waiting to be submerged under something new and transforming billboards planted in the fields like scarecrows marked the way to the casinos in the distance the casinos began to appear, rising out of the fields like ocean vessels on the horizon—a Confederate armada positioned along the Mississippi, protecting the delta from northern invaders

Original Punctuation for Anthony Bourdain's Excerpt from *Kitchen Confidential*

The last cook to arrive is our French fry guy. This is a full-time job at Les Halles, where we are justifiably famous for our frites. Miguel, who looks like a direct descendant of some Aztec king, spends his entire day doing nothing but peeling potatoes, cutting potatoes, blanching potatoes, and then during service dropping them into 375-degree peanut oil, tossing them with salt and stacking the sizzling hot spuds onto plates with his bare hands. I've had to do this a few times, and it requires serious calluses.

Original Punctuation for Annie Dillard's Excerpt from *An American Childhood*

We children lived and breathed our history—our Pittsburgh history, so crucial to the country's story and so typical of it as well—without knowing or believing any of it. For how can anyone know or believe stories she dreamed in her sleep, information for which and to which she feels herself to be in no way responsible? A child is asleep. Her private life unwinds inside her skin and skull; only as she sheds childhood, first one decade and then another, can she locate the actual, historical stream, see the setting of her dreaming private life—the nation, the city, the neighborhood, the house where the family lives—as an actual project under way, a project living people willed, and made well or failed, and are still making, herself among them. I breathed the air of history all unaware, and walked oblivious through its littered layers.

Original Punctuation for Bobbie Ann Mason's Excerpt from "Tunica"

Peyton slept beside her, not waking until they crossed the Mississippi River again, at Memphis. When he stirred, she turned to peer out the window at plow-scarred fields. After Memphis, the delta stretched out flat and blank—old cotton fields waiting to be submerged under something new and transforming. Billboards planted in the fields like scarecrows marked the way to the casinos. In the distance the casinos began to appear, rising out of the fields like ocean vessels on the horizon—a Confederate armada positioned along the Mississippi, protecting the delta from northern invaders.

comma

The comma is slight but not insignificant. Probably the most frequently used mark of punctuation, it is also possibly the least well understood. Although there is a fine logic to placing commas, many writers merely sprinkle commas through text where they think the reader should pause, mentally as well as conversationally. Actually, there is some point to this method of punctuation—one use of the comma is to prevent misreading, to keep apart two words or phrases that, if allowed to elide, might confuse. Bottom line: there are some clear instances where a comma is necessary, obligatory (you are obliged to use one), and where you should learn to insert it. But there are other structures where you may choose a comma, no punctuation, or a different mark. Let's look at the uses of commas.

Commas and Coordinators in Compound Sentences

When you join two (or more) independent clauses in a compound sentence and use a coordinator (*and, but, for, or, nor, yet*), you need a comma **after each pattern** and **before the coordinator separating the patterns**. A schema for this structure might look like this:

Pattern 1, *but* pattern 2.

or

Pattern 1, pattern 2, *and* pattern 3.

"It was unbelievable, but here it was." —Louis L'Amour, "Trap of Gold."

The first independent clause or complete pattern is *It was unbelievable*. The second complete pattern is *here it was*. Here are more examples:

1. "His fingers were stiff, and it took him a long time to twist the lid off the holy water." —Leslie Marmon Silko. From "The Man to Send Rain Clouds."
2. "The market is full of exotic produce, and the prices are being driven up." —Allegra Goodman. From "Variant Text."
3. "There is an accident, and Cruise winds up charged with murder and disfigured." —David Denby, from *The New Yorker*. Rev. of *Vanilla Sky*.
4. "I smiled, but I feared she was right." —Daphne Merkin. From *Enchantment*.
5. "At school boys were thinking of college, and girls were thinking of boys." —Nessa Rapoport, "The Woman Who Lost Her Names."
6. "The edge of the ice sheet lies some ten miles away, and it can be seen—a ghostly white blue in the distance—by climbing just about any hill." —Elizabeth Kolbert. From "Ice Memory."

Commas between Very Short Independent Clauses

If the independent clauses in a compound sentence are **very** short and you want the sentence to move rapidly, it is possible to use only a comma (without its usual coordinator as accompanist) between the two patterns. In addition, in these kinds of sentences, there is typically a very tight relationship between the two clauses, and the two may be structurally quite similar. Be extremely careful when you do this, however: some punctuation purists may consider this a **comma splice** (that is, a compound sentence where two independent clauses are spliced—or held together in a fragile manner—with only a comma, where a comma and coordinator are required). Here are some examples:

1. "His mother was half-English, his father was half-French." —Joseph Conrad. From *Heart of Darkness*.
2. "Certainly there will be work to do, everyone must work here." —Primo Levi. From *Survival in Auschwitz*.
3. "We negotiate the steps, we knock over some books." —Anne Enright. From "My Milk."

Commas Setting Off Introductory Clauses and Phrases

Mark introductory adverbial clauses or introductory long phrases with a comma. The comma is the doorstop that gently prevents the introductory clause from slamming into the main clause.

1. "As if to take another reading of the girl's plain face, I looked again into the coffin on my way out." —Saul Bellow. From *Something to Remember Me By*.
2. "Since George W. Bush took office, there's been a grand total of zero Alaskan oil spills." —Anonymous, from an advertisement for *That's My Bush*, Comedy Central.
3. "If you only had a few days to spare for a Caribbean vacation, where would you spend it?" —Advertisement for Postmark Caribbean.
4. "In memory of him and out of respect for mankind, I decided to live for love." —Grace Paley. From "Goodbye and Good Luck."
5. "Nothing in nature is exhausted in its first use. When a thing has served an end to the uttermost, it is wholly new for an ulterior service." —Ralph Waldo Emerson. From *Nature*.

But No Commas When the Adverbial Clause Concludes

Adverbial clauses that slide in at the end of a sentence are generally **not** set off by a comma. If you listen hard to these sentences, you'll be able to detect that there is no pause, oral or mental, when readers get to the adverbial clause. Here are some examples:

1. "The night was breaking when they got to the house." —Bruce Jay Friedman. From "When You're Excused, You're Excused."
2. "When she lifts her foot to take a step, she no longer trusts the ground to be there when she puts it down." —Francine Prose. From "Electricity."

Note that both adverbial clauses begin with the same subordinator, *when*. The first clause introduces the sentence and is followed by a comma; the second clause concludes the sentence and has no punctuation between it and the main clause *she no longer trusts the ground to be there.*

3. "After that Thanksgiving, Pop gradually sank as if he had a slow leak." —Saul Bellow. From "A Silver Dish."
4. "I was working under my plastic roof when I heard someone shouting." —Nguyen Quang Sang. From "The Ivory Comb."
5. "We stood in the shade of the supply room tent along with the rest while the first sergeant and the supply sergeant filled out forms." —Larry Heinemann. From *Close Quarters.*

The exception to this rule involves clauses beginning with *even though, although, as though, as if, since* and sometimes *while*. These subordinators introduce such a powerful contrast that they generally (but not always) demand some separation from the main clause.

1. "I felt wild and new, as though I could swim the heavens and fly through waves." —Amy Tan. From *The Bonesetter's Daughter.*

2. "There was something almost apologetic in her way of uttering her tender avowal, as if she would beg her listeners not to consider her too bizarre in her taste." —Dorothy Parker. From "Too Bad."
3. "His entire frame jerks and twitches, as if he is taken by a fit." —Rebecca Goldstein. From *The Dark Sister.*
4. "The cleanest water in our country flows from our forested landscapes. The national forests produce about fourteen percent of the runoff, even though they account for only eight percent of the acreage of the lower forty-eight states." —Chuck Sudetic. From "The Forest for the Trees."

Commas, Non-Restrictive Clauses and Restrictive Clauses

Remember adjective clauses? They pattern with nouns, typically begin with *who, whom, that, which,* or *where,* and provide information in noun clusters. You will remember that adjective clauses can be either **restrictive** (providing essential information) or **non-restrictive** (providing interesting but not essential information). Do not separate restrictive clauses from the rest of the sentence with commas; restrictive clauses need to hug their nouns because they are very close to their nouns. Restrictive clauses add essential information; that is, they identify which thing or person is being discussed.

Non-restrictive clauses are, however, another matter. Do use a comma to separate a non-restrictive (or non-essential) adjective clause from the rest of the sentence. A non-restrictive adjective clause presents interesting and informative material —but not information essential to the reader's comprehension of the sentence. Here are some examples of sentences with restrictive and non-restrictive clauses for you to study. First, the sentences with non-restrictive clauses, in bold:

1. "We walked most part of a mile before we came to a house, **which proved to be a sort of a tavern.**" —Elizabeth Ashbridge. From "Account of the Fore-Part of the Life of Elizabeth Ashbridge."
2. "I sit in a psychiatrist's office, **where courtesy reigns**, and begin my story once again." —Daphne Merkin. From *Enchantment*.
3. "He was one of your wary men, **who never laugh but upon good grounds—when they have reason and the law on their side.**"—Washington Irving. From "The Legend of Sleepy Hollow."
4. "Bassett, the young gardener, **who had been wounded in the left foot in the war and had got his present job through Oscar Cresswell, whose batman he had been,** was a perfect blade of the 'turf.'"—D.H. Lawrence. "The Rocking-Horse Winner."
5. "The loud laughs of the musketmen were silenced by the authoritative voice of Richard, **who called to them for attention and obedience to his signals.**" —James Fenimore Cooper. From *The Pioneers*.
6. "Even New York Republicans now admit that it chilled lawmakers from other states, **who smelled pork.**" —Frank Bruni. "Show Us the Money."

And now the restrictive adjective clauses, which restrict or limit the meaning of the nouns they modify:

1. "Soon after our arrival here, our companions **who passed through Cuscowilla** joined us." —William Bartram. From *The Travels of William Bartram*.
2. "The result was a share price collapse **that hastened the demise of the company.**" —Cory Johnson. From "Tools of Self-Destruction."
3. "Rickie Lee Jones is a singer and songwriter **who has performed her blend of smoky, finger-popping music for more than two decades.**" —Anonymous. From *The New Yorker*.

4. "A thirteen-year-old defensive tackle **whose mother was missing and whose father is dead** was found to be raising himself, his guardian grandpa having grown senile." —Katherine Boo. From "After Welfare."

5. "Last August, Dino sent a letter to the town board with a proposal **that, predictably, wasn't well received.**" —Mark Singer. From "Dirty Laundry."

6. "The first people **who interviewed me in white coats from behind a computer** were only interested in my health-care benefits and proposed method of payment." —Audre Lorde. From "A Burst of Light: Living with Cancer."

Commas with Verbals and Absolutes

Use a comma to separate nominative absolutes and long verbal phrases that introduce the sentence (you'll remember that these are called **free modifiers**) from the rest of the sentence. In these sentences the verbal phrases and absolutes are underscored.

1. "There's a softness in the air, **the stench of the river temporarily overwhelmed by the smell of potted chicken wafting from the windows over the shops.**" —Steve Stern. From "The Tale of a Kite."

In Stern's sentence, a nominative absolute is set apart from the base sentence. Notice how the absolute sketches the details of *softness in the air.*

2. "My parents gaze absentmindedly at the ocean, **scarcely interested in its harshness.**" —Delmore Schwarz. From "In Dreams Begin Responsibilities."

This modifier, a past participial phrase, modifies and gives us more detail about *parents.*

3. "And he laid hands upon Sholem Waldman, **pulling him by his vest and flailing him about the side of the head.**" —Wallace Markfield. From "The Decline of Sholem Waldman."

Two present participial phrases explain what happens when *he* lays hands upon Waldman.

4. "But the child, **wholly exhausted**, cried with weariness." — Harriet Beecher Stowe. From *Uncle Tom's Cabin; or Life among the Lowly.*

This interrupting past participial phrase explains why the child cries wearily.

5. "Auda came swinging up on foot, **his eyes glazed over with the rapture of battle**." —T.E. Lawrence. From *Seven Pillars of Wisdom.* This is a nominative absolute that lends more detail to the image of Auda's coming up swinging.

Commas Marking Interrupters

Commas provide one way to separate interrupting phrases from main clauses in which they take up residence. Interrupters may provide transitions (*incidentally, for instance, after that, for example*), or they may present information that the reader needs. You can also use parentheses and dashes to set off interrupters. Of these three ways to punctuate the interruption of a sentence, paired commas (one on either side of the interrupting element, whether it be word, phrase, or clause) is the mildest and least obtrusive. So if you want to create the rhetorical effect of merely pausing the sentence or slowing it down somewhat or if you want to move the sentence along relatively swiftly and not lend the interrupting element considerable weight, use the commas. The pair of dashes will draw the reader up short, gasping (see the section on em dashes). The pair of parentheses sometimes effectively engages the reader as a co-conspirator in the reading. Here are examples of commas setting off interrupters; notice the kind of information presented by the interrupting phrase.

1. "There was no possibility, she decided, of ever working for such a place." —Robin Hemley. From "The 19th Jew."

The interrupting clause *she decided* is set off by commas to provide a momentary slowing around it.

2. "It was a way to make the hours pass, that's for sure, thought Hershleder." —Helen Schulman. From *The Revisionist.*

This sentence interrupter, *that's for sure,* is a clause. Besides the interrupter, which reiterates the validity of Hershleder's perception, this sentence has an inverted structure. Its normal order without the interrupter would be *Hershleder thought it was a way to make the hours pass.* Schulman inverted the sentence to emphasize the thought itself and then added the interrupter to underscore the importance of the idea of making the hours pass.

3. "Hester Prynne, therefore, did not flee." —Nathaniel Hawthorne. From *The Scarlet Letter.*

Here the interrupter is a conjunctive adverb. By cleaving the sentence precisely between subject and verb, the conjunctive adverb gives the sentence more weight and emphasizes the idea that Hester did not flee.

4. "The night's most electric moments, many attendees agreed, came in performances by Solomon Burke and Aerosmith." —Jenny Eliscu and Austin Scaggs. From "Rock's Biggest Night."

The interrupter, *many attendees agreed,* is a clause that provides confirmation of the opinion that is uttered in this same sentence.

5. "I was, strangely enough, indifferent to this news." —Nguy Ngu. From "An Old Story."

Strangely enough is an adverbial interrupter explaining the writer's reflection on the indifference. Interestingly, we learn about the fact that the writer finds the emotion strange in the split second before we learn what the emotion is.

Commas Setting Off Appositives and Nouns of Address

Use a comma to set off non-restrictive appositives from their appositional nouns; this is especially important if the appositive phrase is a long one. If the appositive is one noun falling immediately after its partner noun, it is restrictive and does not need to be set off with a comma.

Also, use a comma to set off nouns of address—that is, when you call someone by name or address someone specifically by name (often at the beginning of a sentence).

1. "They describe a surrealistic landscape, a city without lights, a walk without people." —E.M. Broner. From *Ghost Stories.*

City with its cluster and *Walk* with its cluster comprise two appositives in apposition with *landscape*.

2. "Ida, the retired homemaker, is wearing her reading glasses and flipping through Genesis." —Allegra Goodman. From "Sarah."

In this sentence, *the retired homemaker* explains which *Ida* is referred to.

3. "Do you, my friend, perceive the path I have found out?" —J. Hector St. John De Crevecoeur. From *Letters from An American Farmer.*

Friend is in apposition with *you* in this sentence. In addition, there is an element of address in this appositive. The writer is posing a direct question to the *you*, his reader.

4. "I found myself liking these people, Luu, Khanh, Quang, Ngo Minh." —Lynda Van Devanter. From "Going Back."

Luu, Khanh, Quang, and *Ngo Minh* are all in apposition with *people.* The appositive enumerates and explains *these people.*

5. "Well, I think I'll turn in now, Rainsford." —Richard Connell. From "The Most Dangerous Game."

In this sentence, *Rainsford* is a noun of address. The other character, General Zaroff, is addressing Rainsford or talking to him. The noun of address, *Rainsford,* could just as well have occurred at the beginning of the sentence: *Rainsford, I think I'll turn in now.*

Commas Separating Items in a List

Use commas to separate a series of anything: a series of compound verbs (as in sentences 1 and 2, below), a series of nouns, or anything in a simple list (that is, a list of single items without other words clustered about).

1. "Three hundred faces stared, blinked, squinted, and otherwise engaged the camera while recounting the most awful moments of the century." —Melvin Jules Bukiet. From "The Library of Moloch."
2. "All within my breast was tumult, wildness, and delirium!" —Olaudah Equiano. From *The Interesting Narrative of the Life of Olaudah Equiano.*
3. "Among steam's vocal opponents were the operators of canals, private toll roads and bridges, stagecoach lines, and the

network of merchants and taverns that serviced them." —Wil McCarthy. From "Runaway Train."

4. "I only know she's clever, she deserves an education, and she's going to get one." —Vivian Gornick. From *Fierce Attachments.*

5. "Uncles, cousins, nephews, brother would have looked, too, had they been home between journeys." —Maxine Hong Kingston. From "No Name Woman."

Many magazines follow the style of eliminating the comma before the last item in the series so that Equiano's sentence (c, above) would in this style read like this:

All within my breast was tumult, wildness and delirium!

This is an acceptable style, but be careful that the items are indeed separate when you omit that last comma. Compare these two sentences:

At the grocery store, we bought these items: Doritos, apples, macaroni and cheese.

and

At the grocery store, we bought these items: Doritos, apples, macaroni, and cheese.

The two sentences have slightly different meanings. The first suggests that macaroni and cheese was purchased as a package, the ingredients to be prepared together in an entree. The second suggests that macaroni was purchased and cheese was also purchased—as separate ingredients, not necessarily to be prepared together in a macaroni-and-cheese dish. The comma makes all the difference. Sometimes it is helpful to have the comma simply to prevent misreading.

You will always be correct if you use the comma after each item in the series.

Commas between Coordinate Adjectives

Separate **coordinate adjectives** not joined by *and* with a comma. When more than two adjectives modify a noun separately and their order can be rearranged, they are coordinate adjectives. But if some of the adjectives modify or pattern with some of the other adjectives, then they are not coordinate; they are cumulative. One way to determine whether adjectives are coordinate adjectives is to ask yourself whether the word *and* can be inserted between the adjectives. If it can, you need a comma. Look at these sentences to see the difference:

1. "Spicy, full-bodied filler tobacco is wrapped in a darker reddish-brown Connecticut shade leaf." —From Anonymous. *Georgetown by Post.*

Two noun clusters here have adjectives piled up before them in a cluster: *spicy, full-bodied filler tobacco* is one, and *darker reddish-brown Connecticut shade leaf* is the other. Let's look at the last cluster first. The adjectives in this cluster are cumulative; they lean on one another. We cannot put *and* between each adjective and have the sentence make sense. We don't say a *darker and reddish-brown and Connecticut shade leaf*. Also *darker* patterns with *reddish brown*. The adjectives are cumulative. In the first cluster, *spicy* and *full-bodied* are coordinate: we can say *spicy and full-bodied filler tobacco*. Thus there is a comma between spicy and full-bodied (where an *and* might go). Here are some examples where adjectives are coordinate and commas are used (you can insert an *and* for commas between adjectives):

2. "The New York streets sprawled out, wet, dirty, impenetrably dark." —Isaac Bashevis Singer. "A Wedding in Brownsville."
3. "It had been a scorching, dirty afternoon at a Colorado fairgrounds, the showers dead and dry." —Annie Proulx. From "The Mud Below."

4. "The lieutenant, who was briskly businesslike, introduced me to the director, a young, tall, vigorous engineer who was more businesslike and who evidently had already been told about me." —Primo Levi. *The Periodic Table.*
5. "A wee drop of pure, cool (but not cold) water brings out the subtleties in a dram of fine whiskey." —Glen Waggoner. From "Gaelic Sauce."
6. "I passed all the familiar faces and listened to their harsh, dust-choked greetings." —Amy Tan. From *The Bonesetter's Daughter.*

Commas for Clarification or Contrast

Sometimes you need a comma to separate words just so the reader can process them correctly and understand them. This clarification is especially important when you introduce a contrast. Here are a few examples:

1. "I am only a victim, not a perpetrator." —Nguyen Mong Giac. From "The Slope of Life."
2. "Sloth, by bringing on diseases, absolutely shortens life." — Benjamin Franklin. From "The Way to Wealth."
3. "Soon after, the mutilated deer started to appear: reminders to Wheeler, evidence of crime." —Wayne Karlin. From *Lost Armies.*
4. "Narrowing her eyes, she spun around, but saw nothing." — Louise Erdrich. From *The Last Report on the Miracles at Little No Horse.*
5. "It was as if our daughters were the adults, with friends all their own, and we were the children, too young to be included." — Tova Mirvis. From *The Ladies Auxiliary.*

Commas and Quotations

You often find commas and quotation marks keeping company because they are both associated with quoted material or with transcriptions of what happens. Please note that commas go inside quotation marks when a **metalanguage** tag (*he said,* for instance) follows the quoted material. When, however, the tag introduces the quotation or begins the sentence, the comma remains with the tag and not with the quotation but before it, outside it. Read all the following examples and in your study group explain why the comma goes where it goes.

1. "'Community is the most valuable thing that you have in African-American culture,' he explains." —John Lahr. From "Been Here and Gone."
2. "I awoke to my father shaking his head and saying, 'That kid's got a glass jaw.'" —Naton Leslie. From "Don't Get Comfortable."
3. "'Beyond just the scenics, these amazing locations in the mountains of New Zealand,' says Viesturs, who was one of 50 professional climbers on the set, 'the actors themselves trained for a month with mountaineers.'" —Jason Adams. From "Hollywood Goes Himalayan."
4. "'Leave it be,' broke in the marshal." —Max Brand. From *Happy Jack.*
5. "'Oh, my dear child,' whispered Gitl, pulling her close, 'thank God that your parents are not alive to see you now.'" —Jane Yolen. From *The Devil's Arithmetic.*

More on When Not to Use a Comma

Sometimes writers are tempted to put commas into a sentence for leavening or perhaps for interest; the sentence looks empty, they think, so they sprinkle in a comma or two. Too often, these commas end up near the word *and.* Perhaps some teacher has instructed these writers to pair the comma and *and* in a long sentence, not realizing that what matters is the number and kind of patterns, not the repetitions of *and.* So here is something to remember about using commas: **Don't use a comma between separate parts of a compound subject, compound verb, compound adjectives, compound adverbs, or compound objects.**

1. "I went to meetings in an awful frame of mind and endeavoured to be inwardly acquainted with the language of the True Shepherd." —John Woolman. From *The Journal of John Woolman.*

There is no comma between the two verb chunks *went to meetings* and *endeavoured to be inwardly acquainted with the language of the True Shepherd.*

2. "She tosses her blonde hair back and smiles down at everyone." —Yusef Komunyakaa. From "The Hanoi Market."

Observe: no comma between *tosses* and *smiles down.*

3. "Paule Marshall was both surprised and pleased; she made her son pick up the phone and listen."—Hilton Als. From "Notes on My Mother."
4. "His wife and two children are already asleep."—Max Apple. From "The Eighth Day."
5. "Shy and formal and breathless, my parents are always meeting for the first time."—Le Thi Diem Thuy. From *The Gangster We Are All Looking For.*

A Concluding Comment about Commas

Commas are becoming scarcer. The trend in printed material is to use fewer, not more, commas. So you will see that many editors abjure even the comma after the introductory phrase or clause. Many editors retain the comma chiefly as a guide to reading. Don't be surprised, then, if you find exceptions to the guidelines in this chapter.

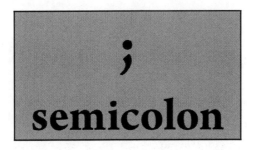

;

semicolon

The semicolon, one of the most misunderstood marks of punctuation, has two primary purposes: separating independent clauses in compound sentences or separating items in a long and grammatically complex list. In both instances, it is a weighty mark that identifies boundaries between major grammatical structures and often has punctuation within *its* boundaries.

Separating Independent Clauses with Semicolons

When you join two (or sometimes more) independent clauses to create a compound sentence and you aren't using any coordinators (conjunctions like *and, or, for, but, nor*), you may use a semicolon. In this case, make sure that you have a complete pattern on both sides of the semicolon, which acts like a fulcrum for the sentence, balancing grammatically equal halves. Here are some examples:

1. "And meanwhile the dust piled up in corners; the refrigerator wheezed and creaked for want of defrosting." —Anne Tyler. From "With All Flags Flying."

Tyler's sentence has two patterns: *dust piled up* (S-V) and *refrigerator wheezed and creaked* (another S-V). No coordinator separates the patterns, so the semicolon is necessary to keep these strong, but related, grammatical elements separate. Did you see the phrasal verb (*piled up*)? And the gerund as object of the preposition (*defrosting*)?

2. "I can work outside all day, breaking ice to get water for washing; I can eat pork liver cooked over the open fire minutes after it comes steaming from the hog." —Alice Walker. From "Everyday Use."

The first pattern is S-V (*I can work*), and the second one is S-V-O (*I can eat liver*). The semicolon separates them. Note how closely related they are; both independent clauses testify to the speaker's endurance and toughness. Did you observe the anaphora in the repeated *I can* phrase? And the participial phrase that contains within it an infinitive phrase whose object is a gerund: *breaking ice to get water for washing*? The second pattern has an adverbial clause, *after it comes steaming from the hog*. This is a very rich sentence.

3. "It smelled of harsh antiseptic; it smelled too clean and hard and metallic." —Ray Bradbury. From "The Pedestrian."

This sentence also has two complete patterns, thus two independent clauses. *It smelled* is an S-V pattern, where *smell* functions as an intransitive verb (there is no complement or completer, nor is one needed). *It smelled clean and hard and metallic* is an S-LV-PA sentence where *clean, hard*, and *metallic* are adjectives describing *it* and *its* smell. The semicolon separates the two patterns and makes the sentence easier to read. Did you notice the anaphora again, the repetition of *smell*? And did you also observe how all the adjectives are themselves filled with hard consonants (*k, d, t* sounds) and dry, hard vowels, particularly the *e* sounds? In this instance, sound definitely echoes sense.

4. "By most standards of literary worth, DeLillo's jewel-like distillation of a novel is very fine; Rayner's overheated melodrama

is rather bad." —Mark Levine. From rev. of *The Body Artist* and *The Cloud Sketcher.*

After the introductory *by* phrase, these independent clauses are parallel and antithetical. The first clause

DeLillo's jewel-like distillation of a novel is very fine

closely matches the grammatical form of

Rayner's overheated melodrama is rather bad.

The ideas, however, are antithetical; Levine likes DeLillo's book but not Rayner's.

5. "We wake and find ourselves on a stair; there are stairs below us, which we seem to have ascended; there are stairs above us, many a one, which go upward and out of sight." —Ralph Waldo Emerson. From "Experience."

This sentence has three independent clauses, separated by semicolons. Notice that each successive clause is longer and more grammatically complicated than the one before it. Did you notice the repetition of *stairs*? What is the effect of the repetition?

Separating Items in a Complex List

Readers can easily get tripped up in long and complicated sentences. That's why we have punctuation: to help them find ways in and to help them interpret the text. In sentences with grammatically complex lists, especially lists where there is internal punctuation, semicolons can help you keep items separate. Notice how the semicolon works in the sentences below:

1. "During those years I was picking coffee on the wet highlands of Venezuela on hills so steep your shoulders almost touched the hillside; staying up all night reciting Pablo Neruda in Syria; going to Catholic christenings, Jewish weddings, and Moslem funerals; looking into the faces of The Disappeared on the Plaza de Mayo in Argentina and seeing the tiny portraits of disappeared children; standing on the steps of a mosque in Beirut and staring at the hands of the old women holding tiny photographs of their sons disappeared in the war; feeling the rasp of stone from a hundred monuments commemorating valor and sacrifice in the service of one's country; standing over an acre of freshly turned earth mixed with common garbage where civilian bodies are buried."—Harry Mattison. From "What Makes Us Think We Are Only Here."

This rich catalog is a complex list of images, each of which is kept separate by virtue of the semicolon barrier.

2. "Three tribes dominate: the Jola, from the country's southwest; the Fula, from the east; and the Serer, from the north, whose fierce and sinewy athleticism makes them the most popular and storied of competitors."—Anonymous. From "Anybody Want Some of This?" *Men's Journal.*

Besides the use of the semicolons to separate the listing of three Gambian tribes, notice also the parallelism of the items listed and the how the sentence is cumulative, that is, how it builds with the longest cluster describing the most famous tribe of wrestlers at the end or at a position of great emphasis.

3. "It takes two hours to get them undressed; two more hours for bathtub, bath tantrums, and bath mop-up; an hour to get them into their Dr. Denton's; and three hours of reading The House

at Pooh Corner to put them to sleep." —P.J. O'Rourke. From "Oh, Baby."

O'Rourke is writing about the time required to get his two toddler daughters to bed. Of course, he's exaggerating quite a bit, but notice how he repeats the key words *bath* and *hours* to reinforce how long he and his wife spend on their daughters' baths. And note how the semicolons keep the different aspects of bath time separate so that you, the reader, can keep them straight.

4. "Before establishing the frame design, consider the information you must include: the title of the presentation, of course; perhaps a subtitle; the speaker's name, title, and affiliation; the company name and corporate logo; the name of the organization or meeting and the date; and funding agencies or other attributions." —Margaret Rabb. From *The Presentation Design Book.*

The items in this straightforward list describe the basic elements of the frame design. Each element is composed of more than one aspect or component, thus requiring internal punctuation of commas. The semicolons are necessary for keeping the items straight in the reader's mind.

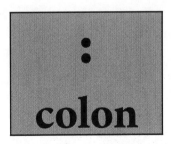

The colon is much like the semicolon, but with even more power. It is more rare and requires more care. The colon is most commonly found in two places. You can find it between two independent clauses that are very closely linked by a cause-effect or call-and-response relationship.

You can also find it after an independent clause announcing a word, phrase, or list to come later in the sentence. Here are some examples.

Colon between Independent Clauses

When you see a colon between two independent clauses, most likely the clauses are extremely closely related. Commonly the first clause sets up the first one or introduces some necessary background or condition for understanding or appreciating the second clause. Sometimes the first clause sets the scene for the second. Often the second clause restates or elucidates the first clause. Here are some examples:

1. "First lay aside your black veil: then tell me why you put it on." —Nathaniel Hawthorne. From "The Minister's Black Veil." *Twice-Told Tales.*

The first clause is the condition for the second: the minister must take off the veil and then explain why he put it on.

2. "I have spoken of the learning of Ligeia: it was immense—such as I have never known in woman." —Edgar Allan Poe. From "Ligeia."

In this sentence, the first clause leads us to the revelation in the second clause. The writer uses the whole first independent clause to remind us of the subject and then the whole second independent clause to comment on the subject. This way the idea is weightier than if he had written *The learning of Ligeia was immense.*

3. "In every stage of these oppressions we have petitioned for redress in the most humble terms: our repeated petitions have been answered only by repeated injuries." —Thomas Jefferson. From *The Declaration of Independence.*

Here the first clause introduces the topic of petitions, which the second clause reiterates with the new information that the petition has been met only with further insults.

4. "That most of us have found adulthood just as morally ambiguous as we expected it to be falls perhaps into the category of prophecies self-fulfilled: I am simply not sure."—Joan Didion. From "On the Morning After the Sixties."

In this sentence, the long and complex first part of the sentence prepares us for the punch line after the colon and emphasizes the uncertainty with which the sentence concludes.

5. "All of a sudden there was silence: the rain had stopped." — Heinrich Boll. From "In the Darkness."

The first clause sets the scene for the revelation of the clause beyond the colon. First the reader "hears" silence; then he realizes that the rain has stopped.

Colon That Introduces

You will also find the colon used as a herald; that is, to announce that something important or significant is approaching at the end of the sentence. The colon brings the reader nearly to a halt; it is not as full a stop as a period, but it is close. Thus you can use it to take your reader right to the brink of something expected, then draw him or her up short and pop the important idea, word, phrase, or list in right after. You can also use the colon to introduce a long or extended quotation or a quotation that you want to make very emphatic. It is important to remember that you must have an independent clause or a full and complete sentence pattern before (or left of) the colon. This is a point that many writers and sign makers miss. Look at these sentences for examples of correct colon use:

1. "Oh yes, I thought, she was like Paul: cold, beautiful, critical." —Lev Raphael. From "History (With Dreams)."

Notice how the colon narrows the reader's attention to those three important words at the conclusion of the sentence.

2. "A cloudy day: do you know what that is in a town of iron-works?" —Rebecca Harding Davis. From "Life in the Iron Mills."

In this sentence the material before the colon frames the material after the colon. The reader is meant to think of a town of iron-works in the context of a cloudy day.

3. "My brother says: 'Thirty years ago, honest to God, I would've been with the guys with the bats. In August, I swear to God, I would have been with the protestors.'" —Barbara Grizzuti Harrison. From *Harper's*.

The colon introduces the quotation from the brother. In this context, a colon is more emphatic than a comma.

4. "Far away, deep in the tunnel of the past, Anton heard the six shots ring: first one, then two, then two more, and finally one last shot." —Harry Mulisch. From *The Assault*.

The introductory material prepares the reader for the emphatic hearing of individual shots in the last half of the sentence. Notice how the many transitions in the second half of the sentence slow the pace and make each cluster of shots distinct: first there is one; then there are two; then there are two more; and finally there is one more. *First, then, then,* and *finally* effectively underscore the number of shots.

5. "When Rodrigo Hertas opened his eyes the morning of October 24, he understood in a flash that he had exhausted all

of his choices save one: suicide." —Luis Lopez-Nieves. From "The Extremely Funny Gun Salesman."

This dramatic use of the colon assembles the whole weight of the sentence to point to one word, one idea, one option for Rodrigo Hertas. The last word is doubly emphatic because of this accumulation.

And don't forget that a colon follows the salutation in a business letter:

Dear Mr. Barney:

Dear Sony Customer:

Honorable Senator Schumer:

Passages to Punctuate: Internal Marks

Copy the passages below, either by hand or by keying them in to your computer, then add internal punctuation. Sentences boundaries are already marked with terminal punctuation, but you will need to add commas, semicolons, and colons inside the sentences where they are needed. You will find each selection as it was originally punctuated at the end of this section.

1. Frank Norris. From *McTeague: A San Francisco Story*.
On week days the street was very lively It woke to its work about seven o'clock at the time when the newsboys made their appearance together with the day laborers The laborers went

trudging past in a straggling file plumbers' apprentices their pockets stuffed with sections of lead pipe tweezers and pliers carpenters carrying nothing but their little pasteboard lunch baskets painted to imitate leather gangs of street workers their overalls soiled with yellow clay their picks and long-handled shovels over their shoulders plasterers spotted with lime from head to foot This little army of workers, tramping steadily in one direction, met and mingled with other toilers of a different description conductors and "swing men" of the cable company going on duty heavy-eyed night clerks from the drug stores on their way home to sleep roundsmen returning to the precinct police station to make their night report and Chinese market gardeners teetering past under their heavy baskets The cable cars began to fill up all along the street could be seen the shop-keepers taking down their shutters

2.   Alvin D. Hall. From *Getting Started with Stocks.*

An asset allocation fund is a variation on the balanced fund that invests in stocks bonds and cash equivalents. There are two types of asset allocation funds fixed and flexible. A fixed asset allocation fund maintains a fixed percentage of its assets in each of the three asset classes stocks bonds and cash equivalents. This type is therefore quite similar to a balanced fund except that the fixed percentages differ. A flexible asset allocation fund adjusts the mix of its assets in response to changing market conditions and investment opportunities. This flexibility is this fund's major advantage. The disadvantage however is that its success depends almost entirely upon the fund manager's skill.

Original Punctuation of Frank Norris Passage

On week days the street was very lively. It woke to its work about seven o'clock, at the time when the newsboys made their appearance together with the day laborers. The laborers went trudging past in a straggling file--plumbers' apprentices, their pockets stuffed with sections of lead pipe, tweezers, and pliers; carpenters, carrying nothing but their little pasteboard lunch baskets painted to imitate leather; gangs of street workers, their overalls soiled with yellow clay, their picks and long-handled shovels over their shoulders; plasterers, spotted with lime from head to foot. This little army of workers, tramping steadily in one direction, met and mingled with other toilers of a different description--conductors and "swing men" of the cable company going on duty; heavy-eyed night clerks from the drug stores on their way home to sleep; roundsmen returning to the precinct police station to make their night report, and Chinese market gardeners teetering past under their heavy baskets. The cable cars began to fill up; all along the street could be seen the shopkeepers taking down their shutters.

Original Punctuation of the Alvin D. Hall Passage

An asset allocation fund is a variation on the balanced fund that invests in stocks, bonds, and cash equivalents. There are two types of asset allocation funds: fixed and flexible. A fixed asset allocation fund maintains a fixed percentage of its assets in each of the three asset classes: stocks bonds and cash equivalents. This type is, therefore, quite similar to a balanced fund except that the fixed percentages differ. A flexible asset allocation fund adjusts the mix of its assets in response to changing market conditions and investment opportunities. This flexibility is this fund's major advantage. The disadvantage, however, is that its success depends almost entirely upon the fund manager's skill.

em dash

The em dash—mostly known as just a dash—is emphatic and attention grabbing. It draws the reader's eye straight to the page and dramatically separates two chunks of text (clause, phrase, word) from one another. It can separate interrupting elements from the main part of the sentence; it can separate examples from generalizations; it can separate a salutation or greeting from the body of a note (but it's breezy, not formal, so be careful). One more thing: when you key in the dash, allow no space between it and the words it butts against.

Take a look at the em dashes in these sentences:

1. "It was not desperation—not exactly that—that she heard in this invocation." —Michelle Herman. From "Auslander."

Notice how the dash interrupts the flow of the sentence to call the reader's attention to the idea that *desperation* is being qualified or clarified.

2. "Always the diction is glorious—ready, with only a bit of memorizing, for Shakespeare." —Norma Rosen. From "What Must I Say to You?"

This dash separates the generalization (that the diction is glorious) from a specific application of it (it is ready for Shakespeare).

3. "He was—it was reduced to this—excited." —Stanley Elkin. From "Among the Witnesses."

In this sentence two dashes separate the interrupter dramatically from the rest of what is a short sentence, emphasizing the idea of his being excited.

4. "After the First World War they had stayed in Italy—in Milan as much as necessary, in a house overlooking Lake Varese as much as possible." —Ann Cornelisen. From *Where It All Began: Italy 1954.*

Here the dash separates assertion (that they had stayed in Italy) and additional detail (in Milan, etc.) to solidify the assertion as if to emphasize where they stayed.

5. "And hospitality and generosity—character—were measured by the amount of meat you served your guests."—Barbara Grizzuti Harrison. From "Women and Blacks and Bensonhurst."

The dashes in this sentence separate an interrupter that is a definition. Here hospitality and generosity are equated with and defined as character.

6. "The world is made up of two classes—the hunters and the hunted." —Richard Connell. From "The Most Dangerous Game."

In this sentence, Connell uses the dash to separate an idea from the elucidation or development or explanation of that idea. *Hunters and the hunted* explain what the *two classes* are.

hyphen

The hyphen (also the en dash) is less weighty than a dash and resides within and between words. Whereas the em dash separates items or entities, the hyphen or en dash connects ideas. Typically, the hyphen connects words too closely related to remain separate words yet not intimate enough to become one word: *commander-in-chief*, for instance. After a period of being hyphenated, many hyphenated compounds become one word, as with apple *turn over*, which became apple *turn-over*, which eventually became apple *turnover*. Here are other examples of the use of the hyphen.

1. "The Black newcomer had been recruited on the desiccated farmlands of Georgia and Mississippi by war-plant labor scouts. The chance to live in two- or three-story buildings (which became instant slums), and to earn two- and even three-figured weekly checks, was blinding." —Maya Angelou. From *I Know Why the Caged Bird Sings*.

Angelou's sentence has many hyphens. Notice in particular the compound determiner-noun hyphenations of *two- and three-story* and *two- and three-figured*: observe that when the hyphenated material is compounded with the same word in the last part of the hyphenation, that last word is not repeated with each iteration. It would be more tiresome for the reader to read *two-story or three-story buildings* than *two- or three-story buildings*.

2. "In a late-summer drizzle, I teeter atop a starting block, my arms swollen as sausages from lactic acid, my head pounding from tension, lack of food, and good old self-loathing." —Jim Thornton. From "Come Get Some, Mark Spitz."

Here *late* is connected to *summer* and qualifies it, and *self* is appended to *loathing*, the object to a verb form, to create a complex noun that fits neatly into the prepositional phrase as an object. The hyphenated structure allows the writer to include in a succinct way the idea of self-loathing as one of the causes of the pounding head. A verbal phrase would have made his sentence more cumbersome.

3. "He has ready such a fresh top-of-the-morning salutation as conjures up the spirits of those days." —Henry David Thoreau. From "Thomas Carlyle and His Works."

Thoreau uses the hyphenated words to create a complicated noun adjunct that does, however, pattern smoothly before the noun *salutation*.

4. "The man was game enough, when his blood was up: but he was no favorite in the mill; he had the taint of school-learning on him—not to a dangerous extent, only a quarter or so in the free-school in fact, but enough to ruin him as a good hand in a fight." —Rebecca Harding Davis. From "Life in the Iron Mills."

Here *school* is attached to *learning* to insinuate that there are other kinds of learning than learning in school, and *free* is attached to *school* to explain the school as a public one in a time when not many schools were public. There are other interesting things about this sentence. Notice the colon which separates two major ideas: that, first, the man was game when he was emotionally ready (when his blood was up); and second, that the man was not a favorite in the mill. The material in the independent clause after the semicolon explains why the man was not popular in the mill: he had had some education. The information after the dash qualifies the extent of his education: he wasn't dangerously educated, but he was spoiled for fighting.

5. "This drew rueful laughter from the crowd, which was made up of family-law types and members of the Trollope society." —Rebecca Mead. From "Lawyers Who Love Trollope."

Family and *law* are hyphenated to describe the kind of law being referred to.

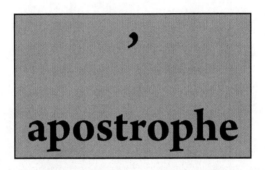

An apostrophe is the sign of something missing; where you see an apostrophe, some part of a word has been omitted. Apostrophes appear in contractions—to indicate that part of a word has been left out—*I'm studying* or *we're too tired*. The apostrophe also indicates possessive nouns and pronouns—*the boy's coat, the water's edge*. And you'll often find it when writers are writing dialect or approximating speech; they typically spell the word phonetically to indicate how it sounds and use apostrophes to indicate omitted letters. The apostrophe is also used in pairs to indicate quoted material within a quotation. Here are some examples of apostrophes.

1. "She had taken the orientation lecture seriously since the one on God. It has been given by a tiny, handsome Scot, a Presbyterian padre who had begun by saying, 'I'm no' here to talk about games, I'm here to talk about God.'" —Mary Lee

Settle. From *All the Brave Promises: Memoirs of Aircraft Woman 2nd Class 2146391*.

The first apostrophe is part of the contraction of *I* and *am: I'm*. The second apostrophe—*no'*—indicates the omitted letter *t* in *not*. This is a representation of a speech dialect; the author is approximating sounds of conversation. And finally, the quotation within the quotation (what the Presbyterian padre below actually says) is framed by single quotation marks.

2. "'Right now your business is not to give any heed to what those folks from Old Sarum tell you—you ain't called upon to contradict 'em, just don't pay 'em any attention—and if you want to know somethin', you just run to old Cal.'" —Harper Lee. From *Go Set a Watchman*.

This excerpt illustrates the popularity of the apostrophe in speech. Two words, *'em* and *somethin'*, have apostrophes to indicate omitted letters (for *them* and *something*). The apostrophe in *don't* signifies an omitted letter *o* from the original *do not*. The style of this conversation is very colloquial and evokes a Deep South dialect.

3. "She said, 'In the retail reality world, it all boils down to one question: Did you sell it? We still don't know.'" —James Collins. From "One Year Later."

Don't has an apostrophe to signify the missing *o* in *do not*. This signals informal diction.

4. "The low, serious drugstore voices that accompanied the Park View's weekly decorum were swept away by revolving, laughing crowds—carnival crowds." —Cynthia Ozick. From "A Drugstore Eden."

The apostrophe in *Park View's* signals possession. This structure is a nod toward informality even as the sentence refers to the sweeping away of decorum.

5. "Here's what they don't tell you about Prozac." —Lauren Slater. From "Black Swans."

The apostrophe in *Here's* indicates an omitted *i* in *Here is,* and *don't* of course is a contraction of *do not.* This is also the mark of an informal utterance.

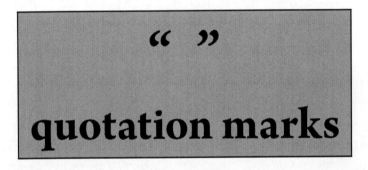

quotation marks

Quotation marks, which come in pairs, embrace a speaker's exact words. They can also be used for emphasis, in effect to underscore a particular word and draw the reader's eye to it. Quotation marks also identify titles of poems, short stories, songs, essays, articles, and brief musical numbers or programs.

1. From Herman Melville's "Benito Cereno," here is an example of a conversation between the ship's captain, Captain Delano, and a sailor, Don Benito. Notice how the quotation marks enclose each speaker's exact words and how the combination of either a new line or a new paragraph means a new set of quotation marks and indicates that another speaker has taken a turn at the conversation:

Glancing towards the hammock as he entered, Captain Delano said, "You sleep here, Don Benito?"

"Yes, Senor, since we got into mild weather."

"This seems a sort of dormitory, sitting-room, sail-loft, chapel, armory, and private close all together. Don Benito," added Captain Delano, looking round.

"Yes, Senor; events have not been favorable to much order in my arrangements."

2. And here's another conversation, from Vivian Gornick's *Fierce Attachments*. Note that the commas remain within the quotation marks and that other end punctuation marks (question marks, exclamation points) are, in this case, also within the quotation marks. These terminal marks are within the quotation marks because they pattern with the quoted material itself, not with the sentence as a whole or with its meta-language (its language about language)—as in *she says* or *I say*:

"Can you believe this?" she says. "A nice Jewish boy shaves his head and babbles in the street. A world full of crazies. Divorce everywhere, and if not divorce, this. What a generation you all are!"

"Don't start, Ma," I say. I don't want to hear that bullshit again.

"Bullshit here, bullshit there," she says, "it's still true. Whatever else we did, we didn't fall apart in the streets like you're all doing. We had order, quiet, dignity. Families stayed together, and people lived decent lives."

3. In the next example, the quotation marks suggest the way that the phrase *side effects* might be read: with an exaggerated irony. The quotation marks call specific attention to the words they enclose.

For seven years I lived with a hand tremor, diarrhea, the possibility of kidney damage and all the other "side effects" of lithium. —Kate Millett. From *The Loony-Bin Trip.*

4. How do the quotation marks tell you to read *slave name* in the sentence that follows?

Bingham met Ali thirty-five years ago in Los Angeles shortly after the fighter had turned professional and before he had discarded his "slave name" (Cassius Marcellus Clay) and joined the Black Muslims. —Gay Talese. From "Ali in Havana."

5. Finally, explain how Joy Williams in "The Case Against Babies" uses the quotation marks in this sentence:

While legions of other biological life forms go extinct (or, in the creepy phrase of ecologists, "wink out"), human life bustles self-importantly on.

( )

parentheses

Parentheses set words, phrases, ideas aside: they cradle them. They often suggest a conspiratorial message, whispered behind a cupped hand. They are an effective vehicle for conveying surprise, disdain, amusement, or confusion. Use them to include definitions, afterthoughts, extra information. Here are some examples:

1. "The girls could not get telephone calls (calls from our families went through Miss Preston, our principal), so it must have been

in one of those letters that he told me when and where to meet him." —Mary McCarthy. From *How I Grew.*

Notice that in this compound-complex sentence, the parenthetical material patterns within the first pattern. Therefore, the comma separating the patterns goes properly **after** the parens.

2. "I didn't go to school, nor had my sister (nine years older) done so except briefly, another thing which set our household apart from others." —Denise Levertov. From "Autobiographical Sketch."

In this sentence the parenthetical material explains how much older the sister was, thus presents information that the reader can use to make more sense of the sentence.

3. "About half the students were Southerners from Louisiana and Arkansas and Mississippi, as well as the farm country of east Texas (with a few city girls from Houston and Dallas mixed in), but the rest were Texans from the high plains, and they were noticeably different from the rest of us." —Shirley Abbott. From "Why Southern Women Leave Home."

The parenthetical material in this sentence provides additional, more specific information about the students.

4. "A compromise was reached by sending a kit of parts to the front-line units so that an extra cannon (20-mm MG151) could be bolted under each wing." —Len Deighton. From *Fighter: The True Story of the Battle of Britain.*

Definition and explanation are the purposes of this parenthetical material, which is more specific than the noun cluster in the text—*extra cannon.*

5. "I am at once repulsed and fascinated by the bullet, which remains lodged in his spine (having done all the damage it can do, the doctors say)." —Debra Dickerson. From "Who Shot Johnny?"

The parenthetical information in this sentence provides the reader a tidbit of information about the bullet. In this sentence it presents a gossipy effect because of the tag, *the doctors say.*

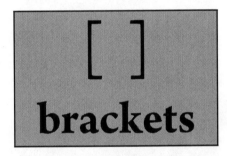

You will use brackets rarely. They enclose editorial remarks or comments inserted into quoted text; sometimes the editor comments on the text, and sometimes the reader inserts something that the author may have omitted. They are also used for stage directions. And if you need to use parentheses within parentheses, you should make the internal set brackets rather than use a double set of parens and confuse the reader with double parentheses. Here are some examples of sentences with bracketed information. Explain why you believe the editor put the information in brackets.

1. "Thus it pleased God to vanquish their enemies and give them deliverance; and by His special providence so to dispose that not any one of them were either hurt or hit, though their arrows came close by them and on every side [of] them; and sundry of their coats, which hung up in the barricado, were shot through and through." —William Bradford. From *Of Plymouth Plantation.*

The editor most likely added the *of* to facilitate reading; it had probably been inadvertently omitted in the original version.

2. "In surveying various responses to plagues in the Middle Ages, Barbara W. Tuchman writes, 'Medical thinking [. . .] stressed air as the communicator of disease, ignoring sanitation or visible carriers.'" —Joseph Gibaldi. From *MLA Style Manual and Guide to Scholarly Publishing*, 2nd ed.

Here the brackets enclose an indication of ellipsis and tell the reader that part of the sentence was omitted.

3. "Graphic artists, multimedia professionals, desktop publishers, and many others use paint software and image editing software to create and modify graphics such as those used in DTP documents and Web pages [Figure 3-29]." —Shelly/Cashman/Gunter. From *Teachers Discovering Computers*.

In this sentence, the bracketed material directs the reader to a figure accompanying the text.

4. "Sharing everything with everyone [was] very difficult because I am a very private person." —Prince William, Duke of Cambridge, describing living conditions on a community-service mission. From "Prince Charming!"

In this example, the writer changed the tense of the verb, most like originally *is*, in the original quotation so that it would fit with the rest of the article, which was written in past tense.

/ slash/virgule

The slash or virgule extends from one side to another and is both vertical as well as horizontal. Its character is equally indecisive. Use the slash to separate a series of words indicating choices for the reader, to point out where a line of poetry ends when you quote it, and to substitute for the word *per* as in miles / gallon. The slash also indicates ratios. And you will find it separating elements of Web addresses. Regardless of where it appears, its purpose is to break up text so that readers can understand it more clearly. Here are some examples of the slash in use:

1. "We have, however, had some real success with cognitive/behavioral treatments." —Lauren Slater. From "Black Swans."

In this sentence the slash separates *cognitive* and *behavioral*, which both modify *treatments*. Slater could have written *cognitive and behavioral treatments*, but the slash suggests a simultaneity that the *and* does not: that the treatments are at once, immediately, both cognitive and behavioral.

2. "But I, for one, can think of a million and one uses for the new hatchback Mini and its folding 50/50 rear seats, against only about 395,000 for the Z3." —Jamie Kitman. From "Major Mini."

Here the virgule separates 50 and 50, to indicate that the rear seat is split and that each half folds.

3. "The NewQ.com/RearViewMonitor"— Infiniti advertisement. *Automobile.*

The slash divides the name of the feature from its description and makes it possible for the reader to perceive almost instantly what TheNewQ.com actually is.

4. For a free action kit on how to end discrimination in the workplace, go to www.aclu.org/gayrights.

Here the slash divides one link—gayrights—from the main web page www.aclu.org (doubtlessly on the ACLU's server). You will also see slashes in the entire Web address, separating the *http:* section from the section denoting the server. The entire Web address for the gayrights site above would be http://www.aclu.org/gayrights.

5. To get information on events that happened on a specific day, go to the "This Day in History" Web site at http://www.historychannel.com/thisday/.

The slashes divide sections of the Internet address and make it easy to readers to identify segments, thus easier to key in or even to remember them.

6. In a large bowl, toss lettuce, arugula, mint, papaya and/or mango, and green onions with the balsamic vinegar/olive oil dressing.

The slash between *and* and *or* is common, suggesting that the writer finds either coordinator appropriate and the reader may choose. In other words, you may add papaya **and** mango. Or you may add either papaya or mango: it doesn't matter. The slash between balsamic vinegar and olive oil suggests the same sort of options. You may use either dressing in this recipe.

7.   "This conflict was sometimes overshadowed by the antago-
nisms of friends and family at home, a situation which under-
standably gave the soldier poets pause. 'Oh hell, he thought,'
writes Siegfried Sassoon in 'Remorse: 'There are things in war
one dare not tell / Poor father sitting safe at home who reads /
Of dying heroes and their deathless deeds.'" —Paul-William
Burch

Here the virgules mark the lines of poetry. Also notice that the name
of the poem is in quotation marks and that the colon introducing the
quoted lines goes outside the quotation marks.

Passages to Punctuate

Copy each of the following passages and add both internal and external
punctuation. Some capitalization may be provided to assist you, but
you will have to supply some capitals as well as all other punctuation.
You will find that there will be several interpretations of how these passages may be punctuated. After you finish, compare your punctuated
version with the original versions at the end of the chapter: Does your
version match the author's? Can you make logical arguments for why
you punctuated as you did?

1.   Donald McCabe. From "Cheating: Why Students Do It and
How We Can Help Them Stop." For Professor McCabe, now
Emeritus from Rutgers Business School, the issue of cheating—why it happens, how it happens, what effects it has on
students and society, and what we can do about it—was the

focus of his life's work. His work inspired an academic integrity award in his name, now awarded annually by the Institute for Ethical Leadership. Here is the passage:

Students find teachers' failings real or supposed useful in justifying cheating the relevance and fairness of assessments are issues students often raise the question here is not the difficulty of the tests or the course material everyone has heard students talk with pride about courses they have taken where despite the difficulty of the course they simply would not cheat however students speak angrily about teachers who give tests that cover material not discussed in class or highlighted in homework assignments and they may find it relatively easy to justify cheating in such cases whatever the truth in individual student complaints there is no question that cheating can be used to express disrespect for a teacher and defiance of the teacher s authority

2. Dr. Race Foster. From "Checklist for Visits to Your Veterinarian."

- Make sure to ask what the prognosis outcome is is it curable will it come back or can you prevent it e g pancreatitis from too much people food

- Is there a special diet your pet has to follow can you get it at any pet store make it at home like a rice ground beef mixture or is it only available at your veterinarians office

- Is this disease or injury common to your pets breed or size

3. Diane Ackerman. From *A Natural History of the Senses.*

The other senses may be enjoyed in all their beauty when one is alone, but taste is largely social humans rarely choose to dine in solitude and food has a powerful social component the Bantu feel that exchanging food makes a contract between two people who then have a clanship of porridge we usually eat with our families so its easy to see how breaking bread together would symbolically link an outsider to a family group throughout the world the stratagems of business take place over meals weddings end with a feast friends reunite at celebratory dinners children herald their birthdays with ice cream and cake religious ceremonies offer food in fear, homage, and sacrifice wayfarers are welcomed with a meal as Brillat-Savarin says every sociability can be found assembled around the same table love friendship business speculation power importunity patronage ambition intrigue if any event is meant to matter emotionally symbolically or mystically food will be close at hand to sanctify and bind it

4.   Karen Armstrong. From *Fields of Blood: Religion and the History of Violence.*

the afghan taliban combined their pashtun tribal chauvinism with Deobandi rigorism an unholy hybrid and maverick form of Islam that expressed itself in violent opposition to any rival ideology after the soviet withdrawal afghanistan had descended into chaos and when the taliban managed to take control they seemed to both the pakistanis and the americans to be an acceptable alternative to anarchy. Their leader mullah omar believed that human beings were naturally virtuous and if placed on the right path needed no government coercion social services or public health care there was therefore no centralized government, and the population was ruled by local taliban *komitehs*, whose punishments for the smallest infringement of Islamic law were so draconian that a degree of order was indeed restored fiercely opposed to modernity, which had, after all, come to them in the form of soviet guns and air strikes the taliban ruled by their traditional tribal norms which they identified

with the rule of God their focus was purely local and they had
no sympathy with bin ladens global vision.

~~~~~~

Original Punctuation of Donald McCabe's Passage

Students find teachers' failings—real or supposed—useful in justifying cheating. The relevance and fairness of assessments are issues students often raise. The question here is not the difficulty of the tests or the course material. Everyone has heard students talk with pride about courses they have taken where, despite the difficulty of the course, they simply would not cheat. However, students speak angrily about teachers who give tests that cover material not discussed in class or highlighted in homework assignments, and they may find it relatively easy to justify cheating in such cases. Whatever the truth in individual student complaints, there is no question that cheating can be used to express disrespect for a teacher and defiance of the teacher's authority.

Original Punctuation of Dr. Race Foster's Passage:

- Make sure to ask what the prognosis (outcome) is: Is your pet's ailment curable? Will it come back or can you prevent it (e. g. pancreatitis, from too much people food)?

- Is there a special diet your pet has to follow? Can you get it at any pet store? Make it at home like a rice ground beef mixture? Or is it only available at your veterinarian's office?

- Is this disease or injury common to your pet's breed or size?

Original Punctuation of Diane Ackerman's Passage:

The other senses may be enjoyed in all their beauty when one is alone, but taste is largely social. Humans rarely choose to dine in solitude, and food has a powerful social component. The Bantu feel that exchanging food makes a contract between two people who then have a "clanship of porridge." We usually eat with our families, so its easy to see how "breaking bread" together would symbolically link an outsider to a family group. Throughout the world, the stratagems of business take place over meals; weddings end with a feast; friends reunite at celebratory dinners; children herald their birthdays with ice cream and cake; religious ceremonies offer food in fear, homage, and sacrifice; wayfarers are welcomed with a meal. As Brillat-Savarin says, "every ... sociability ... can be found assembled around the same table: love, friendship, business, speculation, power, importunity, patronage, ambition, intrigue ... If any event is meant to matter emotionally, symbolically, or mystically, food will be close at hand to sanctify and bind it.

Original Punctuation of Karen Armstrong's Passage:

The Afghan Taliban combined their Pashtun tribal chauvinism with Deobandi rigorism, an unholy hybrid and maverick form of Islam that expressed itself in violent opposition to any rival ideology. After the Soviet withdrawal, Afghanistan had descended into chaos, and when the Taliban managed to take control, they seemed to both the Pakistanis and the Americans to be an acceptable alternative to anarchy. Their leader, Mullah Omar, believed that human beings were naturally virtuous and, if placed on the right path, needed no government coercion, social services, or public health care. There was therefore no centralized government, and the population was ruled by local Taliban *komitehs*, whose punishments for the smallest infringement of Islamic law were so draconian that a degree of order was indeed restored. Fiercely opposed to modernity, which had, after all, come to them in the form of Soviet guns and air strikes, the Taliban ruled by their traditional tribal norms, which they identified with the rule of God. Their focus was purely local, and they had no sympathy with Bin Laden's global vision.

Did your use of commas in particular match the way Armstrong uses them? Are you sure that you capitalized all the proper nouns? This passage is exemplary for its varied and appropriate use of commas.

Chapter 9. A Dozen Prose Passages:Reading for Style and Grammatical Understanding

This chapter concentrates on the relationship of grammar to style, specifically by analyzing passages to understand how writers use grammatical and figurative structures in creating specific stylistic effects. Here you will find a number of stylistically interesting passages to read, enjoy, analyze, discuss.

As you read and talk about these passages, perhaps with your writing group, be especially aware of your initial response to each passage, to its tone and its subject matter. Your first response to the passage will be important to your analysis of the writer's style: you'll want to ask yourself first, "What am I thinking and feeling about what I just read? and then "How did the writer create this effect or response in me?" and "What grammatical structures are at work here?"

Gerald Early on Muhammad Ali. From "Ali, the Wonder Boy."

This passage is from Gerald Early's essay about prizefighter Muhammad Ali; the essay was also one of Philip Lopate's choices of best essays of 1999 and collected in *The Art of the Essay.*

What unnerves us now about Ali and brings out the insipid-ness of victimology is that he has wound up like an old, bro-ken-down prizefighter. The guilt we feel is that we used him as a commodity and that he used us to create great dramas of his fights, dragon-slaying heroics, extraordinary crises of our social order. It mattered greatly whether he won or lost and we are guilty about having been conned into believing a prize-fight means much of anything in this world, guilty about what our being conned did to the confidence man. But Ali, far from being a victim, is perhaps one of the most remarkable examples of triumph over racism in our century. It is not surprising that so many white people hated him; it is surprising that before his career ended a good many had come to love him. (156)

You might begin thinking about this passage by doing a grammatical/rhetorical/stylistic analysis of the paragraph. Such an analysis involves counting paragraph elements (to find out how the paragraph is constructed) and then analyzing them (to determine what grammatical, rhetorical, and stylistic devices the writer used to create the effect). Here are questions to guide your rhetorical analysis:

1. How many sentences are in the passage?
2. How long is the longest sentence (in words)?
3. How short is the shortest sentence (in words)?
4. What is the type (simple, compound, complex, compound-complex) of each sentence?
5. Does a particular sentence pattern dominate this passage?
6. Are there any examples of transformations? Note them.
7. Who (or in some cases, what) is the agent in the passage? What person or force is driving this prose?
8. What grammatical patterns do you observe? Do you see balance? repetition? pairings?
9. Are there repeated words or repeated concepts? Note them.

10. Do you notice any unusual words? Are certain words strategically placed? Is there any unusual punctuation? Note this.
11. What's going on in places of emphasis in the passage—particularly at the end and at the beginning?

Now add up all your responses in about three sentences that describe this writer's style and, for this passage, the effect on the reader. Speculate about the writer's possible aims for the passage and point out specific devices and strategies that lend themselves to the accomplishment of these aims: what does Early make you think and feel about Ali and how does he do it?

Oliver Sacks—From "A Leg to Stand On".

In this passage, Oliver Sacks, former Professor of Clinical Neurology at Albert Einstein College of Medicine and author of many brilliantly readable books about life and medicine, describes a scene where he encounters a bull while hiking alone in the wildness of a Norwegian fjord. As you read, be particularly aware of how Sacks describes the bull, which he had been warned about but whose presence he had disbelieved. In the sentences just before this passage, he describes his feelings of physical competence and well-being as well as his energy and exuberance during the climb, characterizing himself as "strong as a bull." As he climbs, he seems to inhabit a mystical landscape, the mists and clouds around him creating a surreal atmosphere where he's not always sure what is real and what is not. (A note: the italicization and punctuation are of course Sacks's.)

The real Reality was not such a moment, not touched in the least by ambiguity or illusion. I had, indeed, just emerged from the mist, and was walking round a boulder as big as a house, the path curving round it so that I could not see ahead, and it was this inability to see ahead which permitted the Meeting. I practically trod on what lay before me—an enormous animal sitting in the path, and indeed totally occupying the path, whose presence had been hidden by the rounded bulk of the rock. It had a huge horned head, a stupendous white body and an enormous mild milk-white face. It sat unmoved by my appearance, exceedingly calm, except that it turned its vast white face up towards me. And in that moment it changed, before my eyes, becoming transformed from magnificent to utterly monstrous. The huge white face seemed to swell and swell, and the great bulbous eyes became radiant with malignance. The face grew huger and huger all the time, until I thought it would blot out the Universe. The bull became hideous—hideous beyond belief, hideous in strength, malevolence and cunning. It seemed now to be stamped with the infernal in every feature. It became, first a monster, and now the Devil. —Oliver Sacks. From *A Leg to Stand On*

What is Sacks's response to the bull? How does he present the bull? With what words and images does he characterize the bull? What words are repeated? Why are the italics important? And how does punctuation help to create the effect or shape this paragraph? Write a description of Sacks's style in this passage.

Rhonda White—From "Autobiography"

Rhonda White is a native Alabamian with a gift for storytelling. In this excerpt from her autobiography, she recalls her grandfather, Papa Pete:

Now my Papa Pete (grandfather) was what we call a character. He drank his coffee from the saucer; dipped snuff till the day he died; put his feet on the kitchen table after supper (even if everyone else was still eating); hid his liquor from my Big Mamma (grandmother); cussed politicians, the law, and referees on

Saturday Night Wrestling at Boutwell Auditorium via the television; and walked to town every day to catch the local gossip down at the drug store and pick up the latest *Cullman Times*. Now that he is the person described above at the fragile age of around seventy-five, it boggles the mind to think what he was like at around thirty when he married my Big Mamma, but that is another tale altogether best saved for another day. The point is that my Papa Pete was not the most responsible man, even at an age when he had nine little responsibilities running around. After being sent to prison during Prohibition for making moonshine (for the second time), Papa Pete decided with the consensus of all concerned that the time had come for my daddy to obtain gainful employment. After all, he had a seventh-grade education just going to waste.

Look for sentence variation (contrast sentence one with sentence two, for starters) and for patterns of punctuation. Notice the multiple verbs in sentence two and observe how this sentence is punctuated. Listen for alliteration and assonance and consider how the sound of the passage creates coherence. The tone of this piece is decidedly colloquial: how does White create this effect grammatically? Also think about how White makes you feel part of the story, how she creates a comfort zone for the reader.

Mary Roach and the Common Cold. From "How I Blew My Summer Vacation."

Mary Roach is a prolific, celebrated writer of non-fiction about unusual topics; she has written about topics from sex (*Bonk: The Curious Coupling of Science and Sex*) to human cadavers (*Stiff: The Curious Lives of Human Cadavers*). Her latest book is *Grunt: The Curious Science of Humans at War*. The excerpt of her writing here came from her first free-lance assignment, which included a trip to the UK to write about research into the common cold. In England's Common Cold Unit research facility, volunteers are exposed to cold viruses and suffer colds and scientists study "cold" viruses so that one day perhaps the common cold can be eliminated. As Roach describes the unit, it is an all-expense paid vacation in the Salisbury countryside—except for the fact that visitors are subjected to deliberate exposure to at least one of the over-200 cold viruses being studied at the Unit. In this section Roach explains how you catch cold—and how you can prevent colds.

A cold virus is harmless until it gets inside a nose cell—where it takes over and begins replicating itself. Researchers recently discovered how a virus gains entry to our cells: deep openings in the virus particle's surface fit protruding receptors on our nose cells. Researchers are working on two types of drugs, one that plugs the openings on the particle, and one that monopolizes our receptors. Although the main application is prevention— particularly for people with asthma or bronchitis, in whom a cold can trigger a serious attack—these drugs may one day prove useful in treating symptoms.

For now, the only way to prevent colds is to keep the viruses out of our noses. This would be a lot easier if we didn't sneeze. Sneezes—and, to a lesser extent, coughs—launch a mist of virus-laden droplets. (Breathing and talking disperse relatively few virus particles.) The smaller, lighter droplets remain airborne, where they either evaporate or are inhaled by a passing nose. The larger droplets fall to the nearest surface. From there they catch a lift noseward on passing fingertips.

Polite cold sufferers who put hands to face while sneezing or coughing will cut down on airborne transmission; unfortunately, the virus is now all over their hands. If you touch what they've touched before the virus dries up and becomes inactive (several hours with a large droplet), your fingers will pick up the virus.

Bearing all this in mind, there are several ways to minimize your risk, should you find yourself in the company of a cold sufferer.

- Wash your hands often (and have your friend with the cold do the same).

- Try your best not to touch your nose and eyes—the primary transfer points from fingertip to nasal cavity. It happens more often than you'd think. According to University of Virginia cold researcher Jack Gwaltney, people pick their noses and touch their eyes about once every three hours. (These astonishing statistics are based on timed observations of adult Sunday school classes and medical students on rounds.)

- Avoid hand contact. Shaking or holding hands is one of the riskiest things you can do with a cold sufferer—far riskier than kissing. Studies have shown that couples are no more likely than platonic roommates to catch one another's colds.

How to think about this passage: first, ask yourself what you believe to be Roach's purpose for writing this piece. Then consider what pronouns she uses to address you, her reader. Think about the kinds of sentence patterns you find here. Notice all the imperative modes (used for the suggestions). Look at the formatting. Find the transitions that make it easy for the reader to bridge ideas. Look for repeated words. Add everything up; then write a paragraph describing how she uses grammar to accomplish her rhetorical purpose(s).

Thomas Paine's "The Crisis."

Quitting this class of men, I turn with the warm ardor of a friend to those who have nobly stood and are yet determined to stand the matter out: I call not upon a few, but upon all: not on this state or that state, but on every state: up and help up; lay your shoulders to the wheel; better have too much force than too little, when so great an object is at stake. Let it be told to the future world that in the depth of winter, when nothing but hope and virtue could survive, that the city and the country, alarmed at one common danger, came forth to meet and to repulse it. Say not that thousands are gone, turn out your tens of thousands; throw not the burden of the day upon Providence, but "show your faith by your works" that God may bless you.

The passage from 1776 enjoining patriots begins with a fine transition wherein Paine literally quits one association and *turns* to another one. Find the repeated words, antitheses, and exquisite balances. Explain why the imperative mode (*Let it be told*) is effective and why the adverbial phrase *when nothing but hope and virtue could survive*, is an effective interrupter in its sentence. Copy the passage and then explain Paine's stylistic strategies to one of your classmates.

Molly Ivins on America. From "Here's to a Nation Undeterred by Reality." *You Got to Dance with Them What Brung You.*

Molly Ivins was a Texas writer with a sly sense of humor and a barbed wit. Her columns were at one time syndicated from the Ft. Worth *Telegraph-Standard*. In this piece, "A Nation Undeterred by Reality," she fondly catalogs the "lovable stuff about America." This essay is a celebration of the quirkiness, yes the individuality, of the American character. As you read, consider in particular what Ivins accomplishes with the *catalogs* or lists.

For some reason, many people believe that England is the great nation for eccentrics; this is because they see nothing peculiar about people who have dedicated their lives to setting a world record for knocking over dominoes in sequence. Or crocheting toilet paper covers. Or collecting Fiesta-ware. Of course, this means that our [U.S.] teenagers have to dye their hair blue, green or orange in order to be considered odd, but what the hell, it adds color to the streets.

We're the country that put Elvis on a stamp! We buy pink lemonade and striped toothpaste! Sixty-seven point two percent of us believe that Alexis de Tocqueville never should have divorced Blake Carrington! Huge numbers of us believe in flying saucers, horoscopes, palm readers, the lottery and pyramid power, that John Kennedy was killed by the CIA and that you can get AIDS off toilet seats. A nation undeterred by reality—no wonder we went to the moon!

Consider American cuisine: pizza, kungpao chicken, sushi, tacos, bratwurst, tofu burgers and corn on the cob. Who wants to live in a place that favors unanimity and uniformity? Consider American music: jazz, blues, pop, country, folk, opera, heavy-metal rock, Cajun, polka, Gershwin, Sousa, bluegrass, Tejano, baroque, Cole Porter, punk, Latino, industrial rock, Three Tenors, reggae . . . . This is not a case of 37 flavors of the same thing, which is more than anyone needs—this is about possibility.

In this passage you'll find considerably more than just catalogs of words. Look for parallelism, patterns of repetition. Look at the diction, the words, that Ivins uses. Look for alliteration and assonance. What is the effect of the compound sentence that begins the passage? What do you think of Ivins' use of the exclamation point after *moon*?

Kim Hendon, On Learning to Read in a Private Religious School

Kim Hendon attended a private religious academy as an elementary student. She was precocious and learned to read very quickly, devouring all the designated first grade books, second grade books, third grade books, and on through each successive grade. By the time she reached eighth grade, she was close to exhausting Mrs. Rosser's (the librarian's) resources:

I distinctly remember getting to the eighth grade section and Mrs. Rosser's handing me S.E. Hinton's *The Outsiders*. (Students were not allowed to select any book they wanted in Mrs. Rosser's library. Mrs. Rosser selected books and handed them to students). I was happily reading about Ponyboy when I came to a square hole in the novel. I was aghast that anyone would desecrate a book. I pointed out this atrocity to Mrs. Rosser and was horrified to discover **she had done it**! She said there had been a "nasty" word there and she had cut it out of the book. Good Christian children did not read filth and did not question their elders. I thought, "Oh hell!" (That was the only bad word I knew at the time, and that word I had gleaned in chapel service when the older students were called upon to repent for saying or thinking it.)

Did you notice that Hendon uses the possessive case before the gerund *handing*? Notice how Hendon uses interrupters to create effects. What is the effect of the parenthetical comment about book selection? Point out where and how interrupting elements work in this passage. Also, look for specific words that are memorable: consider how you think the diction helps to create a specific emotional effect.

Wilbert Rideau—From "Why Prisons Don't Work."

Wilbert Rideau was sent in 1962 to the Louisiana State Penitentiary for life. In 1994, his essay, "Why Prisons Don't Work," was published in *Time* magazine. In this excerpt from the piece, see if you can discern what rhetorical strategies and devices, what figures and structures, are at work.

Crime is a young man's game. Most of the nation's random violence is committed by young urban terrorists. But because of long, mandatory sentences, most prisoners here are much older, having spent 15, 20, 30 or more years behind bars, long past necessity.

Rather than pay for new prisons, society would be well served by releasing some of its older prisoners who pose no threat and using the money to catch young street thugs. Warden John Whitley agrees that many older prisoners here could be freed tomorrow with little or no danger to society. Release, however, is governed by law or by politicians, not by penal professionals. Even murderers, those most feared by society, pose little risk. Historically, for example, the domestic staff at Louisiana's Governor's mansion has been made up of murderers, hand-picked to work among the chief-of-state and his family. Penologists have long known that murder is almost always a once-in-a-lifetime act. The most dangerous criminal is the one who has not yet killed but has a history of escalating offenses. He's the one to watch.

A suggestion: look for contrasts, opposites. And notice sentence length, one of the ways that Rideau creates interest. What is the effect of the repeated word, *long*? How does the alliteration of *politicians, penal, professionals,* and *pose* function?

John Irving—From "Slipped Away."

In this excerpt from "Slipped Away," as it was named when the *New Yorker* first published it, Irving recalls his prep-school days at Exeter, particularly his wrestling experiences. The first quarter of the piece reports his difficulties at Exeter and his anger at nearly everything.

There was one place at Exeter where I was never angry. I never lost my temper in the wrestling room—possibly because I wasn't embarrassed to be there. It is surprising that I felt so comfortable with wrestling. My athletic skills had never been significant. I had loathed Little League baseball. (By association, I hate all sports with balls.) I more mildly disliked skiing and skating. (I have a limited tolerance for cold weather.) I did have an inexplicable taste for physical contact, for the adrenal stimulation of bumping into people, but I was too small to play football. (Also, there was a ball involved.)

When you love something, you have the capacity to bore everyone about why—it doesn't matter why. Wrestling, like boxing, is a weight-class sport; you get to bump into people your own size. You can bump into them very hard, but the place where you land is reasonably soft. And there are civilized aspects to the sport's combativeness: I've always admired the rule that holds you responsible, if you lift your opponent off the mat, for your opponent's "safe return." But the best answer to why I love wrestling is that it was the first thing I was any good at. And what limited success I had in the sport I owe to my first coach, Ted Seabrooke.

What do you notice in this passage? Pay particular attention to the punctuation in the first paragraph. What is the purpose of the parentheses? Do you see a pattern? What is the effect of the repeated *never*, early on?

George Orwell—From "Marrakech."

This passage describes a funeral procession. After you read this passage, stop a moment to evaluate the emotional effect it creates in you. Then re-read the passage and point to the various rhetorical strategies and devices that work in concert to establish the effect.

As the corpse went past, the flies left the restaurant table in a cloud and rushed after it, but they came back a few minutes later. The little crowd of mourners—all men and boys, no women—threaded their way across the market-place between the piles of pomegranates and the taxis and the camels, wailing a short chant over and over again. What really appeals to the flies is that the corpses here are never put into coffins; they are merely wrapped in a piece of rag and carried on a wooden bier on the shoulders of four friends. When the friends get to the burying-ground, they hack an oblong hole a foot or two deep, dump the body in it, and fling over it a little of the dried-up, lumpy earth, which is like broken brick. No gravestone, no name, no identifying mark of any kind. The burying-ground is merely a huge waste of hummocky earth, like a derelict building-lot. After a month or two no one can even be certain where his own relatives are buried.

Do you see a repeated word or concept? Consider how diction works in the excerpt. Also notice the anaphora near the end of the passage; what is the effect of this device? What is the purpose of the alliterated *corpses* and *coffins*? *Burying, body, broken brick*? *Huge, hummocky*?

Anne Bradstreet—From "Meditation 40, Divine and Moral."

Anne Bradstreet was a devoted Puritan of the 17th century who also happened to be a fine American poet and writer. She used her writing as a way to work through knotty problems in her faith and ultimately to affirm her devotion to God. This brief devotion is an example of her prose.

Meditation 40

The spring is a lively emblem of the resurrection: after a long winter we see the leafless trees and dry stocks (at the approach of the sun) to resume their former vigor and beauty in a more ample manner than what they lost in the autumn; so shall it be at that great day after a long vacation, when the Sun of righteousness shall appear; those dry bones shall arise in far more glory than that which they lost at their creation, and in this transcends the spring that their leaf shall never fail nor their sap decline.

This passage is one long sentence. Begin by finding all the separate independent and dependent clauses; if Bradstreet intends to keep all her ideas collected in one sentence, then she means to keep it tidy and coherent. You'll want to keep this in mind as you analyze the sentence. Next, observe Bradstreet's play with the seasons: what do you think the seasons might symbolize to her? Notice the repetition of *dry, leaf* (or *leafless*), and *sun*. Why do you think Bradstreet wants to emphasize these words for her readers?

Liz Rosenberg. From *Home Repair*.

Liz Rosenberg has written more than thirty books, among them many prize winners. She writes novels, poetry, non-fiction and books for young readers. This excerpt is from her first novel for adults.

She was still asleep even when she realized someone else had answered the phone, a voice down the hall. Then there was a panicked confusion of running footsteps. Suddenly, Marcus was standing in the doorway of her bedroom, backlit by the light in the hall, stock-still as a ghost, looking at her, his mouth opening and closing, not saying anything. He was still holding the cordless phone in his hand but not talking to anyone.

Glossary

A

absolute negatives: one of these negative words: *not, no, none,* or *never.* Any absolute negative effects a negative transformation of a declarative sentence: *Jane never smiles at the parrot.*

adjective: a form class most closely related to nouns and clustering with nouns. The function of adjectives is to describe and to limit, to tell us more about nouns. They demonstrate intensity by degree—the suffixes of *–er* and *–est*. Example: *old, older, oldest.* An adjective will fit in the test sentence: A(n) _____ something is something which is _____. Examples are *old, first, weird, sane, joyous.* See also *predicate adjective.*

adjective clause: a dependent clause that functions as an adjective and clusters around or modifies a noun. Adjective clauses are frequently introduced by subordinators like *who, whom, which,* and *that* and are sometimes called relative clauses. Here is a sentence with an adjective clause: *We moved the car **that had been wrecked**.*

adverb: one of the form classes. Adverbs pattern with verbs to tell how, why, when, or where. A typical adverbial suffix is *–ly;* typical adverbs are *clearly, loudly, sadly.* Adverbs may be single words; in addition, adverbial phrases can explain how, why, when, or where—*in the doorway, around* *the corner, above the ledge*. One distinguishing feature of an adverb is its movability; it may pattern at the beginning, middle, or end of a phrase or clause.

adverb clause: a dependent clause that functions as an adverb. Adverb clauses cluster around verbs and explain *where, how,* or *when.* They are frequently introduced by words like *if, when, although,* and *because.* An example of a sentence with an adverb clause is **When the rain stops,** *we will leave the building.*

adverbial noun: a noun acting adverbially to explain how, why, when, or where: today, yesterday, home: *Today* we went *home.*

agent: a cognate of the Latin verb *ago, agere,* which means *to do.* In a sentence, an agent is a do-er, someone who does something, who acts. The subject is frequently, but not always, an agent. Here is a sentence with an agent as subject: *The African* **bees** *swarmed noisily and dove viciously at the dark canvas target.* The bees are agents, performing an action.

alliteration: the repetition of initial consonant sounds—that is, consonant sounds occurring at the beginning of adjacent words or words that are next to one another: *the big brown bear balanced on the blue ball* is an exaggerated example of alliteration. Example: *The tide shoves and sucks through the islands and makes the current curl in odd patterns.*

anadiplosis: a repetition scheme where a word or group of words is repeated at the *end* of one clause or sentence and then subsequently at the *beginning* of the next clause or sentence. Example: *If David has had Uriah killed with the sword, the sword will rampage among his sons.*

anaphora: a repetition scheme where a word or group of words occurs at the beginning or front of successive clauses or phrases, that is, phrases or clauses that come one right after the other. Example: *The* *reason why I object to Dr. Johnson's style is that there is no discrimination, no selection, no variety in it.*

anastrophe: the inversion of the usual or natural word order. Example: *From America letters came.*

antimetabole: a scheme of balance involving two repeated series. A phrase at the beginning of a passage (usually a sentence) is repeated at the end of the passage—but with its elements reversed. Example: *In fact, Daniel suggests that ideas do not make history but history makes ideas.*

antithesis: the placing of contrasting or opposite ideas within physical proximity. Example: *United there is little we cannot do in a host of cooperative ventures. Divided, there is little we can do.*

apposition: a relationship that occurs when you place two coordinate nouns (that is, two elements that are grammatically equal) side by side. Typically, the second element (called the *appositive*) then explains or limits the first. Example: *Meet the first in-dash personal assistant, the Clarion AutoPC.*

appositives: nouns patterning with and renaming other nouns. Generally, appositives are *in apposition with* the nouns they relate to— this mean that they are literally in position with their nouns, side by side. Here is an example of a sentence with an appositive: *My friend, the championship wrestler, weighs 253 pounds.*

assonance: the repetition of similar vowel sounds in words that are next to or near one another. Although we think of assonance as a device used primarily in poetry, a prose writer may also use assonance to knit sentences together by repeating sounds. Example: *Susskind glanced down at his shabby, baggy knickers.*

asyndeton: a scheme of omission: conjunctions are left out between a series of related words, clauses, or phrases. Example: *Adults have about 10,000, grouped by theme (salt, sour, sweet, bitter), at various sites in the mouth.*

auxiliary verb: also known as a **helping verb**. Auxiliary verbs pattern with forms of the main verb to create the perfect (*have grown*) and progressive tenses (*is growing*), the passive voice (*was grown*), and conditionality (*may grow*).

B

base form: the verb form without any endings. The base form is the same as the present tense form for all verbs except *be*. Also called the *infinitive*.

C

casual style: a style marked by informality and an absence of background information. The writer assumes that the reader or listener does not need background and takes public knowledge and information for granted. Two defining features of casual style are ellipsis (omission of words and phrases) and slang (in the strictest sense, a widely current or popular but short-lived expression).

chiasmus: a figure of speech wherein a phrase at the beginning of a passage (which is usually a sentence) is repeated at the end of the passage or sentence, but with its elements reversed. Antimetabole with parallel elements.

clause: a group of words that contains a sentence pattern, which is a subject and a finite verb. Some clauses are complete sentences, and some are not.

cleft sentence: a sentence that is cut in two, then rearranged with expletives to create emphasis: *Jane bathed Puff* becomes *It was Jane who bathed Puff*. Expletives are place-holding words; they have little meaning, and typically they have no function in a sentence other than to fill a spot so that you can shift the placement of other words. Typical expletives are *it, what, there, here*.

combination sentence: a compound-complex sentence, a sentence containing at least two independent clauses and at least one dependent clause. Also called a *compound-complex sentence*.

comma splice: using a comma to join two independent clauses. This mark is too weak to hold apart the substantial weight of two independent clauses and should be replaced with a semicolon or with the combination of a comma plus coordinator. For instance, the sentence with a comma splice *We saw the woodchucks on the dormitory lawn, they were having a party*, should correctly be punctuated *We saw the woodchucks on the dormitory lawn; they were having a party*.

comparative form: a form of adjective or adverb used when you compare two items. When you compare two things, conditions, or states, use the *-er* degree or comparative form or the word *more* (with most words of more than three syllables). Examples: *This car is slower than a turtle* and *We drove more slowly going home*.

complement: a verb completer. These structures complete the action of the verb, making it sound finished and finite: direct objects, indirect object, predicate nouns, predicate adjectives.

complex sentence: a sentence with one main or base clause (an independent clause) plus one or more dependent or subordinate clauses. Complex sentences express explicit and usually unequal relationships between two or more clauses or patterns. One clause clearly expresses the dominant or main idea, and the other clause or clauses express related but subsidiary ideas or relationships.

compound pattern elements: more than one word occupying a particular slot in a sentence. In this sentence, there are compound *subjects*: **Nathan** *and* **Emily** *did the homework.* Both subjects pattern equally with the verb *did.* The deep structure of this sentence is two sentences: *Nathan did the homework* and *Emily did the homework.*

compound sentence: a sentence composed of two or more independent clauses. All the clauses must be independent; that is, each clause within the compound sentence can be removed and exist as a sentence all by itself.

compound-complex sentence: a sentence that is at once compound *and* complex. That is, it has at least two independent clauses (like a compound sentence) and at least one dependent clause (like a complex sentence). Also called a *combination sentence.*

conditional verbs: verbs that indicate possibility, wish, or a condition contrary to fact—*may, might, can, could, will, would,* and *be* when it is paired with *if.* These sentences have conditional verbs: *We will go if we get tickets, She might want to buy a car, Dad could finish the project tonight.*

conjugation: the recitation of all the parts of a verb through all its tenses and aspects. A conjugation indicates forms appropriate with singular and plural subjects and with first, second, and third person pronouns or nouns. It also indicates the simple tenses, the perfect tenses (or aspect), the progressive tenses. Finally, it also demonstrates forms for active or passive voice.

conjunction: words that join words, phrases, and clauses.

conjunctive adverb: an adverb used as a conjunction, most frequently found in compound sentences paired with a semicolon. Common conjunctive adverbs are *therefore, moreover, however, henceforth, consequently, nevertheless.* Using conjunctive adverbs slows the pace of your prose and makes it sound more serious.

consultative style: a style marked by the explicit giving of information, background, and explanation. Someone writing consultative style does not assume that she or he will be understood automatically and as a result offers context and definition of what might not be clearly comprehended. Indeed, consultative style presents information as fast as it is needed and sometimes anticipates the need for it.

coordinate adjectives: two paired adjectives coming most typically after a noun, as in Wordsworth's line, "'Tis a beauteous evening, calm and free."

coordinator or **coordinating conjunction:** a conjunction that joins two equal grammatical structures, like two subjects, two verbs, two direct objects, two predicate adjectives, two objects of prepositions. A coordinator acts like the equal sign in an equation, mediating the two sides that must balance. The most common coordinators are *and, but, or, not, so, for.*

correlative conjunction: conjunctions that come in pairs, two coordinators that *correlate* or *co-relate with* one another—*either* and *or; neither* and *nor; both* and *and; not only* and *but also.* Correlative coordinators join compound elements.

D

declarative mode: a verb form signifying a simple statement or declaration. The most common mode of verb. Example: *That power saw makes a lot of noise.*

dependent clause: a clause that is a complete pattern with a finite verb that does not sound quite right or complete enough to be a sentence. Also called a **subordinate clause.** Example: *because we ate too much peanut butter.*

degree: the intensity of an adjective, signaled most commonly by suffixes *–er* and *–est.* Example: *friendly, friendlier, friendliest.*

Descriptivist: a linguist more interested in describing usages that occur in the population and understanding how these usages were formed than in correctness in writing and in speech. Descriptivists tend to be academics who note and study language as it is actually used.

determiner: a structure word preceding and signaling a noun. This class of words limits the range of a noun and helps the reader determine the nature of the noun. Determiners help to *determine* or specify nouns. Common determiners include *a, an,* the; *this, that, these,* those; *his, her, my, our, their; much, many, most; first, second, third.*

diction: word choice. Speakers and writers choose a level of diction appropriate to the formality or informality of their purpose and aim for writing.

direct object: a noun that follows the verb and completes its meaning by answering the question *Whom?* or *What.* Example: Izzy (subject) recited (verb) a *slam poem* (direct object) or *Izzy recited a slam poem.*

E

ellipsis: deliberate omission of a word or a cluster of words. Example: *His eye was open to beauty, and his ear to music.* The phrase *was open to* is ellipted in the second independent clause.

emphatic transformation: transforming a sentence pattern to shift emphasis. Emphasis can be shifted by changing word order, changing the verb to passive, using an expletive or cleft structure, or by formatting.

epanalepsis: a repetition scheme where a word or group of words from the beginning of a clause or sentence is repeated at the end of that same clause, sentence, or sometimes passage. Example: *That a famous library has been cursed by a woman is a matter of complete indifference to a famous library.*

epistrophe: a repetition scheme where a word or group of words occurs at the end of successive clauses or phrases. Example: *The lobbyists don't like you. The voters don't like you. The majority doesn't like you. (Our judges will love you.).*

essential clause: an adjective clause necessary for the clear under-standing of the noun with which it patterns, also known as a restrictive clause. Example: *We read the book **that the teacher assigned.***

exclamatory transformation: a transformation that enables the speaker or writer to express surprise, extreme pleasure, or emotion. The exclamatory transformation is punctuated with an exclamation mark, as in *What big teeth you have, Grandma!*

expletive: a word like *there, here,* or *it* that fills a space without contrib-uting any meaning. Expletives are place-holders: they take up space that other words might occupy—and they give the writer a chance to delay using a word, perhaps to gain greater impact by placing it later in the sentence.

extraction: a situation where the listener or reader extracts some pat-tern or meaning from a casual sentence spoken by someone very close to him or her. What the speaker says may not be intelligible to anyone else except the person with whom he or she is intimate. Extraction means deriving some meaning from an expression or utterance that appears to have no relationship at all to ordinary words.

F

figure of speech: a generic term for any artful deviation from the ordinary mode of speaking and writing; a construction that uses balance, repetition, unusual devices of sound, or unusual word orders to enhance plain diction or to create appropriate emphasis.

finite verb: a verb that is complete, that has all parts of a tense structure. Example: *placed* or *will have been going.*

first person: refers to the person speaking, *I* or *we.*

form classes: major sentence building blocks that carry most of the meaning of the sentence. The form classes are *noun, verb, adjective,* and *adverb.* Together, form classes and structure words constitute the English vocabulary.

formal style: a style that informs and maintains a distance between the writer/speaker and the reader/hearer (the opposite of intimate style). The speaker or writer typically absents her- or himself from the text itself (no first person, usually) and depends on a strict form or shape, logical links among ideas, and explicitness. Formal text, characterized by detachment and cohesion, inserts background information in depth and with ordered precision; it assumes a captive, non-responsive audience. It refrains from using ellipsis and contractions. Its sentences tend to be long and complex. It is usually characterized by third person and frequently by words of many syllables derived from Latin.

free modifiers: modifiers and modifying phrases that affix themselves not to any particular word but to the concept expressed in the entire sentence; also known as sentence modifiers. Example: *Tires deflated, frame bent, the bike rested against the wall.*

function words: (also *structure words*). Classes of words that modify and connect the major ideas articulated by the form class words or noun clusters combined with verb clusters.

functional labels: labels that describe the *function* or *job* of each sentence component rather than its appearance or form. *Direct object* is a functional label whereas *noun* is a descriptive label.

G

gerund: a verbal that always end in the *-ing* suffix: *eating, sleeping, reading, thinking.* Gerunds function as nouns only.

get passive: a passive transformation where *get* substitutes for *be:* Example: *The new wallpaper got shredded by Janie's cat.*

give verbs: a rather small class of verbs like *give* that appear in the indirect object pattern.

grammar: a system of thought that describes what a language does and explains how it works.

H

headword: the word at the head or center of the cluster; the word that the other words and phrases cluster around.

hybrid grammatical structure: one word class functioning as another word class; a word that can function, for instance, sometimes as a noun or sometimes as an adjective.

I

imperative mode: verb form signaling a command or desire. The subject *you* is most often ellipted or understood in the imperative mode. Example: *Watch the road! Clean up that kitchen! Wait! Don't do that. Show me.*

incremental anaphora: a repetition pattern where the repeated words or phrases change ever so slightly or incrementally with each repetition.

independent clause: a subject-verb pattern that can stand on its own as a sentence. Example: *The bean plants blossomed overnight.*

indicative mode: the mode of statements, the most common mode. Example: *We washed the dishes.* You can remember the term because *indicati*ve mode *indicates* or points something out or makes a comment.

indirect object: major sentence element intervening between the verb and direct object. Indirect objects receive the indirect action of the verb. They answer the question *To whom was something done or given?* or *For whom was something done or given?*

indirect or reported question: text that reports someone's having asked a question. Example: *Dad asked where the screwdriver was.*

infinitive: a verbal consisting of *to* plus a base verb: *to eat, to sleep, to read, to think.* Infinitives may function as nouns, adjectives, or adverbs and may have their own clusters. Also the base form or stem form of the verb.

intensifier: one of the classes of function words that pattern with adverbs or adjectives (and sometimes verbs) to intensify their meanings, as in words that pattern like *very: quite, hardly, barely, scarcely.*

internal punctuation marks: punctuation marks used within sentences (commas, semicolons, colons, dashes).

interrogative mode: a very form signaling a question. Example: *Why does that power saw make so much noise?*

interrogative question transformation: a question transformation that uses interrogative words and phrases like *who, where, what, when, why, how,* and *how much.* This kind of question demands answers of more content and substance than do yes/no questions. Example: *Where were you at 8:00 on Sunday, July 23?*

intimate style: a level or register of style used between people who know one another extremely well—good friends, family, very close colleagues. Intimate style is characterized by extraction and jargon.

intransitive verb: a verb with no complement whatsoever, no object or predicate complement; also called an **intransitive complete** verb because it is complete in itself. Example: *The sun shone brightly.*

introductory clause: a dependent adverbial clause that introduces a sentence. This clause is set off from the rest of the sentence with a comma: *When she was good, she was very, very good.*

inversion: a grammatical situation that occurs when major sentence elements, especially the subject and verb or complement and verb, are reversed, thus shifting the emphasis of the sentence. Example: *Afraid we were, certainly.*

J, K

jargon: certain words or expressions used among people in close or intimate relationships or work or professional settings. Jargon acts as a kind of shorthand to refer to a vast set of experiences.

L

linking verbs: verbs that join or link the subject to the complement. The most common linking verbs are *am, is, are, was, were, be, being, been, looks, tastes, sounds, smells, feels, seem, appear, become, grow, remain.* Example: *The commercials **were** stupid.*

loose sentence: A sentence that starts with the main idea and finishes with the subordinate one. Example: *The party ended abruptly when the police burst through the apartment door.* Also called a cumulative sentence because modifiers accumulate as the sentence progresses.

M

metalanguage: language about language, the language we use to describe language and to talk about grammar. This book is an example of metalanguage because it contains language written about language.

modal verb: verb forms that express conditions applying to main verbs. Modals are never used as main verbs, only as auxiliaries (except in some sentences where the verb is implied). Modals can help the main verb express the following conditions: possibility (*can, could*); probability (*may, might*); obligation (*shall, should*); necessity (*must, have to*); anticipation (*will, would*).

mode (of verb): also sometimes called **verb mood**. Verb modes signal the intent of the speaker: declarative (intent to make a statement or observation); interrogative (intent to ask a question); imperative (intent to give a command or express a strong desire); and subjunctive (intent to speculate or articulate a situation contrary to fact).

multi-function word: a word that can have different grammatical functions depending on its place or task in the sentence. *Turn*, for instance, can be either a noun (*he took a wrong **turn***) or a verb (*he **turned** down the wrong road*).

N

n-group: noun group or another term for noun cluster, a noun plus its immediate modifiers.

negative transformation: a transformation effected by adding *no, not, never,* or another negative word to a sentence or utterance. The purpose of the negative transformation is to negate, deny, correct, or clarify an incorrect or previously held impression. It is also used to counteract what is said or heard or expected, to call into question someone else's positive or affirming statement.

neologism: new word formations (*neo* = new and *logos*= word) like *computerize.*

nominals: nouns or naming words, from the Latin *nominalis,* name.

nominative absolute: a noun-headed phrase that conveys the notion of a sentence absolutely—yet without a finite verb. A nominative absolute evokes the absolute essence of a sentence and looks like a sentence except that it doesn't have a finite verb. It has a subject or a noun (or nominative) at its head. Example: ***Head held high,*** *Therese strolled calmly out of the room.*

non-essential or **non-restrictive clause**: an adjective clause or a subject-verb pattern that modifies or patterns with a noun and whose information is not required for an understanding of the noun it modifies. Non-essential or non-restrictive adjective clauses are set off with commas. Example: *Julia Child's new cookbook, **which has earned rave reviews**, is sitting on the cabinet.*

non-finite verb: a verb not complete enough to constitute the entire main (or finite) verb in a sentence. A non-finite verb is typically a participle or participial phrase missing an auxiliary verb. Example: *going to the store.*

non-restrictive clause: another name for non-essential clause, an adjective clause whose information is not necessary for identifying the noun it modifies. Example: *The French teacher,* **who spent three years in Paris,** *had a marvelous accent.*

noun: a naming word, one used to label objects, people, and ideas. Examples: *pencil, glass, honesty, friend.*

noun adjunct: a noun functioning in an adjunct position to other nouns (or alongside them physically in a supporting role). Noun adjuncts function only *before* the noun, not in post-noun or post-verb positions as complements. For instance, we can say *The patient has a* **skin** *disease* but not *The patient has a disease* **skin** or *The disease is* **skin.** Other examples are *attention span, computer expert, snow storm, grocery list.*

noun clause: a subject-verb pattern that functions as a noun. Noun clauses may assume any noun's position in a sentence and may function as subject, object, or complement. Example: ***What you left behind*** *was valuable.*

noun cluster: a noun plus its attendants, the words and phrases and clauses that pattern with it, modify it, or describe it; also called an n-group. Example: *the gold* **earrings** *with the pearl insets.*

noun of direct address: a noun or personal name at the beginning of a sentence when a writer or speaker focuses directly on a named audience. Example: ***Frankie,*** *you need a new coat.*

noun suffixes: word endings that signal nouns, such as *–er, -ness, -ity, -dom, -tion*.

number: whether a noun or verb is singular or plural; literally, whether the word refers to one item or to more than one item. *Friend* is singular; *friends* is plural.

O

objective complement: a noun or adjective that completes the direct object, as is *Queen of the May* in the sentence *We chose Hermione **Queen of the May***. The direct object and the objective complement have the same referent.

objects: nouns or noun substitutes that receive the energy of a verb, verbal, or preposition; people, things, or ideas acted upon.

onomatopoeia: a figurative strategy where the sound of words echoes their sense or meaning. Its effect is therefore to create an immediacy, an intimacy, between the reader and the text. Example: *The raindrops plopped and blobbed on the window sill, pooling in a shimmering circle of water.*

P

p-group: another name for a prepositional phrase or a preposition plus its noun object.

parallelism: a rhetorical strategy where pairs or series of related words, phrases, or clauses have very grammatically similar structures. The sentence *We took photos of elephants, giraffes, and cats* has parallel direct objects.

parenthesis: a figurative structure that occurs when a cluster of words interrupts the normal word order of a sentence. The text within the parentheses is called *parenthetical matter*. Example: *The Park View Pharmacy—the drugstore my parents bought—stood on Colonial Avenue between Continental and Burr.*—Cynthia Ozick. From "A Drugstore Eden."

participle: the verb form that patterns with the perfect aspect (past participle like *walked* or *eaten*) or with the progressive tense (present participle like *walking* or *eating*).

particle: a preposition that follows a verb and subtly affects the meaning of the verb. If a particle patterns with a noun, we consider it a preposition. Example of a particle: *up, out, down* as in *turn up, turn out, turn down, turn around, turn in.*

parts of speech: a term associated with traditional grammar, which identified eight kinds of words that compose discourse: noun, verb, adjective, adjective, pronoun, interjection, conjunction, and preposition.

passive voice and passive transformation: a transformation of the direct object pattern characterized by a form of *be* plus the past participle of the verb. In the passive transformation the subject is not an agent; it is acted upon and is passive: *Our team **was beaten** in the playoffs.*

past participle: the form of the verb that patterns with the auxiliary *have* in the perfect tenses (*has eaten, have slept, had read, has thought*) and with *be* to create passive voice (*was torn, is seen*).

past tense: the tense that indicates a time that is immediately past. Past tense typically ends in –*ed*, but it may also end in –*t*, as in *you waited, you dropped the ball, you shot the gun.*

pattern: the basic ways that English sentences fit together. Each of the patterns has a complete subject and a finite verb.

perfect tenses or **aspect**: the form of the verb created by an appropriate tense of the auxiliary *have* plus the past participle of that same verb. Example: We **have eaten** beets.

periodic sentence: a sentence that delays its main idea until the end or period while presenting subordinate ideas or modifiers first. Example: *When the police burst through the apartment door, the party ended abruptly.*

phrasal preposition: a phrase that functions as a preposition, such as *by way of* or *according to*, and that takes an object.

phrasal verb: the combination of a verb plus a particle. Example: *turn on, turn up, turn around, turn down.*

phrase: a group of related words functioning as a grammatical unit, a cluster that does **not** include a complete sentence pattern or that does not contain a subject plus a finite verb.

polysyndeton: a generous use of conjunctions to link a series of phrases or clauses; the opposite of asyndeton. Example: *He was two years old and at first he cried for the shack and the familiar smell of the wood stove and his mother's lean, hard hands.*—Annie Proulx. From *Accordion Crimes.*

possessive form: the form of a noun that indicates possession of a material object (my *sister's* coat, *Janet's* new briefcase). Possessive form, indicated by an apostrophe plus an *s*, can also simply describe—as in *a day's wages for a day's work.* Also called **possessive case.**

predicate adjective: an adjective occurring in the predicate after a linking verb. A predicate adjective describes or modifies the subject and has the same referent as the subject: *The bag is **empty**.*

predicate noun: a noun occurring in the predicate after a linking verb. A predicate noun describes or modifies the subject and has the same referent as the subject: *Cindy is a **nurse**.*

prepositional phrase: a phrase built of a preposition and its object, a noun, and any words that may cluster around the noun object. If the noun object has modifiers of its own, all the modifiers are *constituent*—that is, they *constitute* part of the prepositional phrase and are thus considered part of the prepositional phrase. Example: *of the beans, from the balcony, in the soup, with friends, under the weather.*

prepositions: function or structure words that signal relationships (usually spatial) among part of the sentence. Example: *We went to the moon.*

Prescriptivists: linguists who believe in linguistic tradition, correct usage, and precise syntax; someone who believes, like Bryan A. Garner, that "English usage is so challenging that even experienced writers need guidance now and then." Prescriptivists *prescribe* linguistic practice and set standards for usage.

present participle: a part of the verb that ends in *–ing* and patterns with the auxiliary *be* in the progressive tenses (*eating, sleeping, reading, and thinking*).

principal parts of verbs: principal parts of the verb that constitute the various tenses. They are the base verb (I *do*); the past tense (I *did)*; the past participle, used to create the perfect tense or aspect (I *have done*); and the present participle, used to create the progressive tense (I *am doing*).

progressive tenses: the form of the verb using the appropriate tense of *be* plus the present participle. Example: *Jamal **will be opening** the box tomorrow.*

pronoun: a word that can stand in or substitute for a noun, like *I, you, it, he, she, they, him, her.*

proper noun: a noun that refers to the name of a very specific or particular person, place, organization, or thing: *Mississippi River, Samuel Langhorne Clemens, Missouri, The Adventures of Huckleberry Finn.*

Q

qualifiers: (also called **intensifiers** by some grammarians) intensify or change the degree of meaning of words with which they pattern. The rhetorical effect of words like *too, very, quite, almost, so,* and *extremely* is to mitigate, increase, or reduce the impact of the words they modify. Intensifiers frequently pattern with adverbs in verb clusters.

question mark: the mark of punctuation used to signal the question transformation: ?

question transformation: a transformation that creates a question from a declarative statement. The question transformation can be effected by reversing the order of subject and verb. Only the *be* verb reverses simply, however. With verbs other than *be*, the question transformation requires the addition of an auxiliary verb, usually *do* or a form of *do* appropriate to the tense of the sentence being transformed. Examples: *Do you know the way to the castle? Why are you late for the jousting?*

R

referent: what a word refers to. Two words have the same referent if they refer to the same entity or object.

register of expression: a level of style from casual to formal.

relative clause: a kind of adjective clause that uses a relative pronoun as the subordinator.

relative pronoun: a pronoun that acts as a subordinator to introduce adjective clauses. The relative pronouns relate a dependent clause to the main clause because they articulate and define subordinate relationships: *that, who, whom, whose, which, what.*

restrictive or essential clause: an adjective clause essential to the understanding of the noun it modifies. A restrictive clause is not set off by commas. Example: *The boy **who ate worms** was sent to the hospital.*

retained object: when an S-V-IO-DO or S-V-DO-OC sentence is transformed to passive voice and the direct object is retained or kept in the transformation. Example: *The committee named Jane president* becomes *Jane was named president*—and *president*, the direct object, is retained or kept in the transformation.

rhetoric: a discipline that considers the way that grammatical elements (or parts of sentences) work together to create certain effects in the text. Whether you place a clause at the beginning of a sentence instead of at its end, for instance, you send readers a particular message and you emphasize a specific aspect of your message.

S

S-group: a group of words that constitutes a sentence; a subject and a finite verb: *We ate lunch.*

S-LV-PA: the predicate adjective sentence pattern whose main elements are subject, linking verb, and predicate adjective: *The food was free.*

S-LV-PN: the predicate noun sentence pattern whose main elements are subject, linking verb, and predicate noun: *The students are the winners.*

S-V: the intransitive verb sentence pattern whose main elements are subject and verb: *Birds sing in the lilac bushes.*

S-V-DO-OC: the objective complement sentence pattern whose main elements are subject, verb, direct object, and objective complement (which may be either a noun or an adjective): *The painters painted the woodwork green.*

S-V-IO-DO: the indirect object sentence pattern whose main elements are subject, verb, indirect object, and direct object: *Grandfather gave Sammy his gold watch.*

S-V-O: the direct object sentence pattern whose main elements are subject, transitive verb, direct object: *Everyone saw the alien.*

second person: pronouns that refer to the person spoken to, *you* and *yours*.

simple sentence: a sentence with just one independent clause and no dependent clauses.

skunked term: one whose meaning and use change significantly over an indefinite time; in the middle of this time of change, some people will embrace the change, others will tolerate it, and some will hate it.

slang: a widely current but short-lived, informal expression like the recent *way cool,* which is already passé.

split infinitive: an infinitive phrase where a word intervenes between the *to* and its verb. Example: *to boldly go.*

structure words: the metaphorical cement that joins form class words to one another and makes their relationships clear. Although structure words definitely have meaning, they function more to link, enhance, and clarify the form class words than to present the concepts of the text.

Structure words include these classes of words: *pronouns, prepositions, conjunctions, expletives, intensifiers, auxiliaries, interrogatives.*

subject: a noun that represents what the sentence is about and that is related to the verb in the predicate of the sentence; it is typically found at the first of the sentence. Example: ***Geese*** (subject) fly south for the winter.

subjective complement: a completer of the subject or a complement that modifies the subject and has the same referent as the subject. Predicate adjectives and predicate nouns are subjective complements because they complete the meaning of the subject. In *The nuns were strict, strict* is the subjective complement.

subjunctive mode: the mode or mood used to express situations hypothetical, contrary to fact or expressing wishes. Example: *If I were you, I'd invest in magic carpets.*

subordinate clause: a clause that is a complete pattern with a subject and a finite verb but which does not sound complete enough to be an independent sentence. Subordinate clauses are introduced by subordinators and also called dependent clauses. Example: *although we had plenty of money.*

subordinating conjunction: conjunctions used to link subordinate or dependent clauses to independent clauses. Subordinating conjunctions introduce adjective clauses, adverb clauses, and noun clauses. Also known as *subordinators*. Examples are *when, if, as, although, because.*

superlative form of the adjective: represented by the suffix *–est* or the word *most* (used with most words of more than three syllables): *tightest, poorest, smallest, most lovely, most endearing.* Sometimes we also use *most* with the basic form of the adjective because the sound is more euphonious or pleasing. Example: *The guppy is the **smallest** fish in the tank.*

syntax: the way the words and grammatical parts of a sentence are arranged or put together; the order of the words and the structure of a sentence.

T

tag question: a short question formed from *be* or the auxiliary verb added onto a declarative statement. Example: *He has a big nose, doesn't he?*

tense: the quality that allows verbs to express an element of time.

terminal punctuation: punctuation at the end of a sentence or question; periods, question marks, exclamation marks.

***then* adverbs:** a class of adverb; adverbs of time, like *when* and *then*.

***there* adverbs:** a class of adverb; adverbs of place, like *where*.

There V-S pattern: usually a variation of the intransitive pattern S-V so that an expletive begins the sentence, followed by a verb and then the subject: *There goes the black poodle.*

third person: the pronouns referring to persons spoken about: *he, she, it, they, him, her, it, them* or nouns referring to someone spoken about: *Aunt Ginger, Mr. McGowan, Dr. Malkin, the old lady in the flowery hat.*

***thus* adverbs:** a class of adverb; adverbs of manner, like *slowly*.

transitive verb: a verb that *takes* or requires an object and that *transfers* some kind of action from subject to object. In *Nancy cooked the casserole, cooked* is a transitive verb because it takes a direct object, *casserole*.

U, V

usage: an aspect of grammar concerned with correctness and social approbation or approval. Usage refers to the writer's or speaker's ability to choose and use the most socially acceptable forms of words and to frame linguistic constructions in ways that educated people understand, appreciate, and approve.

verb: one of the two major form classes, verbs express or refer to action in a sentence, to reveal what is happening. Verbs are identified by the ability to have past tense. Sample verbs are *fry, skip, tease, argue, cajole.*

verb aspect: the ability of the verb to indicate the state of an action, whether it is ongoing or complete or yet to be executed. Indicated by perfect and progressive "tenses."

verb-medial language: a language, like English, where the verb typically occurs in the medial or middle position in the sentence.

verb stem or base: the present tense singular form of a verb; the infinitive without the *to.*

verbal: a verb form that doesn't act or function like a verb. Verbals have all the physical characteristics of verbs, but verbals do not function as verbs. Rather they function as nouns or adjectives. The verbals are infinitives, gerunds, and participles.

verbatim recoverability: an aspect of ellipsis where the omitted or understood words are grammatically compatible with the part of the sentence actually on the page. *Jan scored 85 on the test; Ian, 60.* What is omitted from the second clause is *scored*, the verb of the first clause. Thus the sentence has verbatim recoverability.

virtual sentence: a purposeful reduction of any basic sentence pattern. It is not a sentence fragment or an incomplete sentence, for it is used by a writer who is entirely in control and wishes to create a certain effect, particularly a setting. Virtual sentences are used to set a scene or to comment on an event or to describe: **Five o'clock**. *The smell of sizzling sausage penetrated the stairwell.*

WXYZ

yes/no question: a question that can be answered with *yes* or *no*. This kind of question typically begins with *do* or *did: Do you like Cocoa Puffs?*

Permissions and Complete Citations

A

Shirley Abbott. From "Why Southern Women Leave Home." *Womenfolks: Growing Up Down South*. Boston: Houghton Mifflin Harcourt, 1983. Print.

Diane Ackerman. From *A Natural History of the Senses*. New York: Vintage, 1990. Print. Diane Ackerman, "The Social Sense" from *A Natural History of the Senses*. Reprinted with permission of Penguin Random House.

Alice Adams. From "Barcelona." *The New Yorker*, 27 February 1984. Print.

Jason Adams. From "Hollywood Goes Himalayan." Rev. of *Vertical Limit* in *Men's Journal*, December, 2000. Print.

Hilton Als. From "Notes on My Mother." *The New Yorker*, 18 November 1996: 72. Print.

Julia Alvarez. From "The Rudy Elmenhurst Story." *How the Garcia Girls Lost Their Accents*. Chapel Hill: Algonquin Books, 1991. 100. Print. From HOW THE GARCIA GIRLS LOST THEIR ACCENTS. Copyright ©1991 by Julia Alvarez. Published by Algonquin Books of

Chapter Hill. By permission of Susan Bergholz Literary Services, New York, NY and Lamy, NM. All rights reserved.

Maya Angelou. From *I Know Why the Caged Bird Sings*. New York: Random House, 1969. Print.

Anonymous. From "Anybody Want Some of This?" *Men's Journal*, December 2000. Print.

-----. From *Bird Tracks*. Wild Birds Unlimited: N.P., Fall 2000. Print.

-----. From an advertisement for *That's My Bush*, Comedy Central. *That's My Bush!*, created by <u>Trey Parker</u> and <u>Matt Stone</u>, was an American comedy television series that aired on <u>Comedy Central</u> from April 4 to May 23, 2001. Print.

-----. From *The New Yorker*, 9 April 2001, 14a. Print.

Max Apple. From "The Eighth Day." *Ploughshares* 9.4 (1983): 110-21. Print.

-----. From "Joshua." *Congregation*. Ed. David Rosenberg. New York: Harcourt, Brace, Jovanovich, 1987. Print.

Karen Armstrong. From *Fields of Blood: Religion and the History of Violence*. New York: Anchor Books / Penguin Random House, 2015. Print. Excerpt from FIELDS OF BLOOD: RELIGION AND THE HISTORY OF VIOLENCE by Karen Armstrong, ©2014 by Karen Armstrong. Used by permission of Alfred A. Knopf, an imprint of the Knopf Doubleday publishing Group, a division of Penguin Random House LLC. All rights reserved.

Elizabeth Ashbridge. From "Account of the Fore-Part of the Life of Elizabeth Ashbridge." 1774. Print.

Margaret Atwood. From "The Man from Mars." *Dancing Girls and Other Stories*. Toronto: McClelland & Stewart, 1977. Print.

B

Chris Bachelder. From "The Throwback Special, Part 3." *The Paris Review*, Winter 2015. Print.

Russell Baker. From "Make Something of Yourself." *Growing Up*. New York: New American Library, 1984. Print.

Hanson W. Baldwin. From "R.M.S. Titanic." *Harper's Magazine*, January 1934. Print.

James Baldwin. From "Sonny's Blues." *Going to Meet the Man*. New York: Dial Press, 1965. Print.

Charles Barsotti. "Not a Cult." *The New Yorker Collection 1998 Charles Barsotti from cartoonbank.com*. All Rights Reserved.

William Bartram. From *The Travels of William Bartram*. Athens GA: U of Georgia Press, 1998; 1791. Print.

Ann Beattie. From "The Cinderella Waltz." *The New Yorker*, 29 January 1979. Print.

-----. From "That Last Odd Day in L.A." *The New Yorker*, 16 April 2001. Print.

Saul Bellow. From "A Silver Dish." *The New Yorker*, 25 September 1978. Print.

-----. From "Something to Remember Me By." *Something to Remember Me By*. New York: Viking, 1991. Print.

Ambrose Bierce. From "An Occurrence at Owl Creek Bridge." *San Francisco Examiner*, 1890. Print.

Heinrich Boll. From "In the Darkness." *The Stories of Heinrich Boll*. Trans. Leila Vennewitz. Evanston, IL: Northwestern UP, 1986. Print.

Katherine Boo. From "After Welfare." *The New Yorker*, 9 April 2001. Print.

George Booth. "Mr. Woofard." From *The New Yorker Collection 1991 George Booth* from *cartoonbank.com*. All Rights Reserved.

-----. "For the Love of a Good Cat." *The New Yorker Collection 1992 George Booth* from *cartoonbank.com*. All Rights Reserved.

Anthony Bourdain. From *Kitchen Confidential: Adventures in the Kitchen Underbelly*. New York: Bloomsbury: 2007. Print. © Anthony Bourdain, 2013, *Kitchen Confidential*, Bloomsbury Publishing Inc.

Ray Bradbury. From "The Pedestrian." *S is for Space*. New York: Harper Voyager, 2014. Print.

Richard Bradford. From *Red Sky at Morning*. New York: Lippincott, 1968. Print.

William Bradford. From *Of Plymouth Plantation*. Mineola NY: Dover, 2006. Print.

Anne Bradstreet. From "Meditation 40, Divine and Moral." 17th Century. Print.

Max Brand. From *Happy Jack*. South Yarmouth MA: John Curley and Associates: 1980. Print.

Richard Brody. From Rev. of *Under the Sun of Satan*. *The New Yorker*, 13 May 2013. Print.

E.M. Broner. From *Ghost Stories*. New York: Global City Press, 1995. Print.

-----. From *A Weave of Women*. Bloomington, IN: Indiana UP, 1985. Print.

Chip Brown. From "Much About This World." *Wild Stories: The Best of Men's Journal*. New York: Crown, 2002. Print.

Frank Bruni. "Show Us the Money." *NY Times Magazine*, December 16, 2001. Print.

Melvin Jules Bukiet. From "The Library of Moloch." *Nothing Makes You Free*. New York: W.W. Norton, 2002. Print.

Paul-William Burch. "War Poetry." 2002.

Edmund Burke. *An Appeal from the New to the Old Whigs*. Ed. John M. Robson. N.p. The Library of Liberal Arts: 1791, 1962. Print.

C

Ron Carlson. From "Blazo." *Ploughshares* 18.1 (1992): 18-41. Print.

Raymond Carver. "Cathedral." From *Cathedral*. New York: Penguin Random House, 1983. Print.

Dennis Cass. From "Meter Made." *NY Times Magazine,* 16 December 2001. Print.

Louis Ferdinand Céline. From *Journey to the End of the Night*. Trans. Ralph Manheim. New York: New Directions, 1949. Print.

Prince William, Duke Of Cambridge [quoted, describing living conditions on a community-service mission]. From "Prince Charming!" *Good Housekeeping.* July 2001. Print.

Michael Chabon. From "S Angel." *The New Yorker,* 22 October 1990. Print.

Roz Chast. "You Ain't Nothin' But a Hound Dog, etc." From *The New Yorker Collection 1988 Roz Chast from cartoonbank.com. All Rights Reserved.*

John Cheever. From "The Country Husband." *The Stories of John Cheever.* New York: Knopf, 1978. Print.

Anton Chekhov. From "The Lady with the Little Dog." *Anton Chekhov's Short Stories.* New York: W.W. Norton Critical Editions, 2014. Print.

G. K. Chesterton. From "A Piece of Chalk." *Tremendous Trifles.* Mineola, NY: Dover, 2007. Print.

James Collins. From "One Year Later." *The New Yorker.* 16 April 2001. Print.

Richard Connell. From "The Most Dangerous Game" *Collier's Magazine,* 19 January 1924. Print.

Joseph Conrad. From *Heart of Darkness.* New York: Global Classics, 2014;1899. Print.

-----. From *The Secret Sharer and Other Stories.* Mineola NY: Dover Thrift Editions, 1993. Print.

James Fenimore Cooper. From *The Pioneers.* 1823. Print.

Edward P.J. Corbett. From *Classical Rhetoric for the Modern Student*. New York: Oxford UP, 1965. Print.

Ann Cornelisen. From *Where It All Began: Italy 1954*. New York: Dutton, 1990. Print.

J. Hector St. John De Crevecoeur. From *Letters from An American Farmer*. 1782. Print.

D

Rebecca Harding Davis. From "Life in the Iron Mills." *Atlantic Monthly* 7.42 (April 1861). Print.

Len Deighton. From *Fighter: The True Story of the Battle of Britain*. London: Castle Books, 2000; 1977. Print.

David Denby. From "All That Jazz." *The New Yorker*, 13 May 2013. Print.

-----. From "The Lord of the Rings: The Fellowship of the Rings." *The New Yorker*, 14 January 2002. Print.

-----. From *The New Yorker*. Rev. of *Vanilla Sky*, 16 January 2012. Print.

Debra Dickerson. From "Who Shot Johnny?" *Essence* 29.1 (May 1998). 130. Print.

James Dickey. From *Deliverance*. New York: Bantam Dell, 1970. Print.

Joan Didion. From "On the Morning After the Sixties." *The White Album: Essays*, New York: Farrar, Straus, & Giroux Classics, 2009. Print.

Annie Dillard. From *An American Childhood*. New York: Harper, 1987. Print. Brief quotation from p. 74 from AN AMERICAN CHILDHOOD by ANNIE DILLARD. COPYRIGHT © by Annie Dillard. Reprinted by permissions of HarperCollins Publishers.

-----. From *Pilgrim at Tinker Creek*. New York: Harper Perennial, 1974. Print.

E.L. Doctorow. From "Heist." *The New Yorker*, 21 April 1997. Print.

Michael Dorris. From *A Yellow Raft in Blue Water*. New York: Picador Henry Holt, 1987. Print.

Peter Drucker. From "Beyond the Information Revolution." *Atlantic*, October 1999, 52. Print.

Stuart Dybek. From "Pet Milk." *The New Yorker* 13 August 1984. Print.

Bob Dylan. From "Tom's Thumb Blues." *Highway 61 Revisited*. 1965. Audio Recording.

E

Gerald Early. From "Ali, the Wonder Boy." *The New York Review of Books* 45.9 (28 May 1998). Print. Used by permission of Gerald Early, from "Ali the Wonder Boy," *New York Review of Books* 45.9, 28 May 1998.

Jonathan Edwards. From "Sinners in the Hands of an Angry God." 1741. Print.

Albert Einstein. From "Physics and Reality." *Ideas and Opinion*. New York: Crown, 1954; 1982. Print.

Jenny Eliscu and Austin Scaggs. From "Rock's Biggest Night." *Rolling Stone*, 26 April 2001. Print.

Stanley Elkin. From "Among the Witnesses." *Criers & Kibitzers, Kibitzers & Criers*. Victoria, TX: Dalkey Archive Press, 2000. Print.

Ralph Waldo Emerson. From "Experience." *The Spiritual Emerson: Writings of Ralph Waldo Emerson*. Boston: Beacon, 2003. Print.

-----. From *Nature*. Boston: James Munroe and Company, 1836. Print.

-----. From "Thoreau." *The Atlantic*. August 1862. Print.

Anne Enright. From "My Milk." *Harpers,* May 2001. Print.

Louise Erdrich. From *The Antelope Wife*. New York: Harper Perennial, 2012. Print.

-----. From *The Last Report on the Miracles at Little No Horse*. New York, Harper Collins: 2001. Print.

-----. From *Tales of Burning Love*. New York: Harper Perennial, 1996. Print.

Olaudah Equiano. From *The Interesting Narrative of the Life of Olaudah Equiano*. London: Author, 1789. Print.

F

William Faulkner. From "Barn Burning." Harper's, 1939. Print.

------. From *Go Down, Moses*. New York: Random House Vintage, 1990. Print.

Edna Ferber. From *Saratoga Trunk*. New York: Harper Collins, 1968. Print.

Dexter Filkins. From "The Thin Red Line." *The New Yorker*, 13 May 2013. Print.

F. Scott Fitzgerald. From "Babylon Revisited." *Saturday Evening Post*, 21 February 1931. Print.

Richard Ford. From "In the Face." *New Yorker*, 16 September 1996. Print.

Dr. Race Foster. From "Checklist for Visits to Your Veterinarian." *Doctors Foster and Smith Catalog*. N.D. Print.

Janet Frame. From "You Are Now Entering the Human Heart." *The New Yorker*. 29 March 1969. Print.

Benjamin Franklin. From "The Way to Wealth." *Poor Richard's Almanac*. 1758. Print.

Bruce Jay Friedman. From "Lady (featuring Harry Towns)." *The Collected Short Fiction of Bruce Jay Friedman*. New York: Grove Press, 1997. Print.

-----. From "When You're Excused, You're Excused." *The Collected Short Fiction of Bruce Jay Friedman*. New York: Grove, 1997. Print.

Daniel Fuchs. From "A Hollywood Diary." *Jewish American Literature: An Anthology*. Eds. Jules Chametzky and John Felstiner. New York: W.W. Norton, 2001. Print.

G

Donna Gaines. From "Introduction." *Teenage Wasteland: Suburbia's Deadend Kids.* Chicago: U of Chicago Press, 1990; 1998. Print.

John Gardner. From *Freddy's Book.* New York: Knopf, 1980. Print.

-----. From *October Light.* New York: Knopf, 1976. Print.

Bryan A. Garner. *Garner's Modern American Usage: The Authority on Grammar, Usage, and Style, 3rd ed.* New York: Oxford UP, 2009.

William H. Gass. From "In the Heart of the Heart of the Country." *In the Heart of the Heart of the Country and Other Stories.* New York: *New York Review of Books*, 1958. Print.

Nguyen Mong Giac. From "The Slope of Life." *The Other Side of Heaven.* Willimantic CT: Curbstone, 1995. Print.

Joseph Gibaldi. From *MLA Style Manual and Guide to Scholarly Publishing,* 2nd ed. New York: MLA, 1985. Print.

C.S. Godshalk. From "The Wizard." *Agni* 28:1989. 29-45. Print.

Michael Gold. From *Jews Without Money.* New York: Liveright, 1930. Print.

Myla Goldberg. From *Bee Season.* New York: Anchor Random House, 2001. Print.

Paul Goldberger. From "Spiffing Up the Gray Lady." *The New Yorker,* 7 January 2001. Print.

Rebecca Goldstein. From *The Dark Sister.* Madison: U of Wisconsin Press, 2004. Print.

Allegra Goodman. From *Paradise Park*. New York: Dial, 2001. Print.

-----. From "Sarah." *The New Yorker*, 10 January 1994. Print.

-----. From "Variant Text." *Commentary*, 1 June 1986. Print.

Vivian Gornick. From *Fierce Attachments*. New York: Farrar, Straus, & Giroux, 1987. Print. Excerpt from FIERCE ATTACHMENTS by Vivian Gornick. Copyright © 1987 by Vivian Gornick. Used by permission of Farrar, Straus and Giroux, LLC.

Francine Du Plessix Gray. From "Mayakovsky's Last Loves." *The New Yorker*, 7 January 2002. Print.

Gordon Grice. From *The Red Hourglass: Lives of the Predators*. New York: Delta Random House, 1998. Print.

H

Jacob Hacker and Paul Pierson. From "Why Trump Can't Break the GOP." *New York Times*. 3 April 2016. SR3. Print.

Alvin D. Hall. From *Getting Started with Stocks*. New York: John Wiley and Sons, 1992; 1994;1997. Print. Copyright @ 1992, 1994, 1997 by Alvin D. Hall. Published by John Wiley & Sons, Inc. Used by Permission.

J.B. Handelsman. "Unceremoniously Adrift." From *The New Yorker Collection* 1989 J.B. Handelsman from cartoonbank.com. All Rights Reserved.

Barbara Grizzuti Harrison. From "Women and Blacks and Bensonhurst." *Harper's*. March 1990. Print.

Nathaniel Hawthorne. From "The Minister's Black Veil." *Twice-Told Tales*. 1837; 1851. Print.

-----. From *The Scarlet Letter*. 1850. Print.

William Hazlitt. From "On Familiar Style." *The London Magazine*, 1822; rpt. *Table Talk*, 1822. Print.

Benjamin Hedin. From *Studio A: The Bob Dylan Reader*. New York: W.W. Norton, 2004. 238. Print.

Larry Heinemann. *Close Quarters*. New York: Random House, 1977. Print.

Ernest Hemingway. From "The Short Happy Life of Francis Macomber." *Cosmopolitan*, September 1936. Print.

Kim Hendon. From "On Learning to Read." Used by permission of Kim Hendon.

Robin Hemley. From "The 19th Jew." *Reply All: Stories*. Bloomington IN: Indiana UP, 2012. Print.

Michelle Herman. From "Auslander." *A New and Glorious Life: Novellas*. Pittsburgh: Carnegie Mellon UP, 1998. Print.

Michael Herr. From *Dispatches*. New York: Knopf, 1977. Print. Excerpt from DISPATCHES by Michael Herr, copyright © 1977 by Michael Herr. Used by permission of Alfred A. Knopf, an imprint of the Knopf Doubleday Publishing Group, a division of Penguin Random House LLC. All rights reserved.

John Hersey. From *Of Men and War*. New York: Scholastic Trade, 1991. Print.

Allen Hoffman. From "Building Blocks." *Commentary* (May 1974). Print.

Siri Hustvedt. From "A Plea for Eros." The *Art of the Essay*. Ed. Philip Lopate. New York: Anchor, 1999. Print.

Robert Maynard Hutchins. From *Morals, Religion, and Higher Education*. Chicago: U of Chicago Press, 1950. Printed privately for Kenyon College. Print.

I

John Irving. From "Slipped Away." *The New Yorker*, 11 December 1995. 70-77. Print. Used by permission from Skyhorse Publishing. All rights reserved.

Washington Irving. From "The Legend of Sleepy Hollow." 1820. Print.

Molly Ivins. From "Here's to a Nation Undeterred by Reality." *You Got to Dance with Them What Brung You*. New York: Vintage, 1999. Print. "Here's to a Nation Undeterred by Reality" from YOU GOT TO DANCE WITH THEM WHAT BRUNG YOU: POLITICS IN THE CLINTON YEARS by Molly Ivins, copyright © 1998 by Molly Ivins. Used by permission of Random House, an imprint and division of Penguin Random House LLC. All rights reserved. Any third party use of this material, outside of this publication, is prohibited. Interested parties must apply directly to Penguin Random House LLC for permission.

J

Leon Jaroff. From "Nature's Time Capsules." *Time Magazine*. 6 April 1992. Print.

Thomas Jefferson. From *The Declaration of Independence*. https://www. loc.gov/exhibits/jefferson/jeffdec.html. Retrieved 14 March 2016.

Jeremiah 31:33. King James Version of *The Bible*. Print.

Charles Richard Johnson. From "Kwoon." *I Call Myself an Artist: Writings by and about Charles Johnson*. Bloomington: U of Indiana Press, 1999. Print.

Cory Johnson. From "Tools of Self-Destruction." *Wired*, 1 January 2002. Print.

Thom Jones. From "The Black Lights." *The New Yorker*, 2 October 1992. Print.

K

Franz Kafka. From "A Hunger Artist." *A Hunger Artist*. Las Vegas, NE: IAP Publishing, 2010. Print.

-----. From *Metamorphosis*. Trans. David Wyllie. Project Gutenberg, Release Date: August 16, 2005.

Wayne Karlin. From *Lost Armies*. New York: Henry Holt, 1988. Print.

Alfred Kazin. From *A Walker in the City*. Orlando, FL: Harcourt, 1969. Print.

Paula Keisler [Paula Huston]. From "The Singing of Angels." *MSS* (Fall 1983). Print.

James Kelman. From Rev. of *Mo Said She Was Quirky*. *The New Yorker*, 13 May 2013. Print.

John F. Kennedy. From "Inaugural Address." 20 January 1961. http:// www.jfklibrary.org/Research/Research-Aids/Ready-Reference/JFK-Quotations/Inaugural-Address.aspx. Web. 14 March 2016.

William Kennedy. From *Very Old Bones*. New York: Viking Penguin, 1992. Print.

-----. From "Who Are You Now That You're Not Nobody?" *Riding the Yellow Trolley Car*. New York: Penguin, 1993. Print. Excerpt from RIDING THE YELLOW TROLLEY CAR by William Kennedy. Copyright © 1993 by WJK, Inc., used by permission of The Wylie Agency LLC.

Barbara Kingsolver. From *The Bean Trees*. New York: Harpertorch, 1988. Print.

Maxine Hong Kingston. From "No Name Woman." *Warrior Woman: Memoir of a Girlhood Among Ghosts*. New York: Random House Vintage, 1975. Print.

Jamie Kitman. From "Major Mini." *Automobile*. December 2000. Print.

Verlyn Klinkenborg. From "We Are Still Only Human." *New York Times* 29 September 1996. Print.

Stanislaw Kohn. From *The Treblinka Revolt*. http://www.apelslice.com/ books/0-00-Bookshare/0-03-055462-4/revolt.htm. Web. Retrieved 21 March 2016.

Elizabeth Kolbert. From "Ice Memory." *The New Yorker*, 7 January 2002. Print.

Yusef Komunyakaa. From "The Hanoi Market." *Thieves of Paradise*. Middletown, CT: Wesleyan Poetry Series: 1998.

Natalie Kusz. From "Ring Leader." *Best American Essays 1997.* Eds. Ian Frazier and Robert Atwan. New York: Houghton Mifflin, 1997. Print.

L

John Lahr. From "Been Here and Gone." *The New Yorker,* 16 April 2001. Print.

Louis L'Amour. From "Trap of Gold." N.p., n.d. Print.

Richard Lanham. From *Style: An Anti-Textbook,* 2nd ed. Philadelphia: Paul Dry Books, 2007. Print.

Todd Lappin. From "Eureka! Great Moments in the March of Technolust." *Wired,* 1 January 2002. Print.

D.H. Lawrence. "The Rocking-Horse Winner." From *Complete Short Stories of D.H. Lawrence.* New York: Viking Penguin, 1961; 1933. Print.

T.E. Lawrence. From *Seven Pillars of Wisdom.* Ware, Hertfordshire: Wordsworth Editions, 1997;1935. Print.

Harper Lee. From *Go Set a Watchman.* New York: Harper Collins, 2015. 138-39. Print.

Ursula Le Guin. From "The Eye Altering." *The Compass Rose.* New York: Harper and Row, 1982. Print.

-----. From "The New Atlantis." *The New Atlantis and Other Novellas of Science Fiction,* Ed. Robert Silverberg. New York: Grand Central Publishing,1976. Print.

Naton Leslie. From "Don't Get Comfortable." *High Plains Literary Review*: 1996. Print.

Denise Levertov. From "Autobiographical Sketch." *New and Selected Essays*. New York: New Directions, 1992. Print.

Primo Levi. *The Periodic Table*. New York: Schocken, 1984. Print.

-----. From *Survival in Auschwitz*. New York: Orion Press, 1959. Print.

Mark Levine. From rev. of *The Body Artist* and *The Cloud Sketcher*. *Men's Journal,* February, 2001. Print.

Abraham Lincoln. From "The Gettysburg Address." 19 November 1863. http://www.abrahamlincolnonline.org/lincoln/speeches/gettysburg.htm. Web. Retrieved 14 March 2016.

Ryan Lizza. From "The Middleman." *The New Yorker,* 13 May 2013. Print.

Luis Lopez-Nieves. From "The Extremely Funny Gun Salesman." *Journal of Pedagogy, Pluralism, and Practice* 1.1 (Spring 1997). Print.

Audre Lorde. From "A Burst of Light: Living with Cancer." Ann Arbor MI: Firebrand, 1998. Print.

Lee Lorenz. From "I Get Her Heart." *The New Yorker Collection 1992 Lee Lorenz from cartoonbank.com*. All Rights Reserved.

M

Norman Mailer. From "And the Fire Abated," *Jewish American Literature: An Anthology*. Eds. Jules Chametzky and John Felstiner. New York: W.W. Norton, 2001. Print.

Bernard Malamud. From "The Last Mohican." *The Magic Barrel*. New York: Farrar, Straus, and Giroux, 1958. Print.

-----. From "The Magic Barrel." *The Magic Barrel: Stories.* New York: Farrar, Straus, Giroux, 1986. Print.

-----. From "The Silver Crown." *The Stories of Bernard Malamud.* New York: Farrar, Straus, & Giroux, 1983. Print.

Alberto Manguel. From *A History of Reading.* New York: Penguin Putnam 1996. Print.

Robert Mankoff. "Coherent Viewing Policy." *The New Yorker Collection 1992 Robert Mankoff from cartoonbank.com.* All Rights Reserved.

Hilary Mantel. "How to Be Tudor." Rev. of *Charles Brandon: Henvy VIII's Closest Friend,* by Steven Gunn. *The London Review of Books* 38.6 (2016). Print.

Wallace Markfield. From "The Decline of Sholem Waldman." *American Jewish Fiction: A Century of Stories,* Ed. Gerald Shapiro. Lincoln: U of Nebraska Press, 1998. Print.

Bobbie Ann Mason. From *Zigzagging Down a Wild Trail.* New York: Harper, 2002. Print. Reprinted by permission of Penguin Random House. From Bobbie Ann Mason's "Tunica" published in *Zigzagging Down A Wild Trail: Stories.*

Harry Mattison. From "What Makes Us Think We Are Only Here." *Writing Between the Lines: An Anthology on War and Its Social Consequences.* Amherst, MA: U of Massachusetts Press, 1997. Print. Used by permission of the author.

Jane Mayer. From "The House of Bin Laden." *The New Yorker.* 12 November 2001. Print.

Donald McCabe. From "Cheating: Why Students Do It and How We Can Help Them Stop." *American Educator* 25.4 (Winter 2001): 38-43.

Originally published in *American Educator* (Winter 2001), pp. 38-43. Used by oral permission of Professor Donald McCabe, March 3, 2016.

John McCain. From "Commit to Causes Higher Than Yourself." *George Magazine, 1999. 40-41*. Print.

Mary McCarthy. From *How I Grew*. New York: Harcourt, Brace, Jovanovitch, 1986. Print.

Wil McCarthy. From "Runaway Train." *Wired*, 1 January 2002. Print.

Daisann McLane. From "Into the Wild, Wet World of the Everglades." *New York Times*, 14 February 1999. Print.

John McPhee. From *Heirs of General Practice*. New York: Farrar, Straus, and Giroux, 1984. Print.

-----. From "Mini-Hydro." *Table of Contents*. New York: Farrar, Straus, and Giroux, 1985. Print.

Rebecca Mead. From "Lawyers Who Love Trollope." *The New Yorker*, 16 April 2001. Print.

Jonathan Meades. From "Favourite without Portfolio." *London Review of Books*, 4 February 2016. 11. Used by permission of *London Review of Books*.

Mary Mebane. From *Mary: An Autobiography*. New York: Viking, 1983. Print.

Herman Melville. From "Benito Cereno." *The Piazza Tales*, 1856. Print.

Daphne Merkin. From *Enchantment*. New York: Harper Collins, 1988. Print.

Leonard Michaels. From "Murderers." *The Vintage Book of Contemporary Short Stories*. Ed. Tobias Wolff. New York: Vintage, 1994. Print.

Arthur Miller. From "Presence." *Presence: Collected Stories*. London: Bloomsbury, 2010. Print.

Kate Millett. From *The Loony-Bin Trip*. New York: Simon and Schuster, 1990. Print.

Marga Minco. From *Bitter Herbs: The Vivid Memories of a Fugitive Jewish Girl in Nazi Occupied Holland*. New York: Penguin, 1991. Print.

Tova Mirvis. From *The Ladies Auxiliary*. New York: Random House, 1999. Print.

Victor Montejo. From *Testimony: Death of a Guatemalan Village*. Willimantic CT: Curbstone, 1987. Print.

Willie Morris. From "Mississippi." *North Toward Home*. New York: Vintage Random House, 1967. Print.

Bharati Mukherjee. From "The Tenant." *The Middleman and Other Stories*. New York: Grove, 2007. Print.

Harry Mulisch. From *The Assault*. New York: Random House, 1985. Print.

Alice Munro. From "Boys and Girls." *Dance of the Happy Shades*. New York: Random House Vintage, 1998. Print.

N

Nguy Ngu. From "An Old Story." *Writing Between the Lines: An Anthology of War and Its Social Consequences*. Amherst: U of Massachusetts Press, 1997. Print.

Frank Norris. From *McTeague: A Story of San Francisco*. 1899. Book digitized by Harvard University Library. Web. https://archive.org/details/mcteague00norrgoog

O

Joyce Carol Oates. From *Bad Girls*. Dir. Susana Tubert. 11 November 2003. Print drama.

Michael Ondaatje. From *Anil's Ghost*. New York: Knopf, 2000. Print.

P. J. O'Rourke. From "Oh, Baby." *Men's Journal*, December 2000. Print.

George Orwell. From "Marrakech." *A Collection of Essays*. New York: Houghton Mifflin Harcourt, 1950. Print. Excerpt from "Marrakesh" from A COLLECTION OF ESSAYS by George Orwell. Copyright 1950 by Houghton Mifflin Harcourt Publishing Company Copyright © renewed 1978 by Sonia Brownell. Reprinted by permission of Houghton Mifflin Harcourt Publishing Company. All rights reserved.

Cynthia Ozick. From "Bloodshed." *Bloodshed and Three Novellas*. Syracuse UP: 1976. Print.

-----. From "A Drugstore Eden." *The New Yorker*, 16 September 1996. Print.

-----. From "Envy, Or Yiddish in America." *Commentary*. 31 November 1969. Print.

-----. From "Isaac Babel and the Identity Question." *Fame and Folly: Essays.* New York: Knopf, 1996. Print.

-----. From "The Suitcase." *Cynthia Ozick: Collected Stories.* London: Phoenix Orion, 2007. Print.

-----. From "Usurpation." *Cynthia Ozick: Collected Stories.* London: Phoenix Orion, 2007. Print.

P

Thomas Paine. From "The Crisis." 1776. Print.

Grace Paley. From "Goodbye and Good Luck." *The Collected Stories.* New York: Farrar, Straus, & Giroux, 1994. Print.

-----. From "The Loudest Voice." *The Little Disturbances of Man.* New York: Penguin, 1985. Print.

-----. From "Zagrowsky Tells." *Later the Same Day.* New York: Farrar, Straus & Giroux, 1985. Print.

Dorothy Parker. From "Too Bad." *Complete Stories.* New York: Penguin, 1995; *The Smart Set,* 1923. Print.

Ian Parker. From "Navasky Lives," *The New Yorker,* 13 May 2013. Print.

Janice Paskey. From "Mysteries of the Snowpack: Predicting the Unpredictable," *Chronicle of Higher Education,* 16 March 2001. Print.

Edith Pearlman. From "Cul-de-Sac." *Honeydew.* New York: Little Brown, 2015. Print.

Jonathan Penner. From "Emotion Recollected in Tranquility." *The Norton Anthology of Contemporary Fiction*, 2e. Eds. R.V. Cassill and Joyce Carol Oates. New York: W.W. Norton, 1997. Print.

J. Peterman Company. From *Owner's Manual*, No. 136. http://www. jpeterman.com/Marie-Antoinette-Nightshirt). Web. Retrieved 14 March 2016.

Edgar Allan Poe. From "The Casque of Amontillado." *Godey's Lady's Book*, November 1846. Print.

-----. From "Ligeia." *The American Museum*, 1838. Print.

Michael Pollan. From *The Botany of Desire*. New York: Random House, 2001. Print.

Katherine Anne Porter. From "Flowering Judas." *Flowering Judas and Other Stories*. New York: Harcourt, Brace, 1930. Print. Electronic rights granted by The Permissions Company, Inc. and Rights Agency for the Katherine Anne Porter Literary Trust. Print rights: Excerpt from "Flowering Judas" from FLOWERING JUDAS AND OTHER STORIES by Katherine Anne Porter. Copyright © 1930 and renewed 1958 by Katherine Anne Porter. Reprinted by permission of Houghton Mifflin Harcourt Publishing Company. All rights reserved. UK Rights: From *Collected Stories* by *Katherine Anne Porter*, Published by *Jonathan Cape*, Reprinted by permission of The Random House Group Limited.

Francine Prose. From "Electricity." *All Broken Families Are Alike: Women and Children First and Other Stories*. New York: Pantheon, 2003. Print.

Annie Proulx. From *Accordion Crimes*. New York: Scribner (Simon and Schuster), 1996. Print. Reprinted with the permission of Scribner, a

Division of Simon & Schuster, Inc., from *Accordion Crimes* by E. Annie Proulx. Copyright 1996 by Dead Line, Ltd. All rights reserved.

-----. From "The Mud Below." *The New Yorker,* 22 June 1998. Print.

Geoffrey Pullum. From "Lingua Franca" [Blog]. *Chronicle of Higher Education.* 30 March 2016. Web. https://shar.es/1YAJc8. Retrieved 30 March 2016.

R

Margaret Rabb. From *The Presentation Design Book*. Oregon: Ventana Press,1990. Print.

Lev Raphael. From "History (With Dreams)." *American Jewish Fiction,* Ed. Gerald Shapiro. Lincoln: U of Nebraska Press, 1998. Print.

Nessa Rappoport. From "The Woman Who Lost Her Names." *The Woman Who Lost Her Names*. Ed. Julia Mazow. New York: Harper, 1980. Print.

David Remnick. From "The Dreamer." *The New Yorker,* 7 January 2002. Print.

Wilbert Rideau. From "Why Prisons Don't Work." *Time*. 21 March 1994. Print. Wilbert Rideau, excerpt from "Why Prisons Don't Work" from Time (March 21, 1994). Copyright © 1994 by Wilbert Rideau. Reprinted with the permission of the author, c/o The Permissions Company, Inc., www.permissionscompany.com.

Mary Roach. From "How I Blew My Summer Vacation." *In Health,* 1990. Print. Used by permission of Mary Roach. Copyright © Mary Roach. All rights reserved.

Paul Roberts. *Understanding English*. New York: Harper & Row, 1958.

Mary Robison. From "Coach." *The New Yorker*, 14 September 1981. Print.

Norma Rosen. From "What Must I Say to You?" *The New Yorker*. 26 October 1963. Print.

Liz Rosenberg. From *Home Repair*. New York: Avon, 2009. 228-29. Used by permission of the author.

Henry Roth. From *Call It Sleep*. Baltimore: Johns Hopkins UP, 1934; 1962. Print.

Philip Roth. From *Goodbye, Columbus*. Boston: Houghton Mifflin, 1959. Print.

S

Oliver Sacks. From *A Leg to Stand On*. New York: Touchstone, 1984. Print. Electronic Rights: Excerpt from A LEG TO STAND ON by Oliver Sacks. Copyright © 1984 by Oliver Sacks, used by permission of The Wylie Agency LLC. Print Rights: Reprinted with the permission of Simon & Schuster, Inc. From A LEG TO STAND ON by Oliver Sacks. Copyright© 1984. Oliver Sacks. All rights reserved. Print Rights: Reprinted with the permission of Simon & Schuster, Inc. from A LEG TO STAND ON by Oliver Sacks. Copyright 1984 Oliver Sacks. All rights reserved.

Kelefa Sannah. From "Paint Bombs." *The New Yorker*, 13 May 2013. Print.

Nguyen Quang Sang. "The Ivory Comb." From *Writing between the Lines: An Anthology On War and Its Social Consequences*, Ed. Kevin Bowen and Bruce Weigl. Amherst: U Massachusetts Press, 1997. Print.

B. J. Schechter. From "The Buzzer." *Sports Illustrated*, 25 January 1999. Print.

Helen Schulman. From *The Revisionist*. New York: Bloomsbury, 1998. Print.

Michael Schulman. From "Bling Ring." *The New Yorker*, 13 May 2013. Print.

Delmore Schwarz. From "In Dreams Begin Responsibilities." *Partisan Review* 1.1 (1937). Print.

Lynne Sharon Schwartz. From "The Melting Pot." *The Melting Pot and Other Subversive Stories*. New York: Harper Collins, 1987.

Lore Segal. From "Daniel." *Congregation*. Ed. David Rosenberg. New York: Harcourt, Brace, Jovanovich, 1987. Print.

-----. From "II Samuel." *Congregation*. Ed. David Rosenberg. New York: Harcourt, Brace, Jovanovich, 1987. Print.

Mary Lee Settle. From *All the Brave Promises: Memoirs of Aircraft Woman 2nd Class 2146391*. Columbia SC: U of South Carolina Press, 1995. Print.

Leslie Marmon Silko. From "The Man to Send Rain Clouds." *The Man to Send Rain Clouds and Other Contemporary Indian Stories*, Ed. Kenneth Rosen. New York: Penguin, 1974. Print.

David Shapiro. From "Proverbs." *Congregation*. Ed. David Rosenberg. New York: Harcourt, Brace, Jovanovich, 1987. Print.

Isaac Bashevis Singer. From *Gimpel the Fool*. Trans. Saul Bellow. New York: Noonday Press, 1957. Print.

-----. "A Wedding in Brownsville." *Commentary*, 1 March 1964. Print.

Mark Singer. From "Dirty Laundry." *The New Yorker*, 9 April 2001. Print.

Harvey Shapiro. From *A Momentary Glory: Last Poems*. Middletown, CT: Wesleyan Press, 2014. Print.

Paul Sheehan. From "My Habit." *The New Yorker*, 12 February 1996. Print.

Shelly/Cashman/Gunter. From *Teachers Discovering Computers*. Boston: Cengage, 2011. Print.

Charles Simic. From "Dinner at Uncle Boris's." *Creative Nonfiction* 24-25, 2005. Print.

Kate Simon. From "Bronx Primitive." *New York Times*, 23 May 1982. Print.

Lauren Slater. From "Black Swans: The Answer to Illness Is Not Necessarily a Cure." *Missouri Review*. Spring 1996. Print.

Jane Smiley. Used by permission from Jane Smiley, exact source unknown.

Betty Smith. From *A Tree Grows in Brooklyn*. New York: Harper and Brothers, 1943. Print.

Susan Sontag. From "Against Interpretation." *Against Interpretation and Other Essays*. New York: Farrar, Straus and Giroux, 1961. Print.

Michael Specter. From "Postcard From Rome." *The New Yorker*, 5 January 2015. Print.

Steve Stern. From "The Tale of a Kite." *Reform Judaism,* Spring 1997. Print.

Harriet Beecher Stowe. From *Uncle Tom's Cabin; or Life among the Lowly.* 1852. Print.

William Styron. From "Shadrach." *Esquire,* 21 November 1978. Print.

Chuck Sudetic. From "The Forest for the Trees." *Rolling Stone,* 21 June 2001. Print.

T

Margaret Talbot. From "Game Change." *The New Yorker,* 13 May 2013. Print.

Gay Talese. From "Ali in Havana." *The Gay Talese Reader: Portraits and Encounters.* New York: Bloomsbury, 2003. Print.

Amy Tan. From *The Bonesetter's Daughter.* New York: Random House, 2001. Print.

Melanie Thernstrom. From "Pain, the Disease." *New York Times,* 16 December 2001. Print.

Le Thi Diem Thuy. From *The Gangster We Are All Looking For.* New York: Knopf, Borzoi Books, 2003. Print.

Lewis Thomas. From "On Warts." *The Medusa and the Snail.* New York: Penguin, 1979. Print.

Henry David Thoreau. From "Thomas Carlyle and His Works." *Collected Essays and Poems.* New York: Penguin Putnam, 2001. Print.

James Thornton. From *In His Own Words*. U.S. Masters' Swimming. Web. http://www.usms.org/articles/articledisplay.php?aid=1601. Retrieved 14 March 2016.

-----. From "Come Get Some, Mark Spitz." *Men's Journal*, February 2001. Print.

Anne Tyler. From "With All Flags Flying." *Redbook,* June 1971. Print.

Royall Tyler. From *The Contrast*. 1787. Print.

U

John Updike. From "A & P." *The New Yorker*, 22 July 1961. Print.

V

Lynda Van Devanter. From *Home Before Morning: The Story of an American Army Nurse in VietNam*. Boston: U Massachusetts, Boston Press, 1983; 2001. Print.

W

Glen Waggoner. From "Gaelic Sauce." *Men's Journal*, December 2000. Print.

Alice Walker. From "Everyday Use." *In Love and Trouble*. New York: Harcourt, 1973. Print.

-----. From "The Revenge of Hannah Kemhuff." *In Love and Trouble*. New York: Harcourt, 1967. Print.

David Foster Wallace. From "Tense Present: Democracy, English, and the Wars over Usage." *Harper's Magazine*, April 2001, 39-58.

Robert Penn Warren. From *Band of Angels*. New York: Random House, 1955; rpt. LSU Press, 1983. Print.

E.B. White. From "Preposterous Parables: The Decline of Sport." *The New Yorker*, 25 October 1947. Print.

Rhonda White. From "Autobiography." Used by permission of Rhonda White.

Joy Williams. From "The Case Against Babies." *Granta* 55: 26, September 1996. Print.

Carol Winkelman. From "Battered Women's Stories about Life in Schools." *English Education*, December 1996. Print.

Tom Wolfe. From "The Limits of the Envelope." *The Right Stuff*. New York: Farrar, Straus, and Giroux, 1979. Print.

Harold Woodman. From *King Cotton and His Retainers: Financing and Marketing the Cotton Crop of the South, 1800-1925*. Lexington: U of Kentucky Press, 1968. Print.

John Woolman. From *The Journal of John Woolman*. 1774.

Virginia Woolf. From "A Room of One's Own." *Forum*, March 1929. Print.

Y

Jane Yolen. From*The Devil's Arithmetic*. New York: Penguin: 1988. Print.

Z

Alexi Zentner. From *Touch*. New York: W.W. Norton, 2011. Print.

William Ziegler. Used by permission of William Ziegler. From Writing Program Administration listserv, 1 April 2014.

Index

A

Abbott, Shirley 333, 387
abbreviations 48, 276, 281, 285, 286
absolute xiv, 78, 98, 100, 130, 155, 156, 157, 158, 159, 160, 161, 162, 163, 164, 198, 208, 249, 303, 304, 359, 373
absolute negatives 98, 359
Ackerman, Diane 221, 224, 339, 342, 387
acronyms 23, 285, 286
Adams, Alice 292, 387
Adams, Jason 311, 387
adjective 4, 15, 18, 19, 25, 26, 27, 29, 30, 39, 40, 41, 42, 44, 48, 49, 50, 51, 52, 53, 54, 55, 58, 59, 66, 75, 79, 81, 85, 89, 94, 116, 133, 134, 135, 137, 144, 147, 148, 151, 153, 164, 165, 166, 171, 181, 182, 183, 184, 185, 186, 187, 188, 189, 193, 197, 203, 204, 208, 233, 240, 254, 257, 260, 262, 266, 272, 301, 302, 309, 312, 314, 359, 363, 365, 366, 367, 368, 370, 373, 374, 375, 376, 377, 380, 381, 382, 383, 384
adjective clause 89, 181, 182, 183, 184, 185, 186, 187, 189, 197, 204, 208, 240, 272, 301, 302, 359, 367, 373, 374, 380, 382
adjective pairs 50
adverb 4, 15, 19, 27, 29, 30, 39, 40, 41, 42, 77, 79, 80, 81, 82, 84, 89, 90, 91, 94, 103, 116, 134, 135, 137, 153, 164, 165, 171, 173, 175, 176, 180, 188, 190, 191, 192, 193, 194, 234, 255, 258, 260, 276, 277, 305, 312, 359, 360, 363, 365, 368, 370, 379, 382, 383
adverb clause 190, 191, 192, 193, 194, 234, 360, 382
adverbial xiv, 29, 30, 32, 80, 153, 181, 190, 191, 192, 194, 195, 205, 208, 256, 257, 299, 300, 306, 314, 351, 359, 360, 371
adverb of time 80
agent 5, 10, 12, 14, 15, 19, 27, 55, 106, 107, 108, 109, 114, 127, 261, 275, 345, 360, 376
agreement 64, 250, 261
alliteration 208, 226, 227, 228, 239, 348, 352, 355, 360
Als, Hilton 312, 387
Alvarez, Julia 283, 387, 388
ambiguity 95, 346
anadiplosis 226, 232, 233, 360
anaphora 226, 228, 230, 231, 314, 356, 360, 370